T0207257

Lecture Notes in Computer Science 14198

Founding Editors

Gerhard Goos
Juris Hartmanis

The series Lecture Notes in Computer Science (LNCS), including its subseries Lecture Notes in Artificial Intelligence (LNAI) and Lecture Notes in Bioinformatics (LNBI), has established itself as a medium for the publication of new developments in computer science and information technology research, teaching, and education.

LNCS enjoys close cooperation with the computer science R & D community, the series counts many renowned academics among its volume editors and paper authors, and collaborates with prestigious societies. Its mission is to serve this international community by providing an invaluable service, mainly focused on the publication of conference and workshop proceedings and postproceedings. LNCS commenced publication in 1973.

Birgit Milius · Simon Collart-Dutilleul ·
Thierry Lecomte
Editors

Reliability, Safety, and Security of Railway Systems

Modelling, Analysis, Verification, and Certification

5th International Conference, RSSRail 2023
Berlin, Germany, October 10–12, 2023
Proceedings

 Springer

Editors
Birgit Milius **iD**
Technische Universität Berlin
Berlin, Germany

Simon Collart-Dutilleul **iD**
Université Gustave Eiffel
Villeneuve d'Ascq, France

Thierry Lecomte **iD**
CLEARSY Systems Engineering
Aix en Provence, France

ISSN 0302-9743   ISSN 1611-3349 (electronic)
Lecture Notes in Computer Science
ISBN 978-3-031-43365-8   ISBN 978-3-031-43366-5 (eBook)
https://doi.org/10.1007/978-3-031-43366-5

This Springer imprint is published by the registered company Springer Nature Switzerland AG
The registered company address is: Gewerbestrasse 11, 6330 Cham, Switzerland

Paper in this product is recyclable.

Preface

The development of the railway system faces a number of challenges:

- To improve and demonstrate railway system safety, security and reliability
- To reduce production costs, time to market, and running costs
- To increase system capacity and reduce carbon emissions

In the context of the current digital transformation, it requires integrated environments and methods that support different abstraction levels and different views, including:

- System architecture
- Safety analysis
- Security analysis
- Verification tools and methods

It is more obvious than ever that there is a need for close collaboration of industry and academia.

The RSSRail conferences do just that: bringing together researchers and engineers interested in building critical railway applications and systems, as a working conference in which research advances are discussed and evaluated by both researchers and engineers, focusing on their potential to be industrially deployed, keeping in mind the current digital transformation. A key goal is helping the development of advanced methods and tools that will ensure that rail systems meet the safety requirements. To foster this collaboration is at the heart of the RSSRail conference series. Especially after the pandemic, we see huge expectations for a fruitful physical event allowing for networking activities and an informal, but fundamental sharing of knowledge.

The RSSRail conference series started in Paris in 2016 and continued 2017 in Pistoia. In 2019, the conference took place in Lille. In order to adapt to the Covid context, the 2021's occurrence was a special issue of the journal of "Formal aspects of computing", instead of a physical meeting. In 2022, we were back to where we started, in Paris once again. The 2023 meeting was held in Berlin, the fifth RSSRail conference, but the sixth instance of RSSRail, and in a sense we are also back to where the ideas of RSSrail once had a home: If we assume a heritage from the previous Forms/Format cycle of conferences which took place many times in Braunschweig, we should say that formal methods applied to railways is again back in Germany.

This volume contains papers presented at the fifth international conference on Reliability, Safety and Security of Railway Systems: Modelling, Analysis, Verification and Certification (RSSRail 2023) at 10–12 October 2023, organized by TU Berlin.

This occurrence of RSSRAIL attracted 29 submissions from 11 countries. 13 papers were selected after a rigorous review process in which every paper received at least three reviews from committee members or from sub-reviewers of committee members. 3 papers were selected for poster presentation.

The conference covered topics related to all aspects of reliability, safety and security engineering for railway systems and networks including:

- Safety in development process and safety management
- Integrated approaches to safety and security
- System safety analysis
- Formal modelling and verification techniques
- System reliability
- Validation according to the standards
- Safety and security argumentation
- Fault and intrusion modelling and analysis
- Evaluation of system capacity, energy consumption, cost and their interplay.
- Tool and model integration, toolchains
- Domain specific language and modelling frameworks
- Model reuse for reliability, safety, and security
- Modelling for maintenance strategy engineering

Three prominent researchers and leading experts working in railway engineering, Dr. Ing Lydia Kaiser (TU Berlin), Andreas Freese (DB SYSTEL) and Aryldo Russo (GESTE Engineering) kindly agreed to deliver keynote talks. The corresponding abstracts are included in the current volume.

Even more so than before, the Berlin RSSRail conference offered different opportunities for discussion and development of ideas, giving room and time to all participants. We were happy that once again tutorials were offered, covering the topics of human factors, risk assessment, EULYNX and model checking. We very much thank the presenters for sharing their knowledge. The conference was completed by three workshop sessions on specific research questions as well as a concluding panel, discussing the challenges and chances of research: How can we get faster, more efficient, more effective, helping to modernize, digitalise and automate the railway system.

We would like to thank all the committee members and the additional reviewers for all their efforts. We are indebted to TU Berlin for their involvement in the planning and organization of this event and administrative tasks. We particularly thank Theodor Thomas from TU Berlin for his work in preparing the LNCS volume.

We would like to mention the precious advices from Alexander Romanowski and his huge involvement in the publicity activities.

We are very grateful to Ronan Nugent from Springer for supporting the publication of these proceedings in the LNCS series. But most of all, our thanks go to all the contributors and those who attended the conference for making this conference a success.

July 2023

Birgit Milius
Simon Collart-Dutilleul
Thierry Lecomte

Organization

Conference Chairs

Birgit Milius   TU Berlin, Germany
Simon Collart-Dutilleul   Université Gustave Eiffel, France
Thierry Lecomte   CLEARSY Systems Engineering, France

Steering Committee

Anne E. Haxthausen   Technical University of Denmark, Denmark
Alessandro Fantechi   DINFO - Università di Firenze, Italy
Simon Collart-Dutilleul   Université Gustave Eiffel, France
    (President)
Thierry Lecomte   CLEARSY Systems Engineering, France
Alexander Romanovsky   The Formal Route Ltd., UK

Conference Publicity Chair

Alexander Romanovsky   The Formal Route Ltd., UK

Event Organization

Birgit Milius   TU Berlin, Germany
Heiko Herholz   TU Berlin, Germany
Frederik Adebahr   TU Berlin, Germany

Website Design and Management

Stefan Seibt   TU Berlin, Germany

Program Committee

Yamine Ait Ameur	IRIT/INPT-ENSEEIHT, France
Abderrahim Ait Wakrime	UM5r, Morocco
Philippe Bon	Université Gustave Eiffel, France
Jens Braband	Siemens AG, Germany
Nadia Chouchani	IRT Railenium, France
Dalay De Almeida	CLEARSY Systems Engineering, France
Sana Debbech	IRT Railenium, France
David Deharbe	CLEARSY Systems Engineering, France
Alessandro Fantechi	DINFO - Università di Firenze, Italy
Alessio Ferrari	Istituto di Scienza e Tecnologie dell'Informazione "A. Faedo" - Consiglio Nazionale delle Ricerche (ISTI-CNR), Italy
Francesco Flammini	Linnaeus University, Sweden
Barbara Gallina	Mälardalen University, Sweden
Frank Golatowski	University of Rostock, Germany
Alexandra Halchin	Régie autonome des transports parisiens (RATP), France
Anne E. Haxthausen	Technical University of Denmark, Denmark
Akram Idani	Laboratoire d'Informatique de Grenoble - Université Grenoble Alpes, France
Alexei Iliasov	The Formal Route Ltd., UK
Kenji Imamoto	Hitachi Ltd., Japan
Slim Kallel	University of Sfax, Tunisia
Yves Ledru	Laboratoire d'Informatique de Grenoble - Université Grenoble Alpes, France
Michael Leuschel	University of Düsseldorf, Germany
Christophe Limbrée	Université catholique de Louvain, Belgium
Bas Luttik	Eindhoven University of Technology, Netherland
Franco Mazzanti	Istituto di Scienza e Tecnologie dell'Informazione "A. Faedo" - Consiglio Nazionale delle Ricerche (ISTI-CNR), Italy
Marcel Vinicius Medeiros Oliveira	Universidade Federal do Rio Grande do Norte, Brazil
Jan Peleska	Universität Bremen, Germany
Matthieu Perin	Systerel, France
Christophe Ponsard	CETIC, Belgium
José Proença	CISTER-ISEP and HASLab-INESC TEC, Portugal
Alexander Romanovsky	The Formal Route Ltd., UK
Aryldo Russo	GESTE ENGINEERING, France
Marc Sango	SNCF, France

Thai Son Hoang	University of Southampton, UK
Maurice ter Beek	Istituto di Scienza e Tecnologie dell'Informazione "A. Faedo" - Consiglio Nazionale delle Ricerche (ISTI-CNR), Italy
Stefano Tonetta	FBK-irst, Italy
Elena Troubitsyna	KTH Royal Institute of Technology, Sweden
Laurent Voisin	Systerel, France

Additional Reviewers

Bjørnar Luteberget	Sintef, Norway
Simone Soderi	IMT Lucca, Italy
Marielle Stoelinga	University of Twente, The Netherlands
Marco Bozzano	Fondazione Bruno Kessler, Italy
Benjamin Rother	University of Rostock, Germany
Benjamin Beichler	University of Rostock, Germany
Tim Brockmann	University of Rostock, Germany

Sponsors

Abstracts of Keynotes

Unleashing the Potential of Systems Engineering: From Theory to Practice

Lydia Kaiser

Technische Universität Berlin, Fakultät V Verkehrs- und Maschinensysteme, Institut für Werkzeugmaschinen und Fabrikbetrieb (IWF) Chair of Digital Engineering 4.0
lydia.kaiser@tu-berlin.de

Abstract. In an increasingly interconnected and digital world, organizations are facing ever greater challenges in the development and implementation of complex systems. Systems engineering offers an approach to address these challenges and develop innovative solutions. The International Council on Systems Engineering (INCOSE) is dedicated to this topic and brings together actors to develop standards and spread guidelines and best practices. In Germany, the Advanced Systems Engineering (ASE) initiative is addressing the transition of value creation, defining the focus areas and assessing the status Quo in Germany.

One focus of the keynote is to examine the implementation of systems engineering in organizations. For that purpose, the INCOSE activities and the ASE initiative will be presented first. Based on the experiences in the leading-edge cluster it's OWL - Intelligent Technical Systems OstWestfalenLippe, recurring hurdles will be identified and best practices highlighted. Beyond that, the keynote addresses current trends and developments in systems engineering and discusses the role of artificial intelligence and agility for the future of systems engineering.

The keynote will provide the audience with a comprehensive overview of systems engineering and encourage discussion on how systems engineering can become reality in organizations.

Enterprise IT in a Large Organisation is a Challenge. Even More Challenging if the "Large Organisation" is Deutsche Bahn AG in the Middle of the Digital Revolution

Andreas Freese

DB Systel GmbH, Jürgen-Ponto-Platz 1, 60329 Frankfurt am Main, Germany
Andreas.A.Freese@deutschebahn.com

Abstract. DB Systel, the digital partner of Deutsche Bahn, has been on the pioneering fast track for several years: transforming the entire organisation with over 6,000 employees into an adaptive network of self-organising teams. At the same time, IT has been migrated from traditional data centres to the public cloud, and development platforms and DevOps have established modern, scalable IT production. Last but not least, the company has focused on IT-OT convergence due to the intense digitalisation of operational technology (OT) everywhere and the strong growth in OT assets through extensive rollouts, for example through *Digitale Schiene Deutschland*.

State-of-the-art IT production systems and the regulated, highly rules-driven world of railway infrastructure and its supervisory and approval structures come together on this fast track. This raises a number of questions that today's processes and rules may not be able to fully answer — for example, questions about the use of artificial intelligence, cloud technologies and agile methods in software development for security and safety-critical systems. But we will certainly be able to answer these questions using the processes and rules of tomorrow. What will those be? I would like to take you part on this fast track in my keynote address.

Continuous Research for Innovation

Aryldo Russo

Geste Engineering France Sas, 19 Rue Du 4 Septembre, 75002 Paris, France
aryldo.russo@geste.group

Abstract. In several domains, the inertia that can be seen while taking the risk and trying new ideas is bigger than what we could wish for, and tis is stronger as the risk of harming people increases. As we can imagine, this is the case in the railway domain, where a failure might lead to a hazard that potentially can cause several deaths. Luckily, this fear, even if it can slow down the attempts to put in place new ideas, do not block totally the quest for innovation. These ideas are not only disruptive technologies, like hyperloops, or fully autonomous vehicles, but rather new and better ways to do trivial tasks, or even moving some steps away from the problem to have a view outside the box.

In this keynote we will present a bit of the evolution in the railway domain in terms of new technologies that were implemented or that will be, but also in terms of simple measures that could lead to innovation in terms of energy savings and other cool stuff.

Contents

Formal Model and Visual Tooling

Modeling for Security

Automating an Analysis of Safety-Security Interactions for Railway Systems

Ehsan Poorhadi$^{(\boxtimes)}$ and Elena Troubitsyna

KTH – Royal Institute of Technology, Stockholm, Sweden
{poorhadi,elenatro}@kth.se

Abstract. Over recent years, the number of cyberattacks on safety-critical systems, including railways has been rapidly increasing. To analyze the impact of cyberattacks on safety, we need to create methods supporting a systematic and rigorous analysis of system behavior in the presence of cyber threats. In this paper, we propose a methodology and automated tool support for an integrated analysis of the impact of cyberattacks on the safety of railway systems. Our approach relies on graphical modeling in SysML, HAZOP-based analysis of cyber threats and formal modeling in Event-B. The proposed approach allows the designers to identify and visualize the safety requirements that become violated as a result of various cyberattacks.

Keywords: Integrated formal modelling · Safety · Cyberattacks · Automated tool support · Railway networked control systems

1 Introduction

Over recent years, the number and scale of cyberattacks on safety-critical systems have been rapidly growing. Thus it raised a serious concern over the safety of critical infrastructures such as railway signaling systems. Formal modeling and verification are often used to verify the safety of railway signaling systems. Currently, industry practitioners are willing to utilize their expertise and extend it also to reason about safety in the presence of cyberthreats. This motivated our research on integrating safety and security modeling to analyze the potential ways in which cyberattacks could jeopardize system safety.

In this paper, we present a novel extension of our previous work [5] on combining modeling in SysML and Event-B to support a rigorous integrated analysis of the impact of cyberattacks on system safety. Our approach allows the designers to model the system in SysML and then automatically translate it into Event-B, which formally supports the process of identifying safety requirements that are violated by cyberattacks. The safety requirements are formalized as model invariants and the violated requirements are identified via the failed invariant preservation proof obligations. Such an analysis serves as a basis for the consecutive security analysis aiming at defining security control mechanisms and prioritizing their implementation.

Supported by Trafikverket, Sweden.

In this paper, we augment our previous work on formal modeling of safety-security interaction by incorporating HAZOP-based cyberthreat analysis. We use HAZOP (Hazard and Operability Study [17]) to systematically analyze and explicitly model the impact of different types of cyberattacks on the messages exchanged by the system components. Using HAZOP we can identify which kind of deviations from the original message the attacker's actions can cause. They are then represented in the SysML model to analyze their impact on safety.

To support the incorporation of HAZOP-based analysis, we extend our developed *EBSysMLSec* tool to handle the output of HAZOP analysis in SysML models. *EBSysMLSec* enables an automatic generation of Event-B models from the created cyberthreats-explicit SysML models. The Rodin platform [10] is then used to formally verify whether safety requirements defined as a set of model invariants are preserved in the presence of cyberattacks.

To validate the proposed approach and usefulness of our *EBSysMLSec* tool, in this paper, we present security-explicit modeling of moving block case study [16], which is developed in cooperation with the railway industry. Our analysis results in finding necessary and sufficient conditions over the system parameters under which we can guarantee the safety of the system in the presence of cyberattacks.

2   Safety-Critical NCSs: Architecture and Threat Model

An architecture of a networked control system (NCS) is based on the classical feedback control loop "sensing-control-actuation". In NCS, while executing the control loop, the components should communicate with each other over wired or wireless network channels, as shown in Fig. 2. Typically, the high-level safety goal is formulated in terms of some critical parameter P_{real}, which should be maintained within a safe interval while the system provides the intended functionality.

$$Safety: \quad P_{min} \leq P_{real} \leq P_{max}. \tag{1}$$

where P_{min} and P_{max} are the low and high safe thresholds correspondingly.

At each iteration of the control loop, a sensor measures the value of P_{real} and sends a message sen_{out} to the controlling software (usually called controller). The controller receives the sensor measurement, calculates the next required state of the actuator and sends the message $cont_{out}$ to it. The state of the actuator affects the value of P_{real} that enables the system to provide the required functionality and maintain safety. In this paper, we consider fail-safe systems, i.e., the systems that are put in a safe non-operational state if (1) cannot be guaranteed. Railway NCS are typical examples of those.

Our threat model focuses on Man-in-the-middle attacks resulting in compromising messages sent over the communication channels of NCS. Such attacks constitute the main cyberthreat for railway systems due to the wide geographical distribution of the control centers and hence, difficulty to protect the assets [23]. Cyberattacks on the sensor-controller channel would result in incorrect $cont_{in}$. As a consequence, the controller could compute an incorrect, possibly hazardous control command. Similarly, an attack on the controller-actuator channel would result in a discrepancy between act_{in} and $cont_{out}$. It can potentially result in the direct setting of the actuator to a dangerous state.

3   A Case Study: Moving Block

Our case study – a subsystem of the ERTMS/ETCS Level 3 moving block architecture [16]– is a typical example of NCS. The system aims at controlling trains' movement by using as few trackside devices as possible and relying on direct communication with trains. Radio-block centers (RBC) are deployed to deliver signals to trains and receive feedback. Each RBC controls the movement of the trains along a certain area by either authorizing them to move at a certain speed or stopping them.

The authorization is done by sending movement authority messages containing among others the end of the movement authority (EoA) and a danger point to trains. EoA is a position in the track that the train is allowed to reach but not pass. However, depending on the implementation, the RBC defines EoA such that passing the point does not lead to a hazardous situation. This is done by considering a safety margin that defines a danger point to be beyond EoA. This results in a safety property stating that trains must not pass their danger points. An RBC could stop the train from moving by sending an emergency stop message. The message allows the RBC to stop trains from passing the danger point. In this case study, we consider a scenario in which an RBC is controlling a train in its controlling area while the communication channel between them is compromised by an attacker. The goal of the study is to check whether the attacker's actions result in the train passing a danger point.

We consider an attacker who performs a two-phase attack. First, she injects a valid movement authority message to set the value of EoA beyond the danger point defined by RBC. Such an attack constitutes a direct safety hazard since the danger point defined by RBC could be at the rear end of another train. Such an attack is shown to be possible in [19]. The impact of the attack in the first phase is an assumption of our model. It means we consider the stored EoA in the train to be beyond the danger point determined by the RBC. In the second phase, the attacker actively monitors train-RBC communication and takes some actions e.g., dropping a message to prevent the detection of the attack and stopping the train before passing the danger point.

In this study, we model and analyze the communication between the RBC and the train to derive a sufficient and necessary condition to ensure that the train would not pass the danger point. This condition must be met by the RBC when calculating EoA and danger points for the train. Indeed, we show that if the distance between the calculated EoA and the danger point is not large enough then defense mechanisms deployed on both sides do not detect the attacks on time, and the train would pass the danger point. To perform our analysis, we define a control loop including RBC and train subsystems and apply our approach.

In this case study, the controller is distributed between RBC and ATP – an Automatic Train Protection system installed in trains. We define a control loop that will be executed periodically as follows. ATP receives *Odometer* measurement and calculates the train position. Then it forms a position report message to RBC containing positional information. After this, RBC estimates the train position and then does one of the following actions as a response. The RBC may decide not to interact with the train. In this case, the train moves according to its stored movement authority, and the ATP ends the control loop without sending a signal to the train braking system. The RBC may send an *Emergency stop* command that results in the train engaging the brake by sending a signal to the braking system. The RBC might send other messages to the train as a response to the position report within a control loop. In this case, the train moves again according to its stored movement and the control loop ends without engaging the brake. In our modeling, we consider these messages as a heartbeat indicating to the ATP that the communication with the RBC is alive. In our study, the odometer corresponds to the sensor of the generic NCS architecture and the train's braking system to the actuator. Due to the lack of space, in this section, we describe the system only briefly. However, more details will be introduced while demonstrating an application of our approach in the subsequent sections.

4   Integrating HAZOP-Based Analysis of the Impact of Cyberattacks into SysML Modelling of NCSs

System modeling language (SysML) [9] is a general-purpose modeling language often used in the development of safety-critical systems. The graphical nature of SysML models facilitates collaboration between engineers from different domains. In particular, it can help them to visualize component interactions and dynamic behavior under different operating conditions as well as cyberattacks.

To model NCS and represent the impact of cyberattacks, we use a subset of SysML diagrams consisting of the block definition diagram (BDD), the internal block diagram (IBD), the activity Diagram (AD), the state machine diagram (SMD), and the sequence diagram (SD).

4.1   Modeling Guidelines

We define certain modeling guidelines prescribing which aspects of system architecture and behavior should be represented in the corresponding SysML models. They ensure that the resultant SysML models provide a suitable and sufficient basis for the security analysis and subsequent formal modeling. Below we briefly outline them. The detailed description can be found in [5]

Block Definition Diagram. BDD defines the structure of the system model. BDD uses *blocks* to represent a system and its components and *association* to show how the blocks are related. The following rules should be adopted to create the BDD. Figure 3 shows the BDD for our railway case study. A block (block *railway*) is created for the entire system under modeling. It consists of different

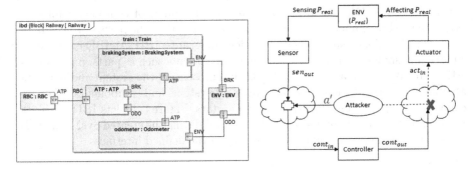

Fig. 1. IBD of Railway block.   **Fig. 2.** An architecture of an NCS.

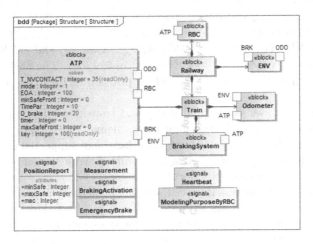

Fig. 3. BDD diagram represents the structure.

blocks modeling sub-systems and/or components. In our case, it has RBC as a component, $Train$ as a subsystem and a composite relation between them. A sub-system block itself can be decomposed into several components in a similar way. In Fig. 3, the components are RBC, ATP, Odometer, BRK, and ENV. To represent safety requirements, as discussed in Sect. 2, we also introduce a block representing the physical environment (block ENV). In our case study, block ENV models the actual position of the train on the track.

At this point, we define internal constants and variables of each component as the *attributes* of the corresponding block, e.g., attributes of the ATP shown in Fig. 3. To model the interfaces between components, we define two *ports* for each pair of blocks (one for each) that communicate with each other. The ports are used to exchange *signals* that are modeled separately in BDD. In our approach, the ports assigned to the block ENV are used to send the monitored parameters and receive the state of the actuator as signals. For the Moving Block system, the Odometer receives the actual position of the train as a signal from block ENV and estimates the distance traveled with some imprecision. Block ENV receives the state of the braking system as a signal sent by block BRK.

Internal Block Diagram. To simulate the dynamics of component interactions, we need to explicitly show the connections between the ports of the components, which is done using the internal block diagram – IBD. An IBD is owned by a block and shows its encapsulated structural contents such as parts, ports, properties, etc. We create an IBD for the block representing the system and instantiate different parts of the system including subsystems and components. Then we connect their ports (interfaces) using *connectors*. Figure 1 depicts IBD for block *railway*. IBD serves as an important tool for validating the created SysML models via simulation, i.e. checking the consistency of the defined interfaces.

State Machine Diagram and Activity Diagram. An SMD is used to represent the internal behavior of blocks. It models both the component functional logic and communication protocols. We create SMD for each block representing a component. Therefore, we create the following SMDs, RBC, ATP, $Odometer$, BRK, and ENV. The SMDs of RBC, ATP, $Odometer$, and BRK model the behavior of the corresponding block within a control loop. The SMD ENV models train movement by updating the actual position of the train at the end of each control loop.

To create SMDs, we use normal states and transitions that can be guarded and/or triggered. To specify the guards, we define the corresponding logical expressions over the block's attributes in a language supported by SysML (in our implementation, Python). A transition may have a trigger – a signal the block receives through one of its ports.

The effect of the transition is described using an activity diagram, which specifies how the block's attributes are updated as a result of the transition. In an AD, we define an *opaque action* as a basis for implementing the corresponding script using *assignment* and *if statement*. In an AD, we can also model sending and receiving signals by defining a *send signal action* or *parameter node*'s, respectively. In a *send signal action*, we specify the signal and the port through which the signal must be sent. To determine the signal parameter, we add a flow of some variables of the opaque action to the signal parameters by adding output pins to the opaque action. To flow signal parameters to the opaque action, we define input pins for the opaque action and connect them to *parameter nodes* of the AD.

As an example, we provide the SMD of ATP in Fig. 4 as well as its two ADs in Fig. 5 and 6. We define four states to model ATP behavior. In state *fullSupervision*, ATP is waiting to receive the Odometer measurements. When the signal is received, the transition is triggered and ATP updates the positional information of the train according to the odometer measurement and determines the mode of the train. This behavior is modeled in AD *estimation* (Fig. 6) assigned to the transition. As can be seen, we define two parameter nodes to get attributes of the measurement signal and use them in the opaque action to update the attributes of the ATP. As a result of the transition, we reach state *odo*. From state *odo*, the ATP either reaches $TrainTrip$ state and stops the train (if $mode \neq 1$) or gets back to $fullSupervision$ (if $mode = 1$). If the ATP is back to the $fullSupervision$ state, it sends a position report message, which is

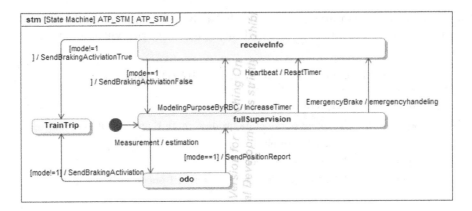

Fig. 4. The SMD of ATP.

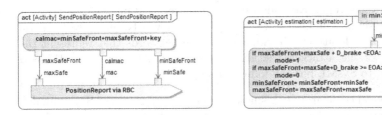

Fig. 5. Sending position report signal   **Fig. 6.** Receiving Odo's measurement

modeled in the AD with a similar name (Fig. 5). At this moment, ATP could receive three different signals modeling RBC responses. If RBC sends an emergency stop message, ATP changes its mode modeled in *emergencyHandling* AD and goes to the *traintrip* state. If RBC sends the heartbeat message then ATP resets its timer showing the connection is alive and back to the *fullSupervision* state. In some cases, RBC might not send a message. In order to complete the control loop and avoid modeling time-constraint behavior, we define an auxiliary (i.e., used only for modeling purposes) signal to indicate that RBC does not send a message in the current control loop. In this case, ATP increases its timer and goes to either *fullSupervision* or *trainTrip* depending on whether the timer passes a threshold ($T_{NVCONTACT}$). Indeed, if the timer passes the threshold then the mode of the train changes to zero. This behavior is modeled in the AD *IncreaseTimer*.

4.2   Integrating SysML Model with HAZOP

HAZOP - HAZard and OPerability Analysis [17] systematically identifies the possible causes and consequences of deviations within the system. The analysis is performed using a set of guidewords and attributes. The original set of guidewords includes *no, more, less, alter, early, late*, etc. The guidewords are applied to the system attributes. HAZOP has been extensively used in safety-critical domain and extended to specifically target security vulnerabilities. In

Table 1. Interpretation of standard HAZOP guidewords

Guideword	Interpretation
Less/More	The signal parameters are less/more than what it is sent
No	No signal is received
Late/Early	The signal is received late/early
Alter	The signal parameter are different from what it is sent

this work, we apply the guidewords to the signals exchanged over the communication channels to systematically identify the attacker's actions and model their impact. Table 1 shows our interpretation of the guidewords. Since we focus on the man-in-the-middle attack, we single out the guidewords that represent the possible effects of the attacker's action of a given signal. Our HAZOP-based analysis applied to SysML has the following steps:

- creating a sequence diagram to visualize signals according to the SMDs model;
- selecting a signal and identifying relevant guidewords that can be applied over the signal by human expertise;
- specifying the applied guidewords and their interpretation in every incident of the signal in the sequence diagram.
- updating state machine diagrams to specify the effect of a deviation or the detection on the receiver behavior;

The modeler can decide to model all deviations altogether or separately to manage the complexity of the model better.

Let us now apply the proposed approach to the moving block case study. Creating the SD is an essential aspect of our analysis. On the one hand, it visualizes the communication protocols and allows us to systematically describe the deviations caused by cyberattacks. On the other hand, it plays a key role in the translation and creation of the Event-B model.

The first step is to create an SD to show the signal exchange. Indeed, in our analysis, the SD provides an abstract view of the communication protocols within a control loop. We create an SD for the block to represent the whole system (*railway* block in Figure 3). In the created SD, we define a lifeline for each component of the system (*RBC, ATP, Odometer, BRK, ENV*) and add a *loop fragment* to represent the control loop. Inside the loop, we create a message for each signal that the components exchange. Note that we define a new message every time that a signal is sent. If there is a conditional interaction within a control loop, we use an *alt fragment.*

In the second step, we identify the signals and relevant guidewords. Since the attacker's aim is the RBC-ATP channels, we only apply guidewords to signals exchanged by ATP and RBC. There are three signals that are exchanged in the channel. We identify that guidewords *less*, *No*, and *delay* could be applied to position report signals. Also, the guidewords *delay* and *No* could be applied to emergency stop signals. Due to the large size of the SD, we provide a part of the diagram in 7 after performing the second step.

At this point, we specify the identified guidewords in SD to visualize the attacker's actions. To do so, for every incident of the signal in the SD, we create an alt fragment with several *operand*, one for each guideword. We also define an extra operand to represent normal signal exchange. In each operand, we interpret the guideword and model the effect of the guidewords on signal parameters. Figure 7 shows the SD after applying the guidewords.

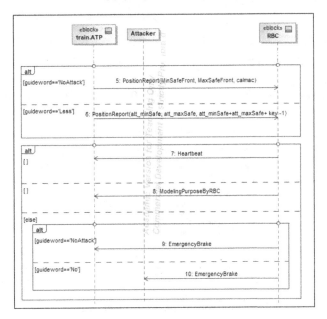

Fig. 7. The integration of SD with HAZOP.

Finally, we need to specify how the guideword affects the receiver behavior. To do so, we update the SMD of the receiver. Particularly, we consider an *if statement* for each defined operand in the AD that the receiver accepts the signal. We define *guideword = w*, where *w* is the guideword of the operand, to be the condition of the branch. Then we model the effect of the deviation and the defense mechanisms inside the branch. Therefore, we update the SMD of ATP and RBC to model the impact of the attacks on the behavior of the components. For brevity, we show how we model the guideword *No* in the SMD of ATP by modifying the *emergencyHandling* AD in Fig. 10.

As a result of the systematic analysis of the cyber threats using HAZOP, we obtain SysML models that explicitly define the deviations cause by an attack on the system behavior. We use these models as the inputs for translation into Event-B. Then the Event-B model is verified to check if the attacks result in safety violations.

5   Formal Analysis of the Impact of Attacks on Safety

We start by briefly overviewing our formal modeling framework – Event-B and outlining the main ideas behind the translation methodology described in full detail in [5] as well as the novel contribution – incorporation of HAZOP with the generated Event-B model. Then we overview the tool support and validation – the moving block case study specification in Event-B.

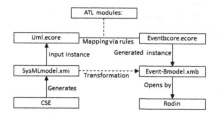

Machine	No. INVs	No. POs	No. Manually proofs	No. Manually proofs with ProB
Abstract	8	44	3	0
ENV	6	62	3	1
Braking system	6	86	2	1
ATP	28	353	39	8
RBC	27	547	43	15
Odometer	32	500	110	30

Fig. 8. The workflow and toolchain.   **Fig. 9.** A summary of generated POs.

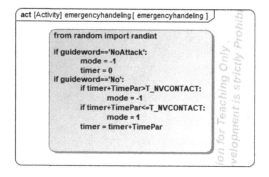

Fig. 10. The guideword impact on the emergency brake.

5.1   Event-B

Event-B is a state-based formal modeling approach that promotes the correct-by-construction development paradigm and formal verification by theorem proving [11]. In Event-B, a system model is specified as an *Abstract State Machine*, which encapsulates the model state represented as a collection of variables and defines operations on the state using a set of atomic *events*. In general, an event e is defined using the list of local variables (parameters) a, the guard G_e, and R_e the next-state relation as follows:

$$e \mathrel{\widehat{=}} \textbf{any } a \textbf{ where } G_e \textbf{ then } R_e \textbf{ end},$$

Usually, a machine has an accompanying component, called *context*, which may include user-defined carrier sets, constants, and their properties given as a list of model axioms. In Event-B, the model variables are strongly typed by the constraining predicates. These predicates and the other important properties that must be preserved by the model constitute model *invariants*.

Event-B employs a top-down refinement-based approach to system development. Development starts from an abstract system specification that non-deterministically models the most essential functional requirements. In a sequence of refinement steps, we gradually reduce non-determinism and introduce detailed design decisions. The consistency of Event-B models, i.e., verification of well-formedness and invariant preservation as well as the correctness of refinement steps, is formally demonstrated by discharging the relevant proof obligations generated by the Rodin platform [10].

5.2   From SysML to Event-B: Translation Methodology

Our translation is incorporated into the Event-B refinement process. This helps us to distribute the complexity of the model into several machines that are easier to verify. Once the refinement process is completed, the SysML models become fully formalized in Event-B and the detailed definition of the impact of cyber attacks on safety emerges via failed proofs of certain safety invariants.

Our translation methodology defines a context C which can be seen by all machines, an abstract specification M_0 which is our starting point in the refinement process, and a machine M_c for each component c that owns an SMD. We use machines M_c's to create the refinement chain discussed later. Therefore, in our case study, an Event-B context is created as well as the following machines, M_0, M_{RBC}, M_{ATP}, $M_{Odometer}$, M_{BRK}, M_{ENV}. In the following, we describe the translation rules for creating the context and the machines.

The Event-B Context. We start by translating the static information of diagrams in an Event-B context C, which is seen by all machines. The context C contains the following information.

The attributes of the blocks that are specified in the SysML model as *Read-Only* will be translated as a constant into the context C. The translation creates an enumeration set,

$$B_{States} = \{state_1, ..., state_s\},$$

for each block B containing all states defined in the block's SMD. This set is later used to type a variable modeling the current state of the block. Indeed, the state transition is modeled in Event-B by giving different values to the variable.

Regarding the signal exchanges, we define two enumeration sets. We define $sig = \{att_1, ..., att_t\}$ for each signal sig containing the signal's attributes if there are any. Indeed, the set shows different fields of the signal. Therefore, sending a signal requires determining some values for the different fields i.e., assigning values to members of the set. We also define an enumeration set

$$Phases = \{s_X, r_X | \ X \ is \ a \ signal\},$$

containing all interaction phases. Here s_X and r_x model signal X are sent and received (or deletion attack performed by the attacker and the signal is dropped), respectively. This set is used later to type a variable that models the current phase of the interaction depicted in the SD.

So far, we translate some static information that we need to specify the behavior modeled in SD and SMDs. In the following, we describe the translation rules that capture the behavior of the model and provide the corresponding Event-B specification.

Abstract specification (M_0). The first machine M_0 is the translation of the SD and some parts of BDD that focuses on modeling sending and receiving signals. The machine models signal exchange according to the SD by defining sending and receiving events. The machine also models the impact of guidewords on the signal. Therefore, the machine provides an abstraction of the whole system without modeling the components in detail.

```
MACHINE AbstractMachine                          grd3:
SEES MainContext                                   (guideword     =     NoAttack  ⇒
EVENTS                                             maxSafe = PositionReport(PositionReport_maxSafe)
Event Sending_PositionReport ⟨⟩ ≙
    when                                           (guideword = Less ⇒ maxSafe <
        grd1: phase = r_Measurement                PositionReport(PositionReport_maxSafe))
    then                                         grd4:
        act1: phase := s_PositionReport            (guideword = NoAttack ⇒ mac =
        act2: PositionReport :∈ PositionReport→    PositionReport(PositionReport_mac))∧
              ℤ
    end                                            (guideword = Less ⇒ mac = 0)
Event Receiving_PositionReport ⟨⟩ ≙              grd5: guideword ∈ {NoAttack, Less}
    any
        minSafe, maxSafe, mac, guideword       then
    where                                          act1: phase := r_PositionReport
        grd1: phase = s_PositionReport             act2: recv_PositionReport       :=
        grd2:                                            {PositionReport_minSafe       ↦
           (guideword = NoAttack⇒minSafe =           minSafe, PositionReport_maxSafe ↦
           PositionReport(PositionReport_minSafe))∧   maxSafe, PositionReport_mac    ↦
                                                       mac}
           (guideword  =  Less ⇒ minSafe <
           PositionReport(PositionReport_minSafe))  end
                                                 END
```

Fig. 11. Two events in $M0$ models sending and receiving position report signals.

Table 2. Python to Event-B translation

Pyhton	Event-B
and, or	$\land, \lor$
$==, <=, >=, <, >, !=$	$=, \leq, \geq, >, <, \neq$
$+, -, *, /$	$+, -, \times, \div$
$randint(v_1, v_2)$	**Any** par **where** $par \in PytoB(v_1)..PytoB(v_2)$
$att = e$	**Any** par **where** par=PytoB(e) **then** att:=par
$var_{local} = e$	**Any** par **where** par=PytoB(e)
$if\ c:$	**Any** par **where** $par = TRUE \Leftrightarrow PytoB(c)\land$
P	$par \Rightarrow PytoB(P).guard$

We start the translation by defining a variable $phase \in Phases$ that points to the current interaction phase. We define two events $sending_{sig}$ and $receiving_{sig}$ for each signal sig modeling sending and receiving the signal. These events update the variable $phase$ to corresponding values. Figure 11 shows a fragment of M_0 for the case study that depicts two events.

The events model sending and receiving the position report signals. In Event $sending_{positionReport}$, Guard $grd1$ specifies the signal can be sent after receiving the odometer measurement. Action $act1$ changes the interaction phase such that the receiving event becomes enabled to fire. Action $act2$ provides a non-deterministic assignment to a variable that models the content of the signal after sending. The variable is of type of function that maps fields of the signal to values.

In the event $receiving_{positionReport}$, we show how the guideword $Less$ is translated. Indeed, we define a guard for each attribute of the signal and specify the impact of guidewords $(grd2 - grd4)$. As can be seen, it corresponds to receiving (i.e., assigning) the value to $recv_{PositionReport}$ (which is a variable with the same type as the $PositionReport$) that is less than the one that has been sent $(act2)$.

Machine. M_c After the translation of the SD and creating M_0, we aim at specifying the behavior of the system components modeled by the corresponding SMDs. We do it by translating the SMD of a block (component) c along with its ADs in a machine called M_c. We aim to specify M_c to mimic the SMD of the block. In the following, we describe the translation for a component C modeled by a block B in the SysMl model.

First We start by defining the variables that we need. We define variables for attributes of B that are not $ReadOnly$, and a variable $BState \in B_{States}$, which designates the current state of the block.

We define an event for each transition of the SMD and specify it according to the source state, the target state, the guard, and the activity of the transition. In the following, we describe how we specify an event e modeling a transition t of the SMD.

We first define a guard $BState = t.source$ and an action $BState := t.target$ that models state transition. Next is to translate the guard of the transition into a guard of e. This includes only translating operators which is done according to Table 2. Finally, We translate the AD of t (if it is defined) as follows.

If AD of t sends a signal sig, then we declare $sending_{sig}$ (defined in M_o) as an abstract event for e. In case sig contains some variables, we refine the abstract assignment to variable $send_{sig}$ according to the AD of t.

If t has a signal sig as a trigger then we declare the event $receiving_{sig}$ (defined in M_0) as an abstract event for e. To consume the signal contents in e, we use the parameters of the abstract event (see the parameters of event $receiving_{PositionReport}$ in Fig. 11).

The final step is to translate the opaque action of the AD, which contains a script. To do so, we start to translate each line of the script as described in Table 2. Due to the lack of space, we skip showing the Event-B model after translating SMDs. In the next section, we will introduce our tool that automates the translation process.

5.3   Automated Tool Support: EBSysMLSec

To facilitate the construction of the Event-B model, we develop a tool *EBSysMLSec* that provides an automatic translation of the SysML models into the Event-B specifications according to the principles discussed above. The implementation can be found in [15]. Figure 8 shows our proposed workflow and the developed tool-chain.

MSSA: Magic Systems of Systems Architect. The first step of the workflow is modeling an NCS in the presence of cyberattacks in Magic Systems of Systems Architect [12] according to the guidelines described in Sect. 3. MSSA supports modeling based on SysML 1.5 standard and provides validation and simulation facilities. Applying model validation and simulation at the early design of the system helps to validate SysML models before their translation. Once the SysML modeling is complete, we export the model as the *Eclipse UML2.5 xmi* file that will be input to our tool *EBSysMLSec*.

EBSysMLSec. Our tool is built using ATL – a model transformation language and toolkit [13]. The ATL IDE, developed on top of the Eclipse platform, provides an environment to develop ATL transformations. In ATL, a model must conform to a meta-model. We use Ecore meta-model technology supported by ATL. A model-to-model transformation involves developing ATL modules that map the source Ecore meta-model (UML meta-model in EBSysMLSec) elements to target Ecore meta-model (eventbcore in EBSysMLSec) elements via defining

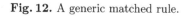

```
rule rule_name {
    from
        source: Type (Condition)
    to
        target_1: Type_1 (Init)
        ...
        target_n: Type_2 (Init)
    do{imperative code}
}
```

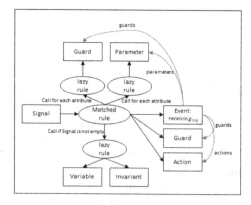

Fig. 12. A generic matched rule.

Fig. 13. A part of a matched rule in EBSysMLSec.

transformation *rules*. In each module execution, rules are called and target elements will be created. A general structure of a rule is shown in Fig. 12. When a rule is applied, for each *source* element of type *Type* that satisfies *Condition* the n target elements of type $Type_1$ to $Type_n$ are generated. Then the imperative code will be executed to initialize the generated elements.

Our tool consists of three ATL modules generating the Event-B context, the abstract specification (M_0), and the refinements (M_c's). The last module takes a block's name as an input and outputs an Event-B machine modeling the block's SMD. Figure 13 shows a part of a rule, which we define to create the events modeling sending and receiving signals in the abstract specification. As can be seen, The rule is called for any signal. When the rule is applied, the event $receiving_{sig}$ along with its guards, parameters, and actions that are defined according to the transition principle mentioned in Sect. 5.2 is generated. As a result of running *EBSysMLSec*, we obtain a complete model in Event-B at different levels of abstraction in xmb files readable by Rodin.

Rodin. The Rodin Platform is an Eclipse-based IDE for Event-B that provides automated support for modeling and proof-based verification [10]. We use the Rose editor plugin [14] to open generated xmb files. After importing Event-B models into Rodin, we manually define the refinement relations between the machines, i.e., define the desired refinement chain. We then augment the specifications with the safety invariant and verify it.

5.4 Formal Verification of Safety of System Under Attack

Let us now discuss our approach to verifying the impact of cyberattacks on safety within the translation-driven refinement process in Event-B. The impact of cyberattacks on safety is analyzed by checking whether a safety property can be proved to be an invariant of the Event-B model under the modeled effect of the cyberattacks on the system behavior. We provide a typical safety property 1 in Sect. 2. However, our approach can be applied to verify any safety property that can be expressed over block attributes using predicate logic.

We follow the relied guarantee style that includes defining some relied condition (R_c) and some guaranteed condition (G_c) for each component c such that the functionality of c guarantees G_c by relying on R_c which itself provided by other components: i.e., other components guaranteed condition satisfy it. We aim to deduce the safety case (proof of Property 1 for example) from R_c's and G_c's. Therefore, we define the safety property as the guaranteed condition of ENV (G_{ENV}). In our verification technique, the guaranteed condition of each component is defined as an invariant of the corresponding machine. Then by analyzing the machine, we find the relied conditions which lead us to define other components' guaranteed conditions. Following this technique require us to create the following refinement chain,

$$M_0 \Rightarrow M_{ENV} \Rightarrow M_{Actuator} \cdots \Rightarrow M_{Sensor}.$$

The above refinement chain allows us to define the safety property as soon as possible and distribute evenly the difficulty of the proof among all machines.

We demonstrate the verification process using our moving block case study. EBSysMLSec takes the SysML model and generates Event-B machines *ENV, BrakingSystem, ATP, RBC,* and *Odometer.* They are imported in Rodin and arranged into the refinement chain in the same order. The detailed model in Event-B is augmented with the safety property,

$$realPosition < dP,$$

where *realPosition* is an attribute of the block ENV points to the actual position of the train, and *dP* is a constant attribute of block *RBC* modeling the danger point determined by the RBC. The event-B model including the invariants can be found in [18]. As a result of the proof-based verification process, we show that safety is preserved even in the presence of the deviations discussed in Sect. 4.2 if the RBC meets a condition stating that the safety margin should be large enough. Figure 9 shows a summary of the invariant and POs that are generated and discharged in the proving process. As can be seen, a large number of invariants are generated, but the majority of them are discharged automatically using ProB, the Event-B model checker, which shows the scalability of our approach.

Discussion. Let us discuss the results of incorporating HAZOP into our methodology and using our extended *EBSysMLSec.* As a result of using HAZOP, we were able to identify how the actions of the attacker can alter the messages exchanged between the components. This allows us to create a SysML model that explicitly represents the cyber threats though it does not attempt to analyze their impact on system safety. Our *EBSysMLSec* tool has been successfully used to automatically generate the corresponding Event-B models. Such translation and tool support reduce the enormous effort to create an understandable formal model. Since our translation supports a refinement-based approach, the complexity of the generated models remained manageable with the majority of proof obligations being discharged automatically. However, the translation has some limitations discussed during the explanation. Notably, it does not provide interesting invariants except for the variable types, and only one instance of a block can be translated.

The moving block case study demonstrated that we can successfully apply the proposed automated approach in practice. We show that the current moving block architecture is resistant against the networked attacker we model in this work if and only if RBC satisfies the proposed condition. In our model, we consider a safety property stating that trains must not pass danger points while other safety properties remain to check such as exceeding the maximum speed. We believe our methodology could be applied to check such properties.

6   Related Work and Conclusions

Related Work. Several previous works proposed different modeling approaches to represent the impact of security attacks on safety within Event-B framework [1] [2]. The authors explored different refinement strategies, as well as the use of HAZOP for requirements elicitation [3]. While our approach adopts the idea of an incremental unfolding system architecture via refinement, we rely on SysML models as an intermediate step between the informal requirements description and formal specification. We have proposed a methodology for using HAZOP to systematically identify the impact of various cyberattacks on component interactions based on SysML model and automate the translation into Event-B. The work on formal modeling of cyberattacks in the railway domain is reported in our previous work [4]. In this paper, we have extended the modeling methodology proposed in [4], on the one hand, to support an integration between SysML and Event-B for generic NCS, and, on the other hand, to include modeling of deletion and tampering attacks on both channels of NCS.

The work on integrating general-purpose graphical modeling and formal specification has been carried out by Snook et al. [6]. Currently, there is also a UML-B plugin available for the Rodin platform that enables an automatic translation of UML-B into Event-B specification [7]. We have adopted similar techniques in translating state machine diagrams but focused on explicit modeling and verification of safety-security interactions.

UML-B has been used in some works to analyze the safety of NCS. For example, in [8], UML-B is used to model hybrid ERTMS level 3. However, our work includes a broader set of SysML diagrams and allows to express a richer set of properties.

The translation of SysML diagrams into formal languages is considered in some works. In [20], the gap between textual requirements and formal specification is filled by using a requirement diagram. In this work, the requirement diagram is used to build hierarchical relationships of requirements. This hierarchical relationship determines the refinement strategy in the translation of the requirement into the Event-B specification. Although using requirement diagrams makes the process of modeling easier, the requirements are still textual. We believe that a combination of the diagrams that we used and requirement diagrams to describe systems can enhance both works. Another work provides an automatic translation of SMDs into Event-B specification for railway application [22]. In another work [21], SysML/KAOS domain model has been integrated into Event-B. They specify a goal model using SysML and KAOS goal language and then translate the model into Event-B.

Conclusions. In this work, we proposed and automated an integrated approach to modeling the impact of cyberattacks on the safety of railway systems. We have defined the principles of modeling the system in SysML and proposed a HAZOP-based methodology for modeling the impact of attacks on component interactions. We utilize EBSysMLSec for translating the SysML model into Event-B.

Our SysML translation into Event-B has been incorporated into the correct-by-construction development process. It allowed us to explicitly analyze the impact of security attacks on the behavior of each component as well as the overall system safety. The resultant model explicitly demonstrates which safety invariants become violated as a result of cyberattacks.

By applying our approach, one can verify any safety property that is express-ible using predicate logic over block attributes. As an example, we model a part of moving block architecture and derive a sufficient and necessary condition under which a train would not pass a danger point determined by an RBC in the presence of an attacker who forges a valid movement authority, tampers with position report, and drops emergency stop signal.

The work on the integration of SysML and Event-B for modeling safety-security interactions in NCSs has been motivated by our cooperation with the railway industry. Since SysML is widely used for system modeling, we believe that the proposed integration approach can facilitate the understanding of formal models and the results of modeling the security attacks by industrial engineers.

In the future, we are planning to investigate the modeling of a broader range of cyberattacks. It would be also interesting to work on visualizing the represen-tation of the results of formal modeling in SysML, e.g. to visualize the attack scenarios.

References

1. Troubitsyna, E., Laibinis, L., Pereverzeva, I., Kuismin, T., Ilic, D., Latvala, T.: Towards security-explicit formal modelling of safety-critical systems. In: Skavhaug, A., Guiochet, J., Bitsch, F. (eds.) SAFECOMP 2016. LNCS, vol. 9922, pp. 213–225. Springer, Cham (2016). https://doi.org/10.1007/978-3-319-45477-1_17
2. Vistbakka, I., Troubitsyna, E., Kuismin, T., Latvala, T.: Co-engineering safety and security in industrial control systems: a formal outlook. In: Romanovsky, A., Troubitsyna, E.A. (eds.) SERENE 2017. LNCS, vol. 10479, pp. 96–114. Springer, Cham (2017). https://doi.org/10.1007/978-3-319-65948-0_7
3. Troubitsyna, E., Vistbakka, I.: Deriving and formalising safety and security require-ments for control systems. In: Gallina, B., Skavhaug, A., Bitsch, F. (eds.) SAFE-COMP 2018. LNCS, vol. 11093, pp. 107–122. Springer, Cham (2018). https://doi.org/10.1007/978-3-319-99130-6_8
4. Poorhadi, E., Troubitysna, E., Dán, G.: Formal modelling of the impact of cyber attacks on railway safety. In: Habli, I., Sujan, M., Gerasimou, S., Schoitsch, E., Bitsch, F. (eds.) SAFECOMP 2021. LNCS, vol. 12853, pp. 117–127. Springer, Cham (2021). https://doi.org/10.1007/978-3-030-83906-2_9
5. Poorhadi, E., Troubitsyna, E., Dán, G.: Analysing the impact of security attacks on safety using SysML and event-B. In: Seguin, C., Zeller, M., Prosvirnova, T. (eds.) Model-Based Safety and Assessment. IMBSA 2022. Lecture Notes in Computer Science. vol. 13525. Springer, Cham (2022). https://doi.org/10.1007/978-3-031-15842-1_13
6. Snook, C., Butler, M.: UML-B: Formal modeling and design aided by UML. ACM Trans. Softw. Eng. Methodol. 15(1), 92–122 (2006). https://doi.org/10.1145/1125808.1125811

7. UML-B Homepage. https://www.uml-b.org/

8. Dghaym, D., Dalvandi, M., Poppleton, M., Snook, C.: Formalising the Hybrid ERTMS level 3 specification in iUML-B and Event-B. Int. J. Softw. Tools Technol. Transf. **22**(3), 297–313 (2019). https://doi.org/10.1007/s10009-019-00548-w

9. SysML Homepage. https://sysml.org/

10. The RODIN platform. http://rodin-b-sharp.sourceforge.net/

11. Abrial, J.-R.: Modeling in Event-B. Cambridge University Press (2010). https://doi.org/10.14236/ewic/ics-csr2014.1

12. Dassault Systèmes. https://www.3ds.com/

13. ATL- a model transformation technology. https://www.eclipse.org/atl/

14. Rose editor. https://sourceforge.net/projects/rodin-b-sharp/files/Plugin_Rose_Editor/

15. EBSysMLSec. https://github.com/Poorhadi/HAZOP-EBSysMLSec

16. ERTMS/ETCS signaling system. https://www.era.europa.eu/domains/infrastructure/european-rail-traffic-management-system-ertms_en

17. Ministry of Defence: Interim Defence Standard 00–58/1: Hazop Studies on Systems. Directorate of Standardization (1994)

18. Case Study including proof. https://github.com/Poorhadi/MovingBlockSysML

19. Chothia, T., Ordean, M., De Ruiter, J., Thomas, R.J.: An attack against message authentication in the ERTMS train to trackside communication protocols. In: Proceedings of the 2017 ACM on Asia Conference on Computer and Communications Security, pp. 743–756. ACM (2017)

20. Zhang, Q., Huang, Z., Xie, J.: Distributed system model using SysML and event-B. In: Gu, X., Liu, G., Li, B. (eds.) MLICOM 2017. LNICST, vol. 226, pp. 326–336. Springer, Cham (2018). https://doi.org/10.1007/978-3-319-73564-1_32

21. Tueno Fotso, S.J., Mammar, A., Laleau, R., Frappier, M.: Event-B expression and verification of translation rules between SysML/KAOS domain models and B system specifications. In: Butler, M., Raschke, A., Hoang, T.S., Reichl, K. (eds.) ABZ 2018. LNCS, vol. 10817, pp. 55–70. Springer, Cham (2018). https://doi.org/10.1007/978-3-319-91271-4_5

22. Salunkhe, S., Berglehner, R., Rasheeq, A.: Automatic transformation of SysML model to event-B model for railway CCS application. In: Raschke, A., Méry, D. (eds.) ABZ 2021. LNCS, vol. 12709, pp. 143–149. Springer, Cham (2021). https://doi.org/10.1007/978-3-030-77543-8_14

23. Masson, É., Gransart, C.: Cyber security for railways – a huge challenge – Shift2Rail perspective. In: Pirovano, A. (ed.) Nets4Cars/Nets4Trains/Nets4Aircraft 2017. LNCS, vol. 10222, pp. 97–104. Springer, Cham (2017). https://doi.org/10.1007/978-3-319-56880-5_10

TrainSec: A Simulation Framework for Security Modeling and Evaluation in CBTC Networks

Amin Fakhereldine[1]([✉]), Mohammad Zulkernine[1], and Dan Murdock[2]

[1] School of Computing, Queen's University, Kingston, Canada
{20amf4,mz}@queensu.ca
[2] Connected Transport, Irdeto, Ottawa, Canada
dan.murdock@irdeto.com

Abstract. Communication-Based Train Control (CBTC) systems are automatic train control systems that improve the efficiency and safety of railway systems. They rely on bidirectional communication between trains and infrastructural components called wayside units (WSUs). CBTC components communicate using wireless protocols; therefore, providing cybersecurity is essential to protect them against cyber attacks. Securing CBTC systems involves designing attack detection and mitigation techniques and assessing their performance. However, it is neither feasible nor practical to perform testing scenarios against real CBTC networks, which proves the need for simulation frameworks. This work presents TrainSec, a simulation framework that simulates components and communications in CBTC networks according to IEEE 1474.1, the standard for CBTC performance and functional requirements. This simulator will facilitate research in the area of CBTC security by providing an environment to model attacks and evaluate defence strategies. TrainSec is an open-source and available for free on GitHub.

Keywords: CBTC Networks · Simulation Framework · Cybersecurity

1 Introduction

Communication-Based Train Control (CBTC) systems help meet the increasing demand for railway services by increasing the capacity of rail lines. Traditional train control systems use fixed-block technologies that allow only one train to occupy a block at a time, which results in long headways between trains [1]. However, CBTC systems employ moving block technologies that allow more than one train to occupy the same block simultaneously. Moving block technologies thus reduce headways between trains and permit more efficient utilization of the railway infrastructure. In addition, CBTC systems integrate Automatic Train Control (ATC) systems [2] and provide continuous safety by ensuring overspeed protection and safe distance separation between trains.

In CBTC systems, trains and wayside units (WSUs) communicate through train-to-wayside (T2W) communications. Trains send their status and mobility

B. Milius et al. (Eds.): RSSRail 2023, LNCS 14198, pp. 22–39, 2023.
https://doi.org/10.1007/978-3-031-43366-5_2

information periodically to WSUs. In return, WSUs respond by sending operational commands. Components and communications in CBTC systems can be subject to multiple cyber attacks and misbehavior techniques that can disrupt the networks or risk the safety of operations.

Providing cybersecurity for CBTC networks involves designing and implementing attack detection and mitigation techniques. The levels of success of such approaches depend on evaluating and assessing their performance in different scenarios. However, it is impractical to immobilize railway infrastructure and rolling stock to utilize them for testing purposes. Building test-specific infrastructure and vehicles can be too expensive as well. Even by assuming the feasibility of these approaches, it is challenging to study high-risk scenarios such as cyber attacks that could cause collisions or derailments of trains. Alternatively, the availability of datasets from CBTC networks can help evaluate security algorithms. However, obtaining such datasets from railway operators is extremely unlikely due to confidentiality and security reasons. This analysis explains the strong demand for a simulation framework that supports research on the security of CBTC networks.

This work presents an open-source simulator that simulates components and communications in CBTC networks according to IEEE 1474.1 [3], the standard for performance and functional requirements of CBTC systems. We call this framework "TrainSec" and implemented it as an extension of VEINS[1], a well-known simulator for vehicular networks. We chose VEINS particularly because it has been used frequently by researchers to study the security of vehicular networks. Several previous works used VEINS to simulate cyber attacks such as denial-of-service (DoS), jamming, flooding, and message replay and to evaluate countermeasures [4,5]. TrainSec provides multiple features that can be summarized as follows:

- Modeling cyber attacks and misbehavior algorithms in CBTC networks.
- Implementing detection and mitigation algorithms.
- Utilizing the provided misbehavior algorithms.
- Evaluating the performance and effectiveness of the implemented algorithms.
- Extracting datasets for data visualization purposes.

The rest of this paper is organized as follows: Sect. 2 presents the related work, and Sect. 3 introduces CBTC systems. Section 4 defines the system model, Sect. 5 explains the TrainSec framework, and Sect. 6 discusses some simulation scenarios. Finally, Sect. 7 concludes the work.

2   Related Work

This section discusses previous approaches to simulate Communication-Based Train Control (CBTC) Systems and their components. It also discusses some simulation frameworks that enable studying the impacts of cyber attacks on the railway and vehicular networks.

---

[1] https://veins.car2x.org/.

Mera et al. [6] presented a simulation test bench for CBTC trackside. Their tool helps reduce the efforts of testing and validating signalling equipment while commissioning or upgrading rail lines. However, it does not implement the essential functional requirements provided in the IEEE 1474.1 standard [3], such as automatic train protection (ATP) and automatic train operation (ATO). Chen et al. [2] introduced a software program that simulates trains' movement in CBTC systems and facilitates performance analysis. The main functions of the simulator are calculating the system headway and the speed profile given a system configuration and a block design. However, it does not implement wayside functionality and train-to-wayside (T2W) communications.

Cho et al. [7] modeled the functionality of the train on-board components. Their system implemented some of the ATO functions required by IEEE 1474.1. However, they did not implement the mandatory ATP functions, wayside functionality, and T2W communications. Dandoush et al. [1] implemented a framework for simulating CBTC systems that helps predict performance. The system implements modules for trains, trackside units, and communications between them. However, it does not consider the essential standardized functional requirements as well.

Xu et al. [8] presented an architecture design for a CBTC simulation platform. It includes the main components of train and trackside modules according to IEEE 1474.1, but it does not provide any implementation. Furthermore, none of the discussed approaches supports security modeling or assessment. None of them allows for implementing attacks or detection and mitigation techniques.

Soderi et al. [9] studied the cybersecurity of railway systems by surveying standards, tools, and technologies used to assess and mitigate cybersecurity risks in railway networks. The survey shows that none of the listed tools is specific to CBTC systems or can be used to evaluate the security of CBTC communications.

Some simulators considered security in railway and vehicular networks. Teo et al. [10] developed a simulation platform that analyzes the impacts of cyber-physical attacks on railway systems. Neema et al. [11] presented a simulation testbed that assesses the resilience of connected railway systems against cyber attacks. However, these simulators are not specific to CBTC systems and do not consider their main requirements.

Kamel et al. [12] introduced a simulation framework known as F^2MD that allows the implementation of cyber attacks and misbehavior techniques against vehicular networks. It also provides the ability to develop misbehavior detection algorithms and assess their effectiveness. F^2MD is an open-source simulator and an extension of VEINS [13], the vehicular networks simulator.

This work presents TrainSec, an open-source simulator for CBTC networks that extends VEINS and supports security modeling and evaluation. TrainSec also considers the functional requirements of IEEE 1474.1 and implements train functionality, wayside functionality, and T2W communications.

3   CBTC Systems

Communication-Based Train Control (CBTC) systems rely on bidirectional and continuous communication between trains and wayside units (WSUs) through high-capacity links. The IEEE 1474.1 standard [3] defines the functional requirements of CBTC systems. This section gives a brief overview of these requirements and the CBTC components and communications, then discusses the security of CBTC systems.

3.1   IEEE 1474.1 Functional Requirements

Functional requirements include automatic train protection (ATP), automatic train operation (ATO), and automatic train supervision (ATS). ATP performs several functions to prevent trains from running into hazardous conditions such as collisions and moving at excessive speeds. ATO controls trains' operations and is responsible for speed regulation and programmed stopping, besides other functionalities. ATS functions include monitoring the behavior of trains by providing schedule and headway regulation, energy optimization, system status information, and controlling stopping at stations.

3.2   CBTC Components and Communications

Components in a CBTC system can be divided into three categories, as shown in Fig. 1. Train-borne components are responsible for computing and fine-tuning a train's position and speed. They also send train status information periodically to the wayside.

Wayside components compute operational messages and send them to their surrounding trains. These components include: zone controllers (ZCs), computer interlockings (CIs), and data storage units (DSUs) [14,15]. ZCs generate limits of movement authority (LMAs) [16]. An LMA determines how far a train can move safely on the railway. CIs set safe routes for trains. DSUs provide storage and retrieval functions of the data exchanged over the network.

DCSs consist of wired and wireless communication systems that facilitate communications between CBTC components. These include IEEE 802.11 for train-to-wayside (T2W) bidirectional wireless communication and Ethernet-based solutions for on-board communications [15].

3.3   Security of CBTC Systems

The security of CBTC systems is an active research area that has been studied from different perspectives [14–20]. A range of attack vectors can affect components and communications in CBTC systems. Attackers against the network can be either insiders or outsiders and disrupt T2W and train on-board communications.

Attacks can be launched against the availability of communications, such as Denial of Service (DoS) attacks that disrupt communications between network

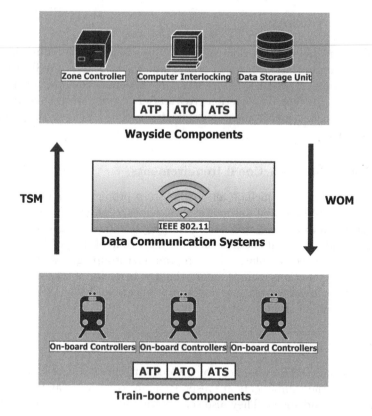

Fig. 1. CBTC components and communications.

entities. They can be achieved by flooding networks, for instance, or jamming using intentional interference. Launching a jamming attack during handoff can fail the process and interrupt the network [16,21]. Attackers can also intercept communications and perform false data injection attacks such as data tampering and message corruption. Impersonation attacks can take place in which an attacker steals the identity of a component and acts on its behalf.

In addition, active network entities could misbehave by sending false data over the network or delaying messages. Misbehavior can be done purposely by malicious entities or involuntarily by failing entities or victims of cyber attacks [12]. These attacks can manipulate or delay critical and essential messages transmitted over the network, which risks the safety of operations.

4   System Model

4.1   CBTC Model

The simulator provides generic modules for trains and wayside units (WSUs) to perform the functionality of their separate components. Figure 1 depicts these generic modules and their underlying components.

TrainSec implements the functional requirements defined in IEEE 1474.1 [3]: automatic train protection (ATP), automatic train operation (ATO), and automatic train supervision (ATS). The simulator implements the functions influenced by T2W communications and directly related to trains' movement and safe operations. Following are the functions implemented in the simulator for each functional requirement.

ATP Functions

- **Determining train location and speed:** The train-borne ATP unit determines the location and speed of a train.
- **Safe train separation:** Wayside ATP ensures that trains remain constantly separated by a defined safe distance.
- **Safe braking model:** A train's safe braking model considers different factors, including the train's length, the allowable overspeed permitted, and the maximum acceleration/deceleration rates.
- **Emergency braking:** Train-borne ATP applies emergency braking as a failsafe mechanism and guides a train to brake to a complete stop whenever it is under dangerous conditions.
- **Overspeed protection and brake assurance:** Trains are not allowed to exceed safety speed limits under any circumstances. If a train exceeds the optimal guidance profile, train-borne ATP must apply service braking. However, if a train exceeds the overspeed detection curve, train-borne ATP must apply emergency braking.
- **End-of-track protection:** Wayside ATP should prevent trains from overtraveling the end-of-track or moving beyond the end-of-track terminus.

ATO Functions

- **Automatic speed regulation:** ATO is responsible for controlling a train's movement and regulating its speed to respect speed limits.
- **Generating guidance profiles:** ATO generates the optimal speed-position guidance profiles.

ATS Functions

- **CBTC train identification and train tracking:** Trains in CBTC systems should be identified along with their specifications.
- **Automatic train regulation:** It adjusts a train's performance through schedule and headway regulation.
- **Station stopping:** It controls a train's stops and dwelling time at stations.

4.2   Train Movement Model

Trains move between stations where they depart, arrive, and stop according to predetermined schedules. The stopping points of each train are defined during its initialization phase. TrainSec adopts the train motion model defined in [20]. According to this model, a train's movement is divided into four phases: (i) an accelerating phase in which a train's speed increases uniformly to reach a predefined cruising speed, (ii) a cruising phase in which a train maintains a constant speed without accelerating, (iii) a coasting phase during which a train decelerates due to friction only, (iv) a decelerating phase where a train's speed decreases uniformly due to service braking until it reaches zero. Figure 2 illustrates changes in position, speed, and acceleration, as a function of time, of a train during normal operation.

Operational messages received from WSUs also influence a train's movement. The Limit of Movement Authority (LMA) determines the last point to which a train can drive safely. WSUs compute an LMA by considering that the train's speed will be zero at this point. Under normal operations, an LMA could be the last safe point before the rear of the preceding train, the station of destination, a switch, or the end of the track. In some abnormal cases, it could be the entrance of an unsafe route, a point of accident, or any object that must be protected [17,22]. Train on-board components use the received LMAs to calculate service braking curves (SBCs) and the emergency braking curves (EBCs). Trains also adjust their speeds and apply emergency braking according to operational messages, or due to lacking these messages for a certain time. TrainSec implements emergency stopping by immobilizing a train for a predefined period.

4.3   Communication Model

Figure 1 represents the communication model considered in TrainSec. T2W communications rely on wireless local area networks (WLANs) and mainly IEEE 802.11 [14,22]. TrainSec thus implements a CBTC network where trains and WSUs communicate using IEEE 802.11. Each train periodically broadcasts its status information in TrainStatusMessages (TSMs) to the closest WSU. A WSU captures TSMs from multiple trains, computes operational commands, and sends them in WaysideOperationalMessages (WOMs). Each WSU is responsible for communicating operational messages only with trains in its vicinity. Figure 3 shows the contents of TSMs and WOMs considered in TrainSec.

4.4   Attack Model

Communications in CBTC networks can be a target for different misbehavior and cyber attacks. Misbehaving entities can send false information in the network or delay sending critical messages. Moreover, the communications can be attacked using various attacks such as data tampering, flooding, jamming, denial-of-service (DoS), or distributed DoS (DDoS).

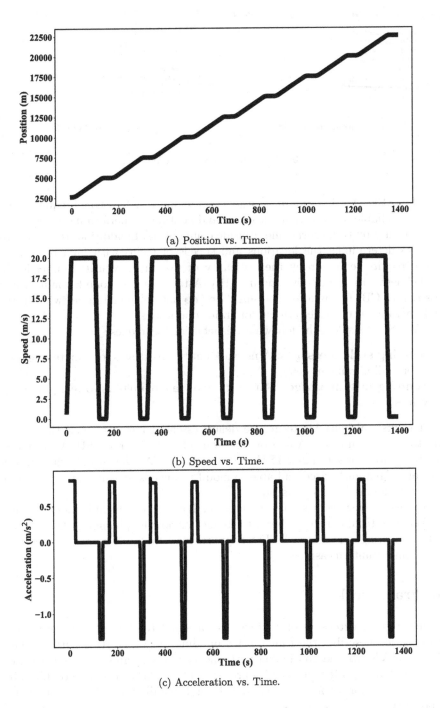

(a) Position vs. Time.

(b) Speed vs. Time.

(c) Acceleration vs. Time.

Fig. 2. Train behavior during normal operation.

```
packet TrainStatusMessage extends BaseFrame1609_4 {     packet WaysideOperationalMessage extends BaseFrame1609_4 {
    simtime_t sendTime;                                     simtime_t sendTime;
    string senderTrainId;                                   string senderWSUId;
    Coord trainPosition;                                    string receiverTrainId;
    double trainSpeed;                                      Coord senderWSUPosition;
    double trainAcceleration;                               double LMA;
    double trainLength;                                     bool reachedEOT;
    double maxSpdStpDist;                                   bool applyEmergencyBraking;
    string opPhase;                                         bool adjustSpeed;
}                                                           double desiredSpeed;
                                                        }
```

(a) Contents of TSMs.   (b) Contents of WOMs.

Fig. 3. Contents of TSMs and WOMs.

The IEEE 1474.1 standard [3] states that supporting functional requirements requires reliable T2W communications and continuous performing of essential functionality by train-borne and wayside components. In addition, the standard requires determining the locations and speeds of trains with high resolution. These requirements convey the criticality of two main security properties in CBTC networks: availability and integrity. Attacks against confidentiality cause less risk to CBTC operations because they do not delay or tamper with status and operational messages critical for trains operations.

TrainSec considers the following misbehavior techniques:

- **Sending stale messages:** A network entity broadcasts legitimate messages after adding random delays.
- **Sending false messages:** An entity adds random offsets to real parameter values.

The first misbehavior technique delays essential messages, and the second involves data tampering. A network entity can be a train or a WSU. A parameter can be position or speed in a TSM or LMA in a WOM. The misbehaving entities are considered authorized and able to modify transmission rates and parameter values in the messages they send.

Future extensions or scenarios based on TrainSec can include more complex misbehavior techniques or cyber attacks such as flooding, jamming, DoS, DDoS, data tampering, and others. VEINS supports modeling such types of attacks and evaluating countermeasures [4,5].

5   Framework

TrainSec is an extension of VEINS [13], a simulator for vehicular networks. This section describes the framework's building blocks, starting with the base simulator VEINS and continuing with the system's components and features. The simulator and its components are available as an open-source on Github[2]. More information about the components and installation are available in the repository.

---

[2] https://github.com/aminfakhereldine/TrainSec.

5.1 VEINS

VEINS is an open-source framework commonly used for simulating vehicular networks [12]. It consists of two simulators: SUMO[3] and OMNET++[4]. SUMO [23] is a road traffic simulator that provides the traffic scenario, while OMNET++ [24] is a network simulator that defines the network configuration. VEINS allows the implementation of various cyber attacks in vehicular networks [4,5].

5.2 Components

Figure 4 presents the framework's architecture. TrainSec Components represent the components added as part of the extension. The nodes represent the network entities: trains, stations, and wayside units (WSUs). The modules define the nodes' behaviors, such as sending and receiving messages and changing states. The messages represent the TrainStatusMessages (TSMs) and WaysideOperationalMessages (WOMs). The simulation manager stores values for parameters that control the simulation, such as trains' dwell time at stations and safety margins.

VEINS Components include a SUMO-ScenarioManager that defines network data (e.g., roads and infrastructure) and traffic demand (e.g., types, attributes, routes, and numbers of vehicles). OMNET-NetworkConfigurator sets the characteristics of the wireless network and launches the simulation scenario. In addition, it defines attacking nodes, attack types, and parameters. Tables 1, 2, and 3 summarize the parameters that can be defined in each component.

In a simulation, trains run between stations and exchange messages with WSUs. The simulation manager controls the trains' movement and stopping at stations. Finally, after the simulation ends, the results component stores the simulation data. This component provides the ability to extract data sets and statistical figures.

5.3 System Features

TrainSec can be easily modified or extended because of the modular nature of VEINS. The simulator allows users to model new attacks on CBTC networks and customize their characteristics. Users can implement attacks by utilizing multiple features, such as modifying the beaconing frequency or the transmission rate and replaying old messages. Security researchers can also evaluate the effects of cyber attacks and detection and mitigation techniques.

SUMO allows modeling traffic demand by defining new vehicle types and routes. It also allows using Netconvert[5] to import road network data from sources

---

[3] https://www.eclipse.org/sumo/.

[4] https://omnetpp.org/.

[5] https://sumo.dlr.de/docs/netconvert.html.

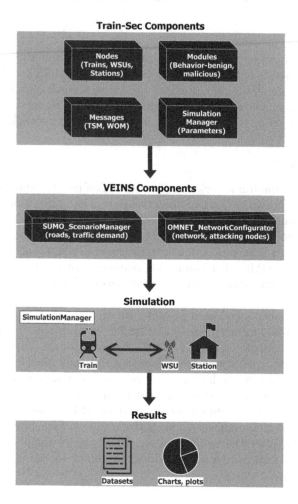

Fig. 4. TrainSec framework architecture.

Table 1. SUMO_ScenarioManager parameters.

Parameter	Value
Train length	139.14 m
Maximum speed	24.44 m/s
Acceleration	0.9 m/s^2
Service braking	-1.35 m/s^2
Emergency braking	-1.5 m/s^2
Headway	90 s

Table 2. OMNET_NetworkConfigurator parameters.

Parameter	Value
Simulation time limit	2200 s
Beaconing interval	1 s
Maximum interference	1250 m m
MAC implementation	802.11p
Thermal noise	−110 dbm
Transmit power	80 mW
Bit rate	6 mpbs

Table 3. SimulationManager parameters.

Parameter	Value
Cruising speed	20 m/s
Safety margin	25 m
Station dwell time	30 s
Emergency stopping time	60 s

like OpenStreetMap[6] and using Netedit[7] to create and edit custom road networks. OMNET++ contains models for the Internet stack and a variety of network protocols. It also includes a model for IEEE 802.11, which is commonly used in vehicular networks. Finally, TraCI[8] can be integrated with VEINS. TraCI [25] allows controlling the behavior of trains during simulation runtime and retrieving characteristics of vehicles, lanes, and other components.

6 Simulation Scenarios

6.1 Simulation Setup

For the simulations, we set up a playground that contains nine train stations and four trains. A train departs from the first station towards the last one and stops for dwell time at the intermediate stations. Train stations are separated by *2.5 kilometers* (km), and each station embodies a wayside unit (WSU) to communicate with the surrounding trains. All WSUs are installed in train stations. To set the stations' separation distance, we referred to the map of subway line 1 of the Toronto Transit Commission[9] (TTC). This line implements CBTC systems, and the long distances between its stations range between *2.5 km* and *2.7 km*.

---

[6] https://sumo.dlr.de/docs/OpenStreetMap_file.html.
[7] https://sumo.dlr.de/docs/Netedit/index.html.
[8] https://sumo.dlr.de/docs/TraCI.html.
[9] https://www.ttc.ca/routes-and-schedules/.

All trains are identical and have the same characteristics. Table 1 presents the adopted values of trains' mobility attributes, lengths, and headways. The values were set based on the features of the Toronto Rocket series[10,11], the most recent TTC train series. The Toronto Rocket trains are CBTC-equipped. Table 2 shows some network configuration parameters, and Table 3 presents some parameters from the SimulationManager module. For example, the cruising speed represents the maximum operating speed, and the safety margin represents the mandatory separation distance between trains.

6.2   Attack Scenarios

Five attack scenarios were implemented to evaluate some misbehavior techniques based on the attack model in Sect. 4.4. Four attack scenarios involve a misbehaving train, and two scenarios involve a misbehaving WSU. The misbehaving entities are chosen to be the second train or second WSU. This criterion helps show the normal behavior of the first entities, demonstrating the malicious behavior of the attacking nodes and reflecting the impact on the following entities. For comparison, Fig. 2a depicts changes in the position of a train operating in normal conditions.

Soderi et al. [9] addressed the aspect of cybersecurity in railway systems and discussed the relationship between safety and security. By surveying various attacks against railway systems and reviewing different techniques, the authors state that disrupting a single train can affect the whole railway schedule and operations. In this section, we demonstrate the effect of misbehavior attacks by showing how misbehaving trains and WSUs affect the operations in the rest of the network.

Figure 5 shows *train_1*'s misbehavior effect by delaying its TSMs by a random offset between *0* and *1 s (s)*. Delaying TSMs caused delaying sending WOMs from the wayside as well, which resulted in frequent applications of emergency brakes to protect the safety of train operations. This behavior affected the operations of *train_2* and *train_3* that were obliged to stop frequently after *train_1* to maintain safe separation.

Figure 6 reflects the consequences of *wsu_1* delaying its WOMs by a random offset between *0 s* and *1 s*. The trains moved properly until the second train station, where *wsu_1* is located. The trains applied emergency braking in the vicinity of the second station due to the delays in receiving operational commands. After that, trains resumed normal operations until reaching the last station.

Figure 7 reflects the effect of *train_1* sending false position information by adding a random value between *250* and *500 meters* (m). Using this attack, the train fooled some WSUs in its vicinity and got farther LMAs that allowed it to avoid stopping at the third and fifth stations. Moreover, all the operations were disrupted after that, and all the trips stopped at the sixth station. Furthermore, Fig. 8 shows the effect of adding a random offset between *2.5 m/s* and

---

[10] https://www.ttc.ca/transparency-and-accountability/Operating-Statistics.

[11] https://www.ttc.ca/about-the-ttc/projects-and-plans/new-subway-trains.

$3.5\,m/s$ to *train_1*'s actual speed. This behavior caused frequent applications of emergency braking due to operational commands to protect the safety of operations. Consequently, *train_2* and *train_3* slowed down and stopped to maintain safe separation from their preceding trains. We can also notice that *train_2* was moving very close to *train_1* due to faulty operational commands.

In addition, Fig. 9 represents the impact of *wsu_1* adding a random offset between *250* m and *750* m to the real LMA. All the trains skipped the second station, where *wsu_1* is located, then continued with normal operation.

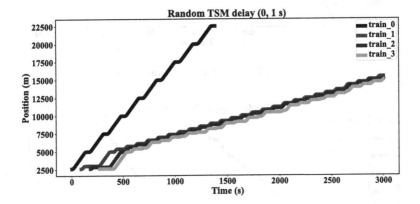

Fig. 5. Train TSM delay.

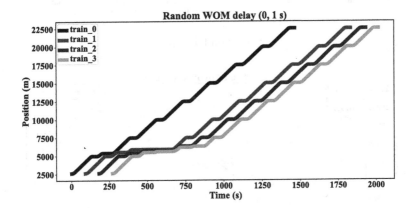

Fig. 6. WSU WOM delay.

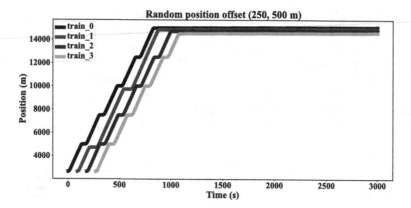

Fig. 7. Train false position.

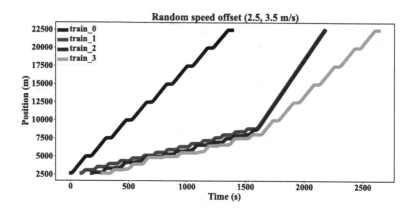

Fig. 8. Train false speed.

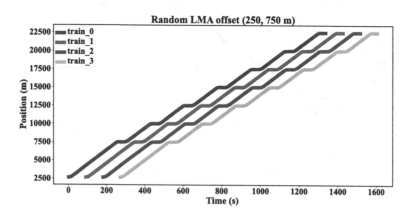

Fig. 9. WSU false LMA.

7 Conclusion

This paper presented TrainSec, a simulation framework that enables security researchers to model and assess the security of Communication-Based Train Control (CBTC) networks. It implements the functional requirements defined in IEEE 1474.1 [3], the standard for CBTC performance and functional requirements.

TrainSec solves the problem of the unavailability of datasets and real testing infrastructure to evaluate the resilience of CBTC networks against cyber attacks. It is an extension of VEINS [13], a vehicular network simulator commonly used in the security of vehicular networks. Like VEINS, TrainSec provides open extensibility due to its modular nature. Users can set their own scenarios and parameters. In addition, they can extract datasets, plots, charts, and other visualization materials.

This work showed how critical and dangerous cyber attacks against CBTC systems could be. The simulator can help find solutions to open challenges in the area of CBTC security. The main contribution of TrainSec is to provide a framework that simulates a CBTC network that can be used for security research. The currently provided scenarios include some misbehavior attacks. However, future extensions and scenarios based on TrainSec can simulate other types of cyber attacks and more complex misbehavior techniques.

The current implementation of TrainSec has some limitations and assumptions that can be addressed in future work. For example, this implementation assumes that trains apply emergency braking by stopping for a predetermined period. In a real-life scenario, a train would wait for a command from the control center to resume its operations. In addition, automatic train protection (ATP) checks for overspeed protection only when a train is in the cruising phase. The rationale is that the speed in the other phases is always less than the cruising speed, which represents the maximum operating speed.

Furthermore, TrainSec implements an ATP module that ensures the safety of trains by reducing speeds or applying emergency braking. Safety can also be achieved by increasing headways as a complementary or supplementary solution. This implementation does not include increasing headways under the assumption of increasing the utilization of the rail line. However, future extensions of TrainSec could implement and integrate it into the system.

Finally, IEEE 1474.1 considers the case when trains with different modes, CBTC-equipped and non-CBTC-equipped, share the same rail line. The scenarios currently provided in TrainSec consider all trains as CBTC-equipped. Future extensions of TrainSec can consider implementing scenarios that allow trains with mixed modes to run on the same line. It would be interesting to study the impact of integrating non-CBTC-equipped trains on the security of CBTC networks.

Acknowledgment. This work is supported by Ontario Centre of Innovation (OCI) and Irdeto Canada. The authors would like to thank them for making this project a success.

References

1. Dandoush, A., et al.: ns-3 based framework for simulating communication based train control (CBTC) systems. In: Proceedings of the 2016 Workshop on ns-3, pp. 116–123 (2016)
2. Chen, R., Guo, J.: Development of the new CBTC system simulation and performance analysis. WIT Trans. Built Environ. **114**, 497–507 (2010)
3. IEEE 1474.1 - 2004: IEEE standard for communications-based train control (CBTC) performance and functional requirements (2004)
4. Kamel, J., Wolf, M., Van Der Hei, R. W., Kaiser, A., Urien, P., Kargl, F.: Veremi extension: a dataset for comparable evaluation of misbehavior detection in vanets. In: ICC 2020-IEEE International Conference on Communications (ICC), pp. 1–6. IEEE (2020)
5. Maleki, M., Malik, M., Folkesson, P., Sangchoolie, B., Karlsson, J.: Modeling and Evaluating the Effects of Jamming Attacks on Connected Automated Road Vehicles. In: 2022 IEEE 27th Pacific Rim International Symposium on Dependable Computing (PRDC), pp. 12–23. IEEE (2022)
6. Mera, J.M., Gómez-Rey, I., Rodrigo, E.: CBTC test simulation bench. WIT Trans. Built Environ. **114**, 485–495 (2010)
7. Cho, C.-H., Choi, D.-H., Quan, Z.-H., Choi, S.-A., Park, G.-S., Ryou, M.-S.: Modeling of CBTC carborne ATO functions using SCADE. In: 11th International Conference on Control, pp. 1089–1093. IEEE (2011)
8. Xu, J., Chen, L., Gao, W., Zhao, M.: CBTC simulation platform design and study. J. Comput. Commun. **3**(9), 61 (2015)
9. Soderi, S., Masti, D., Lun, Y. Z.: Railway cyber-security in the era of interconnected systems: a survey. IEEE Trans. Intell. Transport. Syst. (2023)
10. Teo, Z.-T., et al.: SecureRails: towards an open simulation platform for analyzing cyber-physical attacks in railways. In: 2016 IEEE Region 10 Conference (TENCON), pp. 95–98. IEEE (2016)
11. Neema, H., Koutsoukos, X., Potteiger, B., Tang, C., Stouffer, K.: Simulation testbed for railway infrastructure security and resilience evaluation. In: 7th Symposium on Hot Topics in the Science of Security, pp. 1–8 (2020)
12. Kamel, J., Ansari, M.R., Petit, J., Kaiser, A., Jemaa, I.B.: Urien: simulation framework for misbehavior detection in vehicular networks. IEEE Trans. Veh. Technol. **69**(6), 6631–6643 (2020)
13. Sommer, C., German, R., Dressler, F.: Bidirectionally coupled network and road traffic simulation for improved IVC analysis. IEEE Trans. Mob. Comput. **10**(1), 3–15 (2010)
14. Zhang, W., Bu, B., Wang, H.: An intrusion detection method of data tampering attack in communication-based train control system. In: 2019 IEEE Intelligent Transportation Systems Conference (ITSC), pp. 345–350. IEEE (2019)
15. Fakhereldine, A., Zulkernine, M., Murdock, D.: Detecting intrusions in communication-based train control systems. In: ICC 2022-IEEE International Conference on Communications, pp. 4193–4198. IEEE (2022)
16. Zhu, L., Li, Y., Yu, F.R., Ning, B., Tang, T., Wang, X.: Cross-layer defense methods for jamming-resistant CBTC systems. IEEE Trans. Intell. Transp. Syst. **22**(11), 7266–7278 (2020)
17. Li, Y., Zhu, L., Wang, H., Yu, F.R., Liu, S.: A cross-layer defense scheme for edge intelligence-enabled CBTC systems against MitM attacks. IEEE Trans. Intell. Transp. Syst. **22**(4), 2286–2298 (2020)

18. Li, Y., Zhu, L.: A Bayesian game based defense scheme for CBTC systems under man-in-the-middle attacks. In: 2019 IEEE Intelligent Transportation Systems Conference (ITSC), pp. 2172–2176. IEEE (2019)

19. Kim, S., Won, Y., Park, I., Eun, Y., Park, K.-J.: Cyber-physical vulnerability analysis of communication-based train control. IEEE Internet Things J. **6**(4), 6353–6362 (2019)

20. Lakshminarayana, S., et al.: Signal jamming attacks against communication-based train control: attack impact and countermeasure. In: 11th ACM Conference on Security and Privacy in Wireless and Mobile Networks, pp. 160–171 (2018)

21. Zhu, L., He, Y., Yu, F.R., Ning, B., Tang, T., Zhao, N.: Communication-based train control system performance optimization using deep reinforcement learning. IEEE Trans. Veh. Technol. **66**(2), 10705–10717 (2017)

22. Sedjelmaci, H., Guenab, F., Boudguiga, A., Petiot, Y.: Cooperative security framework for CBTC network. In: 2018 IEEE International Conference on Communications (ICC), pp. 1–6. IEEE (2018)

23. Lopez, P.A., et al.: Microscopic traffic simulation using sumo. In: 2018 21st International Conference on Intelligent Transportation Systems (ITSC), pp. 2575–2582. IEEE (2018)

24. Varga, A., Hornig, R.: An overview of the OMNeT++ simulation environment. In: 1st International ICST Conference on Simulation Tools and Techniques for Communications, Networks and Systems (2010)

25. Wegener, A., Piórkowski, M., Raya, M., Hellbrück, H., Fischer, S., Hubaux, J.-P.: TraCI: an interface for coupling road traffic and network simulators. In: 11th Communications and Networking Simulation Symposium, pp. 155–163 (2008)

Tooled Approaches and Dependability of Highly Automated Transport Systems

Safety Analysis of Automatic Train Operation Based on ETCS

Ziyue Tang[1](✉), Ning Zhao[2], Khalid Khan[3], and Katinka Wolter[1](✉)

[1] Freie Universität Berlin, 14195 Berlin, Germany
ziyuet97@zedat.fu-berlin.de, katinka.wolter@fu-berlin.de
[2] University of Birmingham, Birmingham B15 3SA, UK
n.zhao@bham.ac.uk
[3] Alstom Transportation, Derby DE24 8AD, UK
khalid.khan@alstomgroup.com

Abstract. In Germany and throughout Europe, train operation using the European Train Control System (ETCS) is the most common solution for current trains running on the mainlines. This paper presents a safety analysis of the Automatic Train Operation (ATO) system. The System Modeling Language (SysML) is used to visually model the logical relationships of the mainline ATO system based on ETCS. The Failure Mode and Effect Analysis (FMEA) is used to perform a qualitative safety analysis to identify all possible failure modes of the system. State-space modeling and dynamic quantitative analysis are carried out using a Markov chain model. In order to verify the degree of safety of the ATO model, a real data set from a train operator was used for simulation. We show that using an ETCS-based ATO system to control trains can achieve higher reliability on the mainline with less maintenance than if experienced drivers control trains.

Keywords: ATO · ETCS · SysML · Markov chain · safety analysis

1 Introduction

The advanced development of high-speed railways has made rail travel easier and more popular in both short and long distance trips. Ensuring the consumers' and operators' safety and convenience leads to high requirements for train control as well as railway communication signalling. Existing research and industry reports [1] have indicated that the driver can no longer rely on manual signal recognition to operate safely. The speed of the trains increased to a level where the driver has too short a time to observe and confirm signals on the line side. In order to ensure safe and efficient train operation each country is developing its own Automatic Train Operation (ATO) system. This is well-known in urban railways and receives increasing interest for mainline railways to improve their capacity and punctuality [2].

However, the application of ATO in the main railway lines has stagnated for nearly 30 years, and it has not kept up with the corresponding development of

B. Milius et al. (Eds.): RSSRail 2023, LNCS 14198, pp. 43–61, 2023.
https://doi.org/10.1007/978-3-031-43366-5_3

technology. One of the main reasons could be that various stakeholders do not yet trust the safety and security of ATO on the mainline. Analysing the large-scale safety of ATO on the mainline is not only the direction of the development of global railway operations, but also demonstrates the maturity of ATO. On the other hand, the application of ATO technology on mainlines has not progressed significantly for a long time after the use of GOA2 by the Czech Railways in 1991. For example, it wasn't until March 2018 that the UK implemented the first mainline at Thameslink in London, and the degree of automation was still GOA2 [3].

Even though there are still many open problems academic research on ATO technology still mainly focuses on algorithm updating, aiming to minimise the energy consumption and carbon emissions during automatic train operation. Several papers have discussed simulation studies of automatic train driving systems [4], including a train model [5,6], train control algorithms [7], an adaptive algorithm for ATO control parameters [7,8], the control algorithm and multi-objective optimization of the ATO system of urban rail [9]. In terms of energy saving optimization control one can find search methods for idling control, artificial intelligence network and genetic algorithm for idling control, decision control for energy saving [10,13,14], extreme value control for solving control transformation point to improve energy efficiency [11] and a locomotive handling guidance system based on optimal train operation [12]. In recent years, some papers study the safety of train operation. Enrique Castillo et al. [15] used Bayesian networks to conduct safety analysis on the behavior of drivers and the causes of accidents. A Markov-Bayesian network is used for safety analysis of the driver's attention [16]. A hypothesis and method for analyzing the impact of railway automation on the capacity of the main railway line [17] has been published.

The safety demand for an ATO system is not only important for passengers, but also one of the important indicators for the railway industry to consider its feasibility. For example, after analysing the statistical results of hundreds of thousands of samples, Dea van Lierop et al. [18] concluded that in public transportation the requirement for safety of passengers is even higher than the demand for punctuality.

This paper conducts a detailed safety analysis of the ATO system based on the European Train Control System (ETCS). Simulations were carried out using 6925 h historical fault operation data from a Train operating company to verify that trains with ATO systems on European mainlines are safe enough to be fully driverless.

We use the Unified Modeling Language (UML) to visually model the logical relationship of the ETCS-based ATO system. First, the Block Definition Diagram (BDD) and Internal Block Diagram (IBD) belonging to the System Modeling Language (SysML) are used to display the package structure content of the ATO subsystems and blocks. After the ATO is systematically decomposed, the Failure Mode and Effects Analysis (FMEA) is used for qualitative safety analysis to identify all possible failure modes of the system. Then state space modeling is performed using a Markov chain to obtain dynamic quantitative analysis results. The safety study verifies that the ETCS-based ATO system in the main railway environment is very reliable and safe. Finally, the model is placed in a simulation environment of multiple sets of fault data for validation and verification.

The structure of this paper is as follows. The next section introduces our model of the mainline ATO system based on ETCS, which includes the introduction of the ATO system and the establishment of the structural model. In Sect. 3 FMEA is used for qualitative safety analysis, and the system failure modes are decomposed. Section 4 uses a Markov chain to carry out quantitative safety analysis and determine the reliability of the system. Section 5 shows our validation and verification, placing the model in a failure environment. Section 6 concludes this paper.

2 Modelling the Mainline ETCS Automatic Train Operation System

In this section we will introduce the European Train Control System (ETCS) as well as the functionalities of the Automatic Train Operation (ATO). We will describe different aspects and versions different models which we have developed for the ETCS automatic train control.

2.1 Brief Introduction to ATO with ETCS

The ETCS is a unified and open signalling system organised and developed by the European Railway Authority (ERA) to solve the interconnection and compatibility problems of various national railway signalling systems in Europe. While compatible with the existing signal systems, ETCS realises seamless transition of trains across various countries in the European railway network.

In 2001, the European Union (EU) legislated ETCS as a mandatory technical specification to ensure the interconnection of high-speed trains in the European railway network. With technical innovation and more extensive interconnection requirements the system specification is also constantly updated and extended. In 2008 and 2016, the EU officially released the baseline 2 (2.3.0d) version and the baseline 3 (3.6.0) version of the ETCS system specification, respectively [20]. In recent years, in order to improve the transportation capacity and efficiency of the lines, the ERA began to organise research on superimposing ATO on the basis of ETCS. An ATO system based on ETCS uses a wireless channel independent of ETCS to transmit vehicle-to-ground information.

ETCS is divided into three grades, namely ETCS-Level 1, ETCS-Level 2 and ETCS-Level 3 (Fig. 1). The top shows the one-way transmission of information from L1 to the driver using the signals. The middle one shows L2 using RBC to communicate with the train. The bottom shows L3 using the central controller to get rid of the block occupation by interlocking.

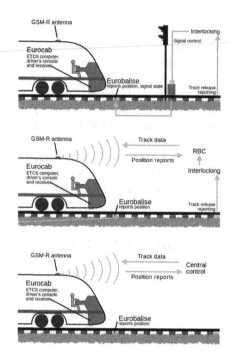

Fig. 1. ETCS design of level 1,2 and 3

Figure 2 shows how the various subsystems of an ATO system with an ETCS system cooperate to complete the entire process of the mission of controlling the movement of the train. The train reads information from trackside and on-board sensors and displays it in the train indicator; the ETCS always synchronises the train's position and speed with the indicator. The ATO system receives the speed limit from the indicator and the ETCS's recommended operating strategy and generates a speed profile for the train to execute.

Trains on the mainline (especially on cross-border lines) railway sections are supported by different operators which may implement different levels of ETCS. Therefore a train may encounter sections of different levels of ETCS on its travel. Such objective conditions require that the on-board ATO system must contain the ETCS level 1–3 full coverage equipment to ensure that the train can switch the communication mode with the lineside facilities anytime and anywhere during the operation. Of course, this design also implicitly increases the redundancy of the ATO system and improves safety.

2.2   The Components of ETCS

The ETCS system is divided into two sub-systems: the on-board and the track-side part. Because different levels of ETCS contain different optional components, they will also be described in different structures and they need to be

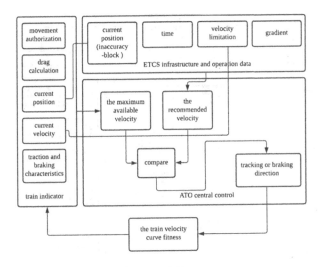

Fig. 2. Functional subsystems

distinguished. According to the subset 125 normative specification [19], among the components that belong to the on-board subsystem are the Euro Vital Computer (EVC), the Driver Machine Interface (DMI), the Train Interface Unit (TIU), the Juridical Recording Unit (JRU), the Balise Transmission Module (BTM), the Loop Transmission Module (LTM), the On-board radio communication system (Euroradio), the Odometry system, and the Specific Transmission Module (STM). Among them, EVC is the core of on-board sub-system, interacts with the driver through DMI, controls the powertrain through TIU, and records data through JRU. BTM and LTM participate in the process of rail-to-train interaction, and euroradio realises two-way interaction. STM is used to switch the ETCS level. Odometry system is a combination of sensors.

The components belonging to the trackside sub-system are the Euro-balise, the Lineside Electronic Unit (LEU), the radio block centre (RBC), interlocking, Euroloop, and Radio Block Interface Unit (RIU). Among them, RBC is the core of the trackside sub-system, interacts with interlocking and balise through LEU, and transmits information to the train through RIU.

Notably, LTM, Euroloop and RIU are equipped in ETCS L1, while RBC is equipped in L2 and L3.

2.3 The ATO Block Definition Diagram

The block definition diagram of the ATO system based on the above component information shown in Fig. 3 for the trackside subsystem. Figure 4 illustrates the components of the on-board system.

The BDD shows the block elements with the corresponding data types and units. The values shows the block's restrictions on the value of certain data.

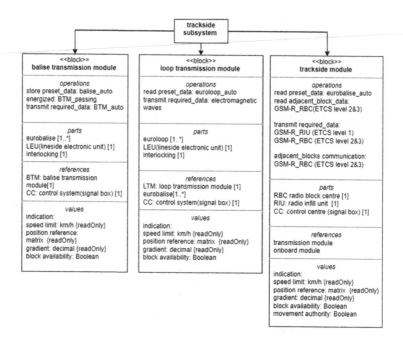

Fig. 3. Block definition diagram (trackside subsystem)

2.4 The Internal Definitions

After the establishment of BDD, the encapsulated blocks of the ATO system based on ETCS can be obtained. Different blocks are responsible for independent tasks, and at the same time they participate in related tasks with different divisions of labour. In order to understand the connections between subsystems at a deeper level (components), especially the interfaces between internal parts, an IBD (internal block diagram) is established as shown in Fig. 5.

According to further deconstructing, the IBD diagram decomposes the ATO system from the subsystem level to the component level. We decomposed the ATO subsystem into six relatively independent modules, analysed the interfaces between the components, and the direction and content of information transmission. Although the IBD diagram is commonly used for static analysis, since most of the information transmission in this example is one-way, part of the sequence of missions can be obtained for the most basic dynamic analysis.

Notably, in order to distinguish the ATO system and the Unattended Train Operation (UTO) system, we use a dotted line to separate the process of driver participation from the equipment. In short, after removing all the dotted lines, the remaining IBD can be used to describe the operation of the UTO system.

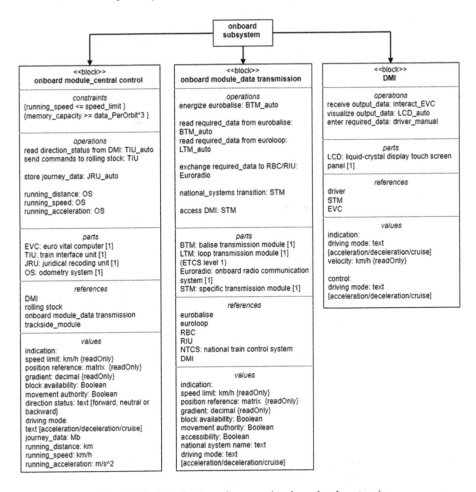

Fig. 4. Block definition diagram (on-board subsystem)

3   Qualitative Safety Analysis by FMEA

After building the structure of the mainline ATO system based on ETCS, the security of the system will be qualitatively analysed. The complexity of the ATO system is manifested in the diversity of components and the number of interfaces. Therefore, in order to be able to review as many components and subsystems as possible during the analysis process, we use the Failure Mode and Effects Analysis (FMEA) for qualitative analysis. One feature of FMEA is that it can examine the potential failure modes in a large number of components and interfaces and analyse the causes and possible effects of different failure modes.

However, the most difficult point is that due to the multi-threaded redundancy in the system, the failure of the system generally is caused by combined

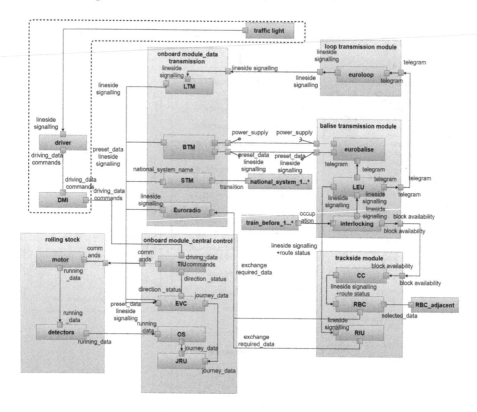

Fig. 5. Internal block diagram

failures of different components. FMEA's is well-suited analyse single-point failures but investigating combined failures is not straight forward.

In order to solve this problem, we have added the combined failure type to the column of system failure effects. Please note that the plus sign (+) means that when the type of failure shown in this line, one of the other failure modes is added, resulting in a combined failure. For simplicity, we only fill in the number after the plus sign (+) to represent the serial numbers of other types of failures listed in this FMEA list.

The main reason why this can be added to the FMEA is that the component failures of the system do not have cascading failures. Each component is relatively independent during operation. For example, the failure of Eurobalise will not cause any failure of EVC. It will only be combined with other single points of failure to cause EVC's mission to fail to complete as expected. The qualitative analysis results are shown in the appendix.

With the FMEA, we identified 29 sets of failure modes for 14 components. Most of the system-level hazards require successive failures of multiple components. This would make the probability of degradation of the ATO system much higher than the probability of downtime. The time between successive maintenance is determined by the probability of degradation or failure. In the next section we will use the failure modes presented in the FMEA to calculate the probability of failure and thus develop a maintenance strategy.

4 Quantitative Safety Analysis Using a Markov Chain

The qualitative FMEA analysis provides us with a series of combinations of component failures leading to system failure. Some of them will lead to the degradation of the system (the system can complete the set missions, but its level of redundancy is reduced). Others will lead to the complete failure of the system (the system can no longer complete any set missions). In order to dynamically and quantitatively analyse the safety of the system, we have derived a Markov chain for the ATO system.

A Markov chain is a probabilistic state transition model that can quantitatively and probabilistically analyse all the enumerated states. Starting from an initial state the probability of reaching all other states at a certain time can be computed. A long-term stationary solution can be obtained if certain conditions hold. Unfortunately, those conditions are not satisfied in our model and therefore we stay with transient analysis.

To ensure the validity of the model, the following assumptions are made. First, the state transition function of the components is constant, hence the failure rate and the maintenance rate follow the exponential distribution. Second, only one event (e.g. failure) can happen at each point in time. Multiple events at the same time are assumed very unlikely and are not considered. The latter assumption seems realistic for an ATO system. Therefore, the ATO system satisfies the requirements of Markov modelling. However, the model has absorbing states (states, which are never again left when being reached) and therefore a stationary solution does not exist.

In order to simplify the model, the quantitative analysis process only analyses the core task of the ATO system, which is to receive the minimum value of the required information and complete the entire process of the algorithm to control the safe operation of the train. It is necessary for the train to receive at least one movement authority and lineside signal at the same time. This is because when the train does not receive the movement authority and lineside signal of the current block, the train must stop immediately to avoid collisions with other trains or obstacles that may exist. In addition, EVC controls basically all algorithms, information collection and train control processes of the ATO system. Therefore, in order to ensure that the ATO system can complete this series of tasks during operation and ensure the safety of train operation, the normal operation of at least one EVC is necessary.

Figure 6 indicates that each state in the Markov chain represents a degraded state of the system in different aspects due to failures of different components. The arrows in the figure indicate the failure rate and repair rate. The combination of failure rates comes from the analysis results of the FMEA. The three states with colors represent the subsystem in a failure state, at which point the system stops operating. As for the value of failure and repair rates, we used existing data from [21], as shown in Table 1.

Table 1. The Reliability Parameter of Components

Name	Failure rate/ h-1	Repair rate/ h-1
EVC_ Internal fault	1.49*10–4 (I9.6)	0.3 (μ9.6)
EVC_disconnection	6.00*10–6 (I9.1–I9.4)	0.0625 (μ9)
Interlocking	2.3*10–6 (I2.1, I2.2)	0.3 (μ2)
RBC	1.45*10–8 (I5.2)	0.3 (μ5)
RIU	1.8*10–5 (I6.1)	0.3 (μ6)
Eurobalise	7*10–8 (I1)	0.25 (μ1)
LEU_RIU disconnection	1.8*10–5 (I3.2)	0.3 (μ3)
LEU_balise&loop disconnection	2.1*10–6 (I3.1, I3.3)	0.3 (μ3)
TIU	2.35*10–5 (I10)	0.3 (μ10)
DMI	5*10–6 (I15)	0.3 (μ15)
OS	2.5*10–9 (I11)	0.25 (μ11)
Euroloop	1*10–6 (I7.1)	0.3 (μ7)
CC	3.4*10–5 (I4.1)	0.3 (μ4)

Notably, the rates in the table have been mapped to the failure modes in the FMEA and are marked in parentheses after the rates. For example, I9.6 means the 9.6 failure of FMEA, which is internal fault of EVC. Since the model is a homogeneous continuous-time Markov chain, to obtain the probability distribution of each state under stable conditions, the reliability parameter of components needs to be brought into the following equation.

$$\pi(t) = \pi(0)e^{At} = \pi(0)\left(1 + \sum_{n=1}^{\infty} \frac{A^n t^n}{n!}\right) \tag{1}$$

where $\pi_x(t)$ represents the probability that the Markov model is in state x at time t. The state probability vector $\pi(t)$ includes 14 elements, π_0 to π_{13}, which is the probability distribution across the states at time t (in hours). Figure 6 shows the simplified notation of the state transition diagram.

Each number in Fig. 6 represents the status of the ATO system. State 0 means that all components of the ATO system are in a successful state. State 6 means that the train is out of service due to loss of movement authorization. State 9 means that the ATO system is out of service due to a total failure of the EVC system. State 13 represents a complete failure of the ATO system and the train system.

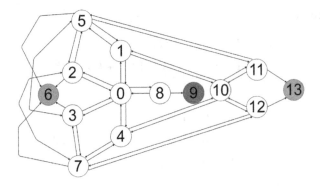

Fig. 6. Numbering of states of the Markov chain

$$A = \begin{pmatrix}
\Lambda_0 & I_A & I_B & I_C & I_D & 0 & 0 & 0 & 2I_E & 0 & 0 & 0 & 0 & 0 \\
\mu_A & \Lambda_1 & 0 & 0 & 0 & I_B & 0 & 0 & 0 & 0 & I_D & 0 & 0 & 0 \\
\mu_B & 0 & \Lambda_2 & 0 & 0 & I_A & I_D & I_D & 0 & 0 & 0 & 0 & 0 & 0 \\
\mu_C & 0 & 0 & \Lambda_3 & 0 & I_B & I_B & I_D & 0 & 0 & 0 & 0 & 0 & 0 \\
\mu_D & 0 & 0 & 0 & \Lambda_4 & 0 & 0 & I_C & 0 & 0 & I_A & 0 & 0 & 0 \\
0 & \mu_B & \mu_A & \mu_A & 0 & \Lambda_5 & I_C & 0 & 0 & 0 & 0 & I_D & 0 & 0 \\
0 & 0 & 0 & 0 & 0 & 0 & 0 & 0 & 0 & 0 & 0 & 0 & 0 & 0 \\
0 & 0 & \mu_D & \mu_D & \mu_C & 0 & I_B & \Lambda_7 & 0 & 0 & 0 & 0 & I_A & 0 \\
\mu_E & 0 & 0 & 0 & 0 & 0 & 0 & \Lambda_8 & I_E & 0 & 0 & 0 & 0 & 0 \\
0 & 0 & 0 & 0 & 0 & 0 & 0 & 0 & 0 & 0 & 0 & 0 & 0 & 0 \\
0 & \mu_D & 0 & 0 & \mu_A & 0 & 0 & 0 & 0 & 0 & \Lambda_{10} & I_B & I_C & 0 \\
0 & 0 & 0 & 0 & 0 & \mu_D & 0 & 0 & 0 & 0 & \mu_B & \Lambda_{11} & 0 & I_C \\
0 & 0 & 0 & 0 & 0 & 0 & \mu_A & 0 & 0 & \mu_C & 0 & \Lambda_{12} & I_C \\
0 & 0 & 0 & 0 & 0 & 0 & 0 & 0 & 0 & 0 & 0 & 0 & 0 & 0
\end{pmatrix}, \qquad (2)$$

A is a square matrix used to describe the transitions of a continuous-time Markov chain. It adds up to zero for all elements in each row. And each row in A represents a state in the Markov model. All states can be collected in the vector π and the transitions between states form the matrix A. The transition matrix is a $14 * 14$ square matrix as shown in Eq. (2).

Where Λ_i is the negative sum of all other elements in column i of the matrix.

The values from IA to IE and μA to μD are as follows. Among them, letter 'I' represents the failure rate, 'μ' represents the repair rate, and the naming of A to E enumerates the different operational modes. Since the failure factors are independent of each other, the failure rate required for a failure mode is the sum of the failure rates of each component in the minimal cut set. The calculation method of the maintenance rate is not a simple addition. This is because the unit of the repair rate is h^1, so it is necessary to calculate the repair time and take the reciprocal.

$$I_A = I_{7.1} + I_{3.3} + I_{9.1}$$
$$= 1 \times 10^{-6} + 2.1 \times 10^{-6} + 6 \times 10^{-6} \tag{3}$$
$$= 9.1 \times 10^{-6}$$

$$I_B = I_{3.2} + I_{6.1} + I_{9.4}$$
$$= 1.8 \times 10^{-5} + 1.8 \times 10^{-5} + 6 \times 10^{-6} \tag{4}$$
$$= 4.2 \times 10^{-5}$$

$$I_C = I_{5.2} + I_{4.1} + I_{9.4}$$
$$= 1.45 \times 10^{-8} + 3.4 \times 10^{-5} + 6 \times 10^{-6} \tag{5}$$
$$= 4.00145 \times 10^{-5}$$

$$I_D = I_1 + I_{2.2} + I_{3.1} + I_{9.2}$$
$$= 7 \times 10^{-8} + 2.3 \times 10^{-6} + 2.1 \times 10^{-6} + 6 \times 10^{-6} \tag{6}$$
$$= 10.47 \times 10^{-6}$$

$$I_E = I_{9.6} = 1.49 \times 10^{-4} \tag{7}$$

Notably, since the link between the EVC and the on-board module consists of the bus, when the EVC is disconnected from any of the LTM, BTM, STM and Euroradio modules, the repair process will take 4 times the time of fixing a single line. In addition, since system operation stops with system-level failure, states $6, 9$ and 13 are absorbing states.

$$\mu_A = \frac{1}{1/\mu_3 + 1/\mu_7 + 4/\mu_9} = 3/212 \tag{8}$$

$$\mu_B = \frac{1}{1/\mu_3 + 1/\mu_6 + 4/\mu_9} = 3/212 \tag{9}$$

$$\mu_C = \frac{1}{1/\mu_4 + 1/\mu_5 + 4/\mu_9} = 3/212 \tag{10}$$

$$\mu_D = \frac{1}{1/\mu_1 + 1/\mu_2 + 1/\mu_3 + 4/\mu_9} = 3/224 \tag{11}$$

The maintenance interval of the current railway system can take on two values according to whether a small or full maintenance is performed: one week and one month. ATO failure corresponding to state 9 is subsystem failures and defaults to a maintenance interval of 28 days. In contrast, train failures corresponding to state 6 and state 13 result in a complete system shutdown. This is a system level failure and defaults to a maintenance interval of one week.

In order to analyse whether the current railway system maintenance strategy meets the needs of the ATO3 class system, the probabilities of the three different failure states are calculated.

$$U_i = [-Q]^{-1} * R_i, \tag{12}$$

where U_i represents a vector which contains the probability of absorption in the i−th absorbing state when starting from a non-absorbing state. Q represents the transition matrix for the transitions from non-absorbing states to non-absorbing states. Hence, Q is obtained from A by removing the rows where all entries are zero, as well as the corresponding columns. R_i denotes the vector of probabilities of a transition from the non-absorbing states to the absorbing states.

$$U = \begin{pmatrix} 0.1743 & 0.8257 & 0.0000 \\ 0.1743 & 0.8257 & 0.0000 \\ 0.1749 & 0.8251 & 0.0000 \\ 0.1767 & 0.8233 & 0.0000 \\ 0.1743 & 0.8257 & 0.0000 \\ 0.1760 & 0.8239 & 0.0000 \\ 0.1761 & 0.8239 & 0.0000 \\ 0.1738 & 0.8262 & 0.0000 \\ 0.1743 & 0.8257 & 0.0000 \\ 0.1749 & 0.8237 & 0.0015 \\ 0.1749 & 0.8237 & 0.0014 \end{pmatrix} \quad U^* = \begin{pmatrix} 0.1743 & 0.8257 \\ 0.1743 & 0.8257 \\ 0.1749 & 0.8251 \\ 0.1767 & 0.8233 \\ 0.1743 & 0.8257 \\ 0.1761 & 0.8239 \\ 0.1761 & 0.8239 \\ 0.1738 & 0.8262 \\ 0.1743 & 0.8257 \\ 0.1763 & 0.8237 \\ 0.1763 & 0.8237 \end{pmatrix} \quad P = \begin{pmatrix} 33.1712 \\ 33.1700 \\ 33.0306 \\ 32.6162 \\ 33.1699 \\ 32.7613 \\ 32.7501 \\ 33.2670 \\ 33.1685 \\ 32.6983 \\ 32.6943 \end{pmatrix} \tag{13}$$

When the ATO system is in state i, the probability of the type of fault being a train fault, a system fault, or a double fault in the event of failure is shown in row i of U. Considering that state 13 has the same maintenance needs as state 6, the first and third columns have been combined to the first column of U^*.

State 9 corresponds to a time interval of 7 days for maintenance of major failure. Considering that the probability of the system falling into an absorbing state should be inversely proportional to the maintenance interval, states 6 and 13, which have a lower probability of absorption, could have longer maintenance intervals. The expected interval of the maintenance of minor failure in each state is determined as shown in P. It is therefore proposed to adjust the system level maintenance interval from 28 days to 33 days, which will reduce maintenance costs.

5 Experimental Validation and Verification

We evaluate the developed Markov chain model for perform safety analysis of the ETCS-based ATO system. The objective is to compare the reliability of the ATO system with that of the conventional ETCS system. We have implemented the model in Python to simulate the Markov chain which represents the operation of the ATO system. The results are compared with the respective failure probabilities in the data set.

Table 2. Frequency statistics by failure mode of ETCS

Sort	Times	Fault mode
T	4	BC/FC (Battery Charger/Fault Condition): MVB-PD-communication from battery charger faulty
T	1	C: MVB-PD-communication from TCU faulty
E	1	Shutdown profile: battery off after transfer to emergency operation
E	1	BCU (Brake Control Unit)-speed EC (Electronic Control) implausible
E	1	EC: MVB-PD(Multifunction Vehicle Bus- Protocol Data)-communication from TCU faulty
E	2	MCB (Main Circuit Breakers) ETCS accordingly ATP2TCR switched off
E	1	VCB (Vacuum Circuit Breaker) OFF from slave-CCU
E	3	No automatic train protection active
E	3	Emergency brake for 48 h
T&E	1	Automatic train stopping DNRA (Driver's Notification of Route Acquisition)
T&E	1	Failure CCU (Central Control Unit)

Based on a train operating company's ETCS fault dataset for a particular train, a data pattern frequency statistics table was created as shown in Table 2. The dataset contains 6925 h of train operation fault history. As different systems have completely different downgrade logic, it is not possible to compare them in this aspect. Therefore the graphs do not include degradation modes but only failure modes. Failure modes are classified as T and E. T means that the failure mode comes from the Traction Control module and E means that the failure mode comes from the Electronic Control module.

Car number: 104177
Diagnostic code: 6148h : EC: MVB-PD-communication from ETCS faulty
Reset time: 26.10.2017   13:46:17
Set in maintenance mode

Car number: 104177
Diagnostic code: 6148h : EC: MVB-PD-communication from ETCS faulty
Set time: 26.10.2017   13:46:14
Set in maintenance mode

Fig. 7. Diagnostic code example of the MVB Data

The model parameters are estimated based on real-world failure data that has been collected from 2:25AM 26/10/2017 to 2:12AM 28/10/2017. A severe fault could be detected at the beginning of the period. The MVB-PD(Multifunction Vehicle Bus- Protocol Data) communication had a serious failure during the operation of the train, which prevented the train from receiving the information of railway authorization and line-side signals from both RBC and RIU (cf. Fig. 7).

The above fault data is represented that the ETCS has lost its movement authority and lineside signal. Therefore, in order to balance the objective factors of the ATO system with the ETCS system. We set the initial state in the model to state 5, which means that the RBC and RIU systems of the ATO system are lost. In the initial state, the ATO is in the same degraded state as the ETCS.

The simulation results are shown in Fig. 8. Since the train needs to run a round trip before the vehicle can enter maintenance, considering the capacity of the line, it will take at least the next day for the train to reach the depot of the starting station. Therefore, we have decided to evaluate the model after two days (48 h) of operational time.

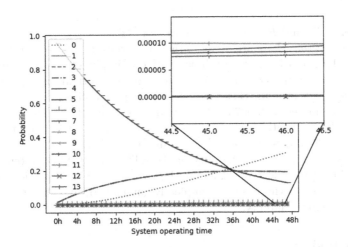

Fig. 8. The ATO system probability of state 0 to 13

After 48 h of operational time the state probabilities are shown in Table 3. The three states 6, 9 and 13 are the failed states where the systems stops. Hence all three are absorbing states. The sum of the probabilities that the system is in states 6, 9 and 13 is the probability that the target ATO system will completely fail. The results show that the probability that the system is relatively reliable within the first 48 h is 99.88%.

Table 3. State Probabilities at time $t = 48$

π_0	0.3037	π_1	0.1896	π_2	0.1899	π_3	0.1896	π_4	9.519E$-$5	π_5	0.1247	π_6	1.202E$-$3
π_7	7.664E$-$5	π_8	8.909E$-$4	π_9	1.968E$-$6	π_{10}	8.3662E$-$5	π_{11}	9.614E$-$5	π_{12}	6.480E$-$8	π_{13}	1.737E$-$7

To conduct a reliability comparison between an experienced driver and the ETCS-based ATO system, the reliability of the driver must be estimated. According to research results, the reliability R_0 of the driver's operation of the train is affected by three factors: the received information reliability R_1, the judgment reliability R_2 and the execution reliability R_3 Their relationship is shown in the following equation.

$$R_0 = R_1 \times R_2 \times R_3 \tag{14}$$

Table 4. The Reliabilities of R_2 AND R_3

Category	Description	R_2	R_3
Easy	Only a few variables, comprehensive consideration of ergonomics	0.9999	0.9995–0.9999
General	No more than ten variables	0.9995	0.9950–0.9995
Complex	More than 10 variables, incomprehensive ergonomic considerations	0.9900	0.9900–0.9990

The values of R_2 and R_3 are shown in Table 4 [22].

Considering that there are no more than 10 variables commonly used in train operation, the operation of the train is relatively simple, so we set R_2 to 0.9999, and R_3 to 0.9997. R_1, the reliability of the received information reliability from the system ETCS system. Based on the failure probabilities shown in Table 2, R_1 can be calculated as 0.9973, which means the value of R_0 can be calculated as 0.9969. This is slightly less reliable than with the ATO system that continues to operate for 48 hours after a serious failure occurs.

It can be seen that the reliability of the ETCS-based ATO system running on the mainline is almost the same as the reliability of the experienced driver driving the train in the case of completely unmanned, and it can even show higher continuous reliability.

6   Conclusion

As of yet, the ETCS-based ATO Level 3 (L3) system, which will operate driverless, has not been deployed in the mainline railroad environment. This is due to the fact that the safety of driverless train systems cannot be effectively guaranteed at the operational level. Therefore system-level safety analysis is necessary. In this paper, we conducted a qualitative and quantitative analysis of the ATO system on the mainline railway.

We have formulated the system in SysML and FMEA to perform a qualitative analysis. Since there is no cascading fault environment a combined fault analysis could be added for analysing the impact of subsystem failures. The results of the FMEA tables show that avoiding signal loss between subsystems is the best safety measure to prevent system degradation.

We have developed a continuous-time Markov chain to calculate the failure mode ratio of the ATO system. We propose to adjust the default maintenance interval to 33 days, saving 17.86% in maintenance costs.

Using real railway data we have simulated the ATO system. We found that the probability of failure of the ATO system operating on the mainline railway is 0.12%, which corresponds to the safety level of the current railway system. Therefore, we could confirm that in the context of the current ETCS applying an ATO will maintain the current level of safety on the mainline.

In future work the parameters of the model can be further improved. Due to time and economic constraints, it is impossible to personally do experiments to obtain model-related data. All data used in the paper are taken from references. In addition, we want to extend the model to capture larger topologies as well as interoperation between trains.

A FMEA

See Figs. 9 and 10.

NO	Unit	Failure mode	Mission phases	Local failure effect	Higher failure effect	System failure effect	Root failure mode causes
1.1	Eurobalise	Disconnection with LEU	Cruise	Eurobalise cannot receive the lineside signalling	BTM cannot receive the lineside signalling	- Degradation& Basic information (preset data) of the block lost +7.1 or ETCS L1 =Lost all passive line side signalling	-Physical disconnection with LEU
1.2	Eurobalise	Power lost	Entering the block	Eurobalise cannot send message	BTM cannot receive route status & lineside signalling	- Basic information (preset data) of the block lost	-Eurobalise single failure -BTM single failure
2.1	Interlocking	No occupation signal generated	After last train entering the block	No occupation signal generated	No occupation signal transmission	Collision	- interlocking single failure - railway brake
2.2	Interlocking	Disconnection with LEU	After last train entering the block	LEU cannot receive the lineside signalling	LTM&BTM cannot receive lineside signalling	- Degradation +5.1 or 5.2 = Lost all wireless line side signalling	- Physical disconnection with LEU
2.3	Interlocking	Disconnection with CC	After last train entering the block	CC cannot receive the block status	Changes in the availability of the block cannot affect the signal processing process	- It is possible that the train receives two different signals	- Physical disconnection with CC - power supply of CC failure
3.1	LEU	Disconnection with eurobalise	Before entering the block	Eurobalise cannot receive the telegram	BTM cannot receive lineside signalling	- Degradation +1.1 or 1.2 = Lost all passive line side signalling	- Physical disconnection with Eurobalise
3.2	LEU	Disconnection with RIU	Cruise	RIU cannot receive the lineside signalling	Euroradio cannot receive lineside signalling	- Degradation +5.1 or 5.2 = Lost all wireless line side signalling	- Physical disconnection with RIU
3.3	LEU	Disconnection with euroloop	Cruise	Euroloop cannot receive the telegram	LTM cannot receive the lineside signalling	- Degradation +1.1 or 1.2 = Lost all passive line side signalling	- Physical disconnection with euroloop
4.1	CC	Disconnection with RBC	Cruise	RBC cannot receive the lineside signalling & route status	Euroradio & RBC_adjacent cannot receive the lineside signalling & route status	- Signal& movement authority logic incorrectly affecting adjacent RBCs	- Physical disconnection with RBC
4.2	CC	Internal fault	Cruise	Error/no signal generated to RBC	Error/no signal to Euroradio	- Degradation +6.1 = Lost all wireless line side signalling	- CC single failure - power supply of CC failure
5.1	RBC	Disconnection with other adjacent RBCs	Cruise	Other RBCs cannot receive the selected data	Signal& movement authority logic incorrectly affecting adjacent RBCs	- Signal& movement authority logic incorrectly affecting adjacent RBCs + 6.1 = Lost all wireless line side signalling	- Physical disconnection with other adjacent RBCs
5.2	RBC	Disconnection with Euroradio	Entering the block	Euroradio cannot exchange train position &movement authority with RBC	-Euroradio cannot receive the movement authority from RBC -RBC cannot receive train position	- Stop or Degradation - without further movement suggestion +6.1 = Lost all wireless line side signalling	- Signal interference of GSM-R - RBC single failure - power supply of RBC failure
6.1	RIU	Disconnection with Euroradio	Entering the block	Euroradio cannot receive wireless information from RIU	The train cannot receive the information from Eurobalise in advance	- Degradation + 5.1, 5.2 or ETCS L1= Lost all wireless line side signalling	- Signal interference of GSM-R - RIU single failure - power supply of RIU failure
7.1	Euroloop	Disconnection with LTM	Entering the block	LTM cannot receive lineside signalling	The train cannot receive the lineside signalling	- Degradation + 1.1 or 1.2 = Lost all passive line side signalling	- Euroloop single failure
8.1	STM	Disconnection with national system	Entering the block under other national system	STM cannot receive data from National Train Control system	National Train Control system has not access to DMI &EVC	Lost control interface standard of certain national train control system	- STM single failure
9.1	EVC	Disconnection with LTM	Cruise	EVC cannot receive the lineside signalling	The train cannot receive the lineside signalling in advance	- Degradation + 9.2, 1.1 or 1.2 = Lost all passive line side signalling	- Part or whole of the bus is physically broken - Interface damaged
9.2	EVC	Disconnection with BTM	Cruise	EVC cannot receive the lineside signalling & preset data	The train cannot receive the lineside signalling & preset data	- Degradation + 9.1or 7.1= Lost all passive line side signalling	- Part or whole of the bus is physically broken - Interface damaged
9.3	EVC	Disconnection with STM	Cruise	EVC cannot receive data from National Train Control system	National Train Control system has not access to DMI &EVC	Lost control interface standard of certain national train control system	- Part or whole of the bus is physically broken - Interface damaged

Fig. 9. FMEA-1

9.4	EVC	Disconnection with Euroradio	Cruise	EVC cannot receive the lineside data& route status	The train cannot receive the lineside signalling & route status	- Degradation - Lost all wireless line side signalling	- Part or whole of the bus is physically broken - Interface damaged
9.5	EVC	Disconnection with JRU	Cruise	JRU cannot receive data and variables from train journeys	Huge negative impact on train maintenance	Slow down the maintenance process and reduce the quality of maintenance	- JRU single failure - Physical disconnection between JRU and EVC
9.6	EVC	Internal fault	Cruise	Most components of the train cannot receive any instructions	The ATO system has lost the ability to process data through algorithms.	The train loses primary control	EVC single failure
10.1	TIU	Disconnection with motor	Cruise	Motors cannot receive the latest driving instructions	ATO system cannot control motor	The ATO system is completely malfunctioning which may cause a collision.	Physical disconnection between motor and TIU
10.2	TIU	Disconnection with EVC	Cruise	Failed to distribute information from EVC	DMI and motor lose interface	- Affect the driver's judgment - Degradation	Physical disconnection between EVC and TIU
11.1	OS	Disconnection with JRU	Cruise	JRU cannot receive train data from OS	Seriously affect the judgment and repair time	No impact on system operation	OS single failure
12.1	JRU	Internal fault	Cruise	JRU loses recording function	Seriously affect the judgment and repair time	No impact on system operation	JRU single failure
13.1	Motor	Disconnection with TIU	Cruise	Motor cannot receive commands from the ATO system.	Unable to complete train acceleration or power regeneration as expected	- Degradation +Multiple motors lose connection at the same time, causing the ATO function to be completely lost.	- Physical disconnection between motor and TIU - Control element failure
13.2	Motor	Internal fault	Cruise	Motor does not have the ability to complete ATO commands	Unable to complete train acceleration or power regeneration as expected	- Degradation +Multiple motors fail at the same time, causing the ATO function to be completely lost.	Motor single failure
14.1	Detectors	Disconnection with OS	Cruise	The train cannot self-test the motion parameters	Seriously affect the judgment and repair time	No impact on system operation	Physical disconnection between detectors and OS
14.2	Detectors	Internal fault	Cruise	Unable to produce raw driving data	The driver or EVC cannot get the current speed and acceleration parameters.	Make the algorithm lack the original data	Detector single failure

Fig. 10. FMEA-2

References

1. Staino, A., Suwalka, A., Mitra, P., Basu, B.: Real-time detection and recognition of railway traffic signals using deep learning. J. Big Data Anal. Transport. (2022). https://doi.org/10.1007/s42421-022-00054-7
2. Assessment of architectures for Automatic Train Operation driving functions. https://www.sciencedirect.com/science/article/pii/S221097062200052X. Accessed 11 May 2023
3. Automatic Train Operation Takes to the main line. https://www.railjournal.com/in_depth/automatic-train-control-takes-to-the-main-line/. Accessed 8 May 2023
4. Huang, Y., Su, S., Liu, W.: Optimization on the driving curve of heavy haul trains based on artificial bee colony algorithm. In: 2020 IEEE 23rd International Conference on Intelligent Transportation Systems (ITSC) (2020). https://doi.org/10.1109/itsc45102.2020.929421
5. Cai, C.: Research on methods for urban rail transit train operation regulation. Appl. Mech. Mater. **536–537**, 820–823 (2014). https://doi.org/10.4028/www.scientific.net/amm.536-537.820
6. Zhu, X., Liu, X.: The modeling of test systems of Automatic Train Operation (ATO) in Urban rail transit based on LABVIEW. In: 2010 International Conference on Computer Application and System Modeling (ICCASM 2010) (2010). https://doi.org/10.1109/iccasm.2010.5620785
7. Dong, H., Li, L., Ning, B., Hou, Z.: Fuzzy tuning of ATO system in train speed control with multiple working conditions. In: Proceedings of the 29th Chinese Control Conference (2010)

8. Luo, H.Y., Xu, H.Z.: Model reference adaptive algorithm designed for automatic train braking control. Appl. Mech. Mater. **253–255**, 1374–1379 (2012). https://doi.org/10.4028/www.scientific.net/amm.253-255.1374

9. Liu, K.-W., Wang, X.-C., Qu, Z.-H.: Research on multi-objective optimization and control algorithms for automatic train operation. Energies **12**, 3842 (2019). https://doi.org/10.3390/en12203842

10. He, T., Xiong, R.: Research on multi-objective real-time optimization of Automatic Train Operation (ATO) in urban rail transit. J. Shanghai Jiaotong Univ. (Sci.) **23**, 327–335 (2018). https://doi.org/10.1007/s12204-018-1941-x

11. Watanabe, S., Koseki, T., Isobe, E.: Evaluation of automatic train operation design for energy saving based on the measured efficiency of a linear-motor train. Electr. Eng. Jpn. **202**, 50–61 (2017). https://doi.org/10.1002/eej.23059

12. Luo, M., Ke, Q., Li, J.: Research on automatic braking and traction control of high-speed train based on neural network. J. Phys. Conf. Ser. **1952**, 032048 (2021). https://doi.org/10.1088/1742-6596/1952/3/032048

13. Gallo, M., Botte, M., Ruggiero, A., D'Acierno, L.: A simulation approach for optimising energy-efficient driving speed profiles in metro lines. Energies **13**, 6038 (2020). https://doi.org/10.3390/en13226038

14. Carvajal-Carreño, W., Cucala, A.P., Fernández-Cardador, A.: Fuzzy train tracking algorithm for the energy efficient operation of CBTC equipped metro lines. Eng. Appl. Artif. Intell. **53**, 19–31 (2016). https://doi.org/10.1016/j.engappai.2016.03.011

15. Castillo, E., Grande, Z., Calviño, A.: Bayesian networks-based probabilistic safety analysis for railway lines. Comput.-Aided Civil Infrastruct. Eng. **31**, 681–700 (2016). https://doi.org/10.1111/mice.12195

16. Castillo, E., et al.: A Markovian-Bayesian network for risk analysis of high speed and conventional railway lines integrating human errors. Comput.-Aided Civil Infrastruct. Eng. **31**, 193–218 (2015). https://doi.org/10.1111/mice.12153

17. Venkateswaran, K.G., Nicholson, G.L., Roberts, C., Stone, R.: Impact of automation on the capacity of a mainline railway: a preliminary hypothesis and methodology. In: Proceedings of the 2015 IEEE 18th International Conference on Intelligent Transportation Systems (ITSC '15). IEEE Computer Society, USA (2097–2102). https://doi.org/10.1109/ITSC.2015.339

18. van Lierop, D., Badami, M.G., El-Geneidy, A.M.: What influences satisfaction and loyalty in public transport? A review of the literature. Transp. Rev. **38**, 52–72 (2017). https://doi.org/10.1080/01441647.2017.1298683

19. UNISIG, ATO over ETCS - system requirements specification., Subset-125 (2018)

20. Geng, H., Zhang, C., Sun, Y., Li, Q., Ke, C., Liu, Z.: Technical analysis of the ETCS architecture development. Control Inf. Technol. **2**, 80–84 (2020). https://doi.org/10.13889/j.issn.2096-5427.2020.02.015

21. Chen, R.: The Safety and Reliability Analysis Methods for Train Operation Based on Hybrid Automata. Beijing Jiaotong University, Beijing (2019). https://doi.org/10.26944/d.cnki.gbfju.2019.001655

22. Jianqiang, J.: Research on Training Method of High-Speed Railway ATO On-Board Subsystem Based on Human Reliability Analysis. Beijing Jiaotong University, Beijing (2020). https://doi.org/10.26944/d.cnki.gbfju.2020.001919

Remaining Useful Life Estimation for Railway Gearbox Bearings Using Machine Learning

Lodiana Beqiri[✉], Zeinab Bakhshi, Sasikumar Punnekkat,
and Antonio Cicchetti

Mälardalen University, Västerås, Sweden
{lodiana.beqiri,zeinab.bakhshi,sasikumar.punnekkat,
antonio.cicchetti}@mdu.se

Abstract. Gearbox bearing maintenance is one of the major overhaul cost items for railway electric propulsion systems. They are continuously exposed to challenging working conditions, which compromise their performance and reliability. Various maintenance strategies have been introduced over time to improve the operational efficiency of such components, while lowering the cost of their maintenance. One of these is predictive maintenance, which makes use of previous historical data to estimate a component's remaining useful life (RUL). This paper introduces a machine learning-based method for calculating the RUL of railway gearbox bearings. The method uses unlabeled mechanical vibration signals from gearbox bearings to detect patterns of increased bearing wear and predict the component's residual life span. We combined a data smoothing method, a change point algorithm to set thresholds, and regression models for prediction. The proposed method has been validated using real-world gearbox data provided by our industrial partner, Alstom Transport AB in Sweden. The results are promising, particularly with respect to the predicted failure time. Our model predicted the failure to occur on day 330, while the gearbox bearing's actual lifespan was 337 days. The deviation of just 7 days is a significant result, since an earlier RUL prediction value is usually preferable to avoid unexpected failure during operations. Additionally, we plan to further enhance the prediction model by including more data representing failing bearing patterns.

Keywords: Railway · Gearbox bearing · Predictive maintenance · Remaining useful life · Machine learning

1 Introduction

The maintenance of a railway system plays an important role in ensuring its safety, dependability, and efficiency [1]. Train reliability is a daily requirement for millions of people, and as such, it is a perpetual challenge for all vehicle manufacturers. The reliability expectation is met by using electrical and mechanical components such

© The Author(s), under exclusive license to Springer Nature Switzerland AG 2023
B. Milius et al. (Eds.): RSSRail 2023, LNCS 14198, pp. 62–77, 2023.
https://doi.org/10.1007/978-3-031-43366-5_4

as robust pantographs, transformers, and an optimized propulsion system. These components are subject to significantly demanding operation conditions, and to preserve their operational performance, effective maintenance strategies are essential. In the context of predictive maintenance, safe and efficient train operation [2] is relied on accurate estimation of RUL of railway components. In this respect, traditional methods, like model-based prediction, leverage complex models, such as non-linear ones [3] or temperature models [4], which can potentially impact the accuracy of the prediction [5]. Machine learning (ML) techniques, on the other hand, offer increasingly popular alternatives that provide improved efficiency and accuracy [2,6,7]. ML models can utilize sensor data and other operational parameters to predict the remaining lifespan of bearings, enabling proactive maintenance and minimizing downtime. Data analytics, feature extraction, and ML techniques have shown promising potentials for predicting component failures and estimating RUL [5,8]. The use of ML techniques for RUL estimation has been explored in various fields, such as wind turbines [5,9,10], where high operation and maintenance costs make it essential to predict component failures. However, these techniques have been rarely applied to train propulsion systems or their components. In fact, although there are some similarities between gearbox bearings in different contexts, there exist significant differences. Train propulsion systems operate under specific operational conditions and encounter various environmental variables, including temperature, vibration levels, humidity, etc. As a result, the wear patterns and degradation mechanisms exhibited by train propulsion systems differ from those observed in other domains, influencing the various methods used to assess them. Typically, vibration data from propulsion system gearbox bearings are analyzed using techniques such as Fourier or time-frequency analysis to detect anomalous patterns associated with bearing problems. There data can then be fed to further steps of anomaly detection system, such as, ML algorithms to classify and locate bearing problems.

The current study focuses on the challenges presented by train propulsion system gearbox bearings and their wear. Due to the limitation in obtaining real-world gearbox bearing data, existing works usually depend on simulated data or controlled operating condition data in laboratory settings. Instead, this paper presents a method that has been validated using real data from a train propulsion system with a maximum speed of 300 km/h given by our industrial partner Alstom. The approach proposes a preprocessing phase that uses low pass filtering to reduce oscillations in raw data [11] and increase RUL estimation accuracy. The obtained data is employed in a regression model to predict RUL. The proposed techniques also includes a change point algorithm, necessary to derive thresholds for assessing degradation trends. By going into more details, the process begins with an analysis of sensor data acquired from a real-world propulsion system. A combination of one class support vector machine (One-class SVM) and interpolation is used, allowing signal outlier identification and trend analysis. In the case of deteriorating trends, a change point technique, Pruned Exact Linear Time (PELT) is applied to the data to identify the signal's variation instances. Based on the variation points thresholds are built. To develop a prediction model, regression models such as the polynomial and the exponential ones are created and trained on the data. The RUL of the bearings is then determined by using the best-performing model. The obtained prediction results are promising, as our prediction model is very close to the actual bearing failure, with only a 7-day difference[1]. In other words, in real-life condition the bearing lasted an additional 7 days before failing. In fact, such a margin would prevent downtime due to in-service failures, while at the same time avoiding excessive waste of remaining lifespan. Moreover, in contrast to previous research, the proposed approach enables the provision of explanations about how thresholds for degradation trends are established through the application of a change point algorithm without the use of domain-specific knowledge. The remainder of the paper is structured as follows: Sect. 2 provides background information about the research effort, including railway maintenance, the propulsion system, and estimation of RUL. Moreover, Sect. 3 discusses existing related works and the proposed solutions. Section 4 presents an overview of the adopted research methodology and discusses the data preparation, exploratory data analysis, and prediction models. A summary of the obtained results and findings is illustrated in Sect. 5, while Sect. 6 provides conclusive remarks and discusses the possibilities for further development.

2   Background

2.1   Railway Maintenance

Railway maintenance focuses on boosting operating availability and safety of its components, while reducing expenses and downtime [12], and detecting potential issues. To achieve these goals, maintenance should be systematic, with thorough planning and continual monitoring of different components conditions. The maintenance activities are broadly categorized into: reactive, preventive, predictive [13,14], as further discussed below. Historically, train maintenance has been **reactive**, also known as run-to-failure maintenance. This technique entails simply examining and repairing equipment after it has failed. This is the most basic but least effective strategy, as the cost of interventions and accompanying downtime after failure will be prohibitively expensive, including the potential growth of safety concerns. **Preventive maintenance** is planned and scheduled to reduce the chance of equipment failure while also enhancing production efficiency; in particular, inspections and replacement of components on specific pieces of equipment are performed on a regular basis. Even if better than the reactive approach, preventive maintenance is still more expensive than the predictive one, since while most failure issues are avoided, there exists a high chance of carrying out unneeded remedial activities. **Predictive maintenance** seeks to estimate the failure time of a system or its components based on experience and/or historical data and replace them before they fail. By predicting the need for maintenance in advance, this strategy also helps in improving maintenance planning, which takes time and resources. **Condition-based maintenance** (CBM) is a form of predictive maintenance that shifts the scope of

---

[1] Our model forecasts the failure to occur on day 330, and in reality, the gearbox bearing lasts for 337 days.

inspections towards changes that could indicate possible failures rather than performing general inspections at regular intervals. In particular, CBM aims at detecting early symptoms of oncoming failures and hence predicting the need for maintenance; typically, it employs sensors measuring variables that may affect the machine's efficiency. Moreover, to assess when/if a defect is detected CBM leverages thresholds to preclude unnecessary replacements and carry out maintenance activities only when required.

2.2   The Propulsion System

The propulsion system of a train generates the required power and force to propel the train, allowing it to move and assuring efficient transportation. The propulsion mechanism comprises of a traction motor attached to the bogie and a gearbox linked to the wheel axle. The method proposed in this paper is validated using data from a train propulsion system provided by the world-leading train manufacturer Alstom. There are eight carriages on the train where the data is collected from, four of which are traction cars. Each of these cars has two bogies. A bogie is a train component that sits beneath the train's body and holds and links all of the locomotive's parts, including axles and wheels. Each bogie has two axles, each with its own traction motor and gearbox. Figure 1 depicts a simplified representation of components in the electric propulsion system analyzed in this study, such as the traction motor, gearbox, and the respective sensor placement. Gearbox bearings have an important role in the functioning of the train propulsion system. Bearings are key components that facilitate the smooth operation and transmission of power within the gearbox. They support the rotating shafts and gears, ensuring proper alignment and reducing friction, thus enabling efficient power transfer. Bearings must withstand frequent movement, varied speeds, and severe loads while retaining performance. They are, however, prone to wear, fatigue, lubrication contamination, and other potential damage. Contact fatigue is the most common cause of bearing failures [15]. Other factors include oxidation, fatigue on the rolling elements, and misalignment of bearings during installation [16]. Many challenges exist in maintaining and ensuring the performance of propulsion system gearbox bearings. Understanding the challenges is crucial for designing effective maintenance and optimizing their performance which ensures the train runs efficiently.

2.3   Estimation of Remaining Useful Life (RUL)

RUL estimate plays a pivotal role as an aspect of predictive maintenance, contributing to the effectiveness of maintenance procedures. RUL for gearbox bearings has attracted considerable attention in the literature, not only in the railway industry, but also in other manufacturers who rely on machinery [5,11,17–19]. Models such as similarity, degradation, and survival models have emerged as tools for forecasting the remaining lifespan of essential railway components. These models aim to anticipate the RUL based on criteria such as wear, deterioration patterns, and historical data. *Similarity models* are based on the RUL

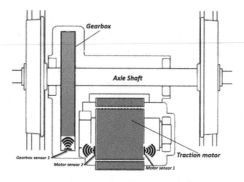

Fig. 1. Components within the Electric Propulsion System

forecast of a testing machine based on a historical comparison of known behavior of other similar machines. They use run-to-failure data describing the degradation profile. *Degradation models* extrapolate previous behavior to predict future conditions. If the condition indicator is known to signal failure, regression models are adopted, and the remaining time calculated till some predetermined threshold is reached. In this paper we leverage a degradation model to estimate the RUL. *Survival analysis* is a method for analyzing data based on the time it takes for an event to occur and estimates the probability distribution of failure.

Machine learning approaches and data-driven techniques like as regression models, neural networks, and support vector machines can be used to analyse historical data and trends of bearing degradation. In the following section, we will discuss some of the prior research done in the aforementioned context.

3   Related Work

Carvalho et al. [20] conducted a systematic literature review on predictive maintenance using ML techniques. They explored the equipment types studied and the ML methods used, concluding that there is an increasing trend in using ML for predictive maintenanced, which helps reduce the cost of unnecessary equipment replacement in various applications. Based on Carvalho et al.'s work, we identified related works that explored different ML methods. Amruthnath et al. [21] focused on early failure identification on vibration data from an exhaust fan. They evaluated various algorithms such as T^2 statistics, PCA, hierarchical clustering, K-means, and fuzzy C-means clustering. The authors suggested that clustering techniques can be a cost-effective solution when maintenance costs are high. By monitoring machine health regularly using clustering, expenses on machine maintenance can be saved until a critical level is reached. In another study [22], the same authors proposed an unsupervised learning approach for fault class prediction and detection in a predictive maintenance system. They utilized Gaussian Mixture Models (GMM) and K-means algorithms to forecast the machine state and achieved an 82.96% accuracy for error prediction. Kundu et al. [23] proposed a method for predicting the RUL of rolling bearings using a combination of K-means clustering and change point detection algorithms. By identifying failure patterns in the data, the authors improved the accuracy of their RUL predictions. They suggested that their method could be extended to other applications of predicting RUL and state interference where changing a state shows degradation of the bearing. This method is useful for calculating the probability of shifting from a healthy state to damage by using a state matrix. Hong et al. [24] proposed a method for predicting the RUL of bearings using Gaussian Process Regression (GPR). They utilized RMS, kurtosis, and crest factor as input features to construct the minimum quantization error (MQE) through a self-organizing map (SOM). The authors found that using a composite kernel improved the prediction accuracy and reduced the variance of the RUL in comparison to using a single kernel, highlighting the importance of kernel selection in GPR for RUL prediction in machine health monitoring. Elasha et al. [11] proposed a bearing prognosis approach that used regression and back-propagation neural networks to estimate the RUL of high-speed shaft bearings of a wind turbine. They demonstrated the effectiveness of the regression model in improving the predictive performance of the neural network model, with the proposed ANN model exhibiting strong performance in predicting the remaining useful life of a bearing. Li et al. [25] improved the exponential model and utilized particle filtering to eliminate random faults in bearing degradation process. Their method was demonstrated on four tests and outperformed the original exponential model used in their previous work in predicting RUL of rolling element bearings. While this study enhanced prediction accuracy of the exponential model by selecting optimal FPT and minimizing random errors, failure threshold remains subjective and few studies have been done to determine them dynamically in RUL prediction. The authors in [26] developed a method for estimating the RUL of rolling element bearings in induction motors using dynamic regression models. They used a gradient-based approach to build failure thresholds and developed the time to start prediction (TSP) metric to detect the onset of bearing degradation, after which the trend in the bearing health indicator should be continuously monitored to estimate the RUL. The proposed methodology was evaluated on run-to-failure data, nevertheless, the authors state that further study is required to confirm its efficacy since it was limited to a single dataset.

The studies in this subsection focus on unsupervised learning for fault detection, RUL prediction, and improving exponential model accuracy. Techniques like clustering algorithms, change point detection, Gaussian process regression, adaptive first prediction time selection, and particle filtering can save costs by reducing equipment replacements and improving machine uptime [27,28]. However, selecting the appropriate technique depends on the equipment, data, and maintenance goals [20].

4   Methodology

This section describes the methodology used in the course of the work. The approach includes exploratory data analysis, trend analysis, and the use of one-class SVM and interpolation to identify and handle the outliers. Following the deployment of the prediction model, PELT is used to detect changes in signal trend and establish state-definers thresholds. The prediction model is applied to the signals that are identified as degrading. Using the training data, multiple regression models are trained, and the best model is chosen to forecast the RUL of gearbox bearings[2]. The whole procedure is presented in Fig. 2, and the subsections that follow describe each step.

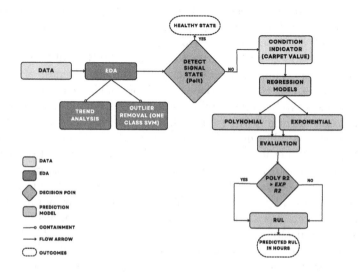

Fig. 2. Proposed Methodology

4.1   Dataset

Accelerometers are mounted on the motor and gearbox casings to capture vibration signals. Two sensors are installed in the traction motor, and two more are installed in the same location in the gearbox, also shown in Fig. 1. The sensors are programmed to transmit data to a controller unit, which is then analyzed to determine the prognosis. Data was collected from a train over a 10-month period, and specifically from the four traction cars on the train, with the goal of identifying concerning patterns. The prediction model was constructed using

---

[2] While the source code remains proprietary, the GitHub repository includes a pseudocode representation https://github.com/lodianabeqiri/BearingRUL-Estimation-Pseudocode.

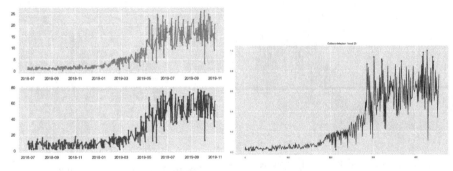

Fig. 3. Carpet and Max Values: Damaged
Gearbox Bearing (Color figure online)

Fig. 4. Outlier Detection

data from another train's damaged gearbox bearing. The gearbox was removed
for inspection by Alstom engineers, and a problem with the transmission's bearing was discovered. The signals received through the sensors were further filtered
by the engineers to produce two features called as the carpet value and the maximum value. The carpet value reflects the energy level of the signal, while the
maximum values represent the signal's peak values. If there is no damage, the
carpet values can be used to reveal the amount of vibration, or energy inside
the motor and gearbox bearing. Based on domain expertise, when there is bearings deterioration, the carpet value rises as the damage worsens. On the other
hand, the maximum values do not always imply component damage, since they
depend on both external noise and component degradation. For these reasons,
the carpet value is employed as a prediction indication in this paper to uncover
data variation associated to failure.

4.2   Exploratory Data Analysis (Eda)

Eda is a crucial step in comprehending the data, making it easier to spot trends
and anomalies. The data has been partitioned into training and test sets in a
80/20 proportion. The MinMaxScaler normalization technique has been used on
the training set for transforming the numerical values to a common scale without distorting the values range or removing information. The test data has been
used to evaluate the model. Figure 3 depicts the maximum value in green and
the carpet value in pink from the damaged bearing[3].

Visualization is a useful tool for understanding the data trends. A time series
trend refers to the pattern or direction of change that can be observed across
time. The moving average and Bollinger Bands were examined in the analysis.
Bollinger Bands are standard deviation envelopes that appear above and below a

---

[3] GitHub repository https://github.com/lodianabeqiri/RULforBearings_images contains all the figures presented in this paper.

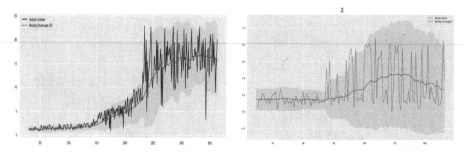

Fig. 5. Trend Analysis: Damaged Gearbox Bearing

Fig. 6. Trend Analysis: Signal 2

simple moving average. A moving average represents the average value of preceding data points without weighting. The trend of the failed bearing is illustrated in Fig. 5. The moving average with a 30-day time window is represented by the red line, while the green zone depicts the Bollinger Bands. The signal does not vary significantly at first, but when the degradation process begins, the values begin to rise. The signal appears to have a stagnant pattern with consistently high values as it approaches the failure phase. Figure 6 illustrates another signal, which shows a slight shift in the trend with a considerable increase in values.

4.3   Outliers

Outliers are observations, also known as abnormalities, that do not fit with the rest of the data. Summary statistics, including mean and variance, can be affected by outliers. Traditional deterministic methods are often applied in practice for outlier identification, such as displays of the distribution and labeling each observation over or below a specific threshold as an outlier. One-class classification is a subfield of ML that focuses on identifying outliers. In this paper we use one-class SVM. It is a SVM variant that captures the density of the majority class and classifies outliers as examples at the density function's extremes. It learns the distribution's bounds referred to as "support" and can thus classify any points outside the boundary as outliers. The algorithm parameter include *nu* that is used to fine-tune the trade-off between overfitting and generalization, parameter *gamma* and the *kernel function*. The decision boundary will be increasingly "linear" as the gamma increases, and the more complex the model, and the greater the risk of overfitting. The *kernel function* changes the training set of data so that a non-linear decision surface can be translated into a linear equation in a larger number of dimension spaces. Figure 4 depicts the outliers as red dots discovered by one-class SVM with the optimized parameters: nu = 0.05, kernel = "rbf", gamma = 0.01. Data distribution could be drastically altered by removing outliers. Therefore linear interpolation was chosen to estimate the missing value by directly linking points in the ascending order.

4.4   Models

This subsection provides an overview of the models used. We examine the rationale for selecting these models and provide a brief explanation of each.

Regression analysis is a type of curve fitting optimization problem, where the objective is to find the best line or curve that fits the data in a way that minimizes the difference between the predicted and actual values. We investigated polynomial and exponential regression models and compared their results to determine the best fit. *Polynomial regression* is a version of linear regression in which a polynomial equation is used to describe the data in order to capture the curvilinear relationship between the independent and dependent variables. The polynomial equation of degree n is represented as:

$$y = \theta_0 + \theta_1 x + \theta_2 x^2 + \cdots + \theta_n x^n + \epsilon \tag{1}$$

where y is the dependent variable, x is the independent variable, $\theta_0, \theta_1, \ldots, \theta_n$ are the regression coefficients or weights, ϵ is the error term, and n is the degree of the polynomial. The 1-degree polynomial is a simple linear regression, therefore the degree value must be greater than 1. If the n value is low, the model will struggle to fit the data properly, and if it is high, the model will easily overfit the data.

Exponential regression is the process of determining the best exponential function equation for a set of data. The exponential equation is given as:

$$y = \theta_0 e^{\theta_1 x} + \epsilon \tag{2}$$

where y is the dependent variable, x is the independent variable, θ_0 and θ_1 are the exponential regression coefficients, and ϵ is the error term.

PELT is a change point algorithm that can be used to detect performance declines [29]. There is no unique definition for the term "change point". They can be regarded as time series points with statistical characteristics that differ from the data distribution. For a given cost function, penalty score, and model, PELT is used to locate the change points in a data set by computing the segmentation of the data that minimizes the cost function. The algorithm uses the pruning rule where many indices are deleted, resulting in a significant reduction in computational cost while maintaining the ability to determine the best segmentation. To find multiple change points, PELT is first applied to the entire dataset and then iteratively and independently applied to each partition until no change points are found.

The bearing degradation process due to measurement noise is vulnerable to a variety of fluctuations, which may affect the model's ability to evaluate the degradation trend [11]. In this case, the data is smoothed before being used as input to the prediction models. The *Savitzky-Golay* is a low pass filter that smooths out data with certain oscillations using a polynomial function, resulting in a signal that is easier to understand and analyze. The technique is repeated for all data points, yielding a new set of data points that closely resembles the original data.

The following paragraphs discuss the practical application of the discussed models on the data. We investigate the process of optimizing these models to ensure their effectiveness in capturing data patterns and discuss their outcomes.

4.5 Setting the Thresholds

The PELT algorithm locates the points in the damaged gearbox bearing carpet value where there is a change or an obvious rising trend. These identified points are used as reference thresholds to assess the health of other signals. The premise behind this approach is that if any other signals have degraded or failed, they may exhibit a similar pattern to the damaged bearing. This assumption was made due to a paucity of data on different failure behavior, and we relied on known failures to detect the similar failure trend. The PELT model was fed with the carpet value and a penalty score and detects the variation point of the signal to build the thresholds. The best parameters for PELT were the Gaussian kernel as a model with a penalty score of 10 and as the cost function the constrained sum of approximation errors. To enhance the signal, the Savgol filter was applied using a window size of 51 and a polynomial order of 3. Subsequently, the filtered signal was passed to PELT. Three vertical lines in Fig. 7 represent the detected thresholds for illustration reasons. The red line represents the degradation threshold, and the degradation zone extends from the red to the blue line. When the signal exceed the blue line, it reaches failure. These thresholds are used to determine whether we proceed to compute the RUL for other signal. Based on the thresholds, most of the signals that were evaluated for each car were categorized as healthy. The method was then applied to the damaged bearing signal, the result is that the signal has already failed, and no RUL calculation is required.

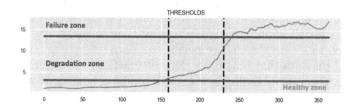

Fig. 7. Thresholds (Color figure online)

However, when compared to signal 2 presented in Sect. 4.2 it is classified as degraded, and for this signal the RUL can be determined. Figure 8 shows in green the filtered signal 2. The x-axis represents the time at which the signal was acquired, while the y-axis represents the carpet value of the signal. The signal exhibits an increasing pattern that begins after 2000 h and ends before 5000 h. Unlike the damaged signal in Fig. 3, which has a growing tendency over time until failure, the signal 2 is susceptible to the "healing phenomenon" [30]. After the values increase, possibly due to a defect, the signal returns to low values. For instance this could happen as a result of newly formed surface defects caused by the rolling elements of the bearings. Assuming signal 2 will eventually fail after recovery, we employed extrapolation using numpy polyfit in python to forecast future data points and observe the potential trend the signal might follow. Extrapolation is the process of assuming values outside the range of the currently available data by using data from existing points. It is important to note that extrapolation might result in inaccurate results, owing to the variety of gearbox bearing degradation patterns. However, in scenarios with a sufficient number of samples exhibiting the same failure pattern, or multiple failure cases for more complex extrapolation tasks, insights into the signal's future behavior become possible. We conclude that there is insufficient data to calculate the RUL for signal 2.

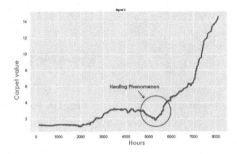

Fig. 8. Signal 2 Extrapolation (Color figure online)

4.6   RUL

To determine the RUL, three main functions were developed: *actual or true RUL*, another to estimate the *RUL*, and yet another to calculate the *prediction error*. The *actual RUL* is defined as the time elapsed between the true failure of the bearing and the actual time we consider for each point on the training set. The RUL is calculated in terms of hours. We used the last instance of our provided data as the time when the bearing failed, which was 8092 h in the training data. For the *estimated RUL*, we used the polynomial regression that best fitted the data, calculating the estimated RUL as the difference between the estimated time of bearing's failure and the time determined by our polynomial function for each data point on training set by projecting the point to the hour axes. The estimated time is to be around 7928 h in the training set by extrapolating the data and finding this value when the data exceeded the failure threshold. Finally, the *prediction error* is defined to determine how well the prediction model performed, as the difference between the actual and predicted RULs.

5   Results

The polynomial and exponential functions applied to the damaged bearing signal are shown in Figs. 9 and 10, respectively. Figures 11 shows the model constants and assessment metrics for each regression model. Evaluation tables indicate that the polynomial function exhibited the lowest Root Mean Square Error (RMSE) and the highest R squared (R2) value, indicating the best fit to the data. Consequently, we employ polynomial regression to calculate the RUL. Similar results can be observed when it comes to the test data.

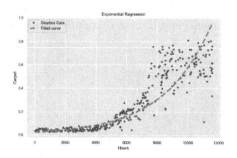

Fig. 9. Exponential Function   **Fig. 10.** Polynomial Function

TRAINING SET

REGRESSION MODELS	Model coefficients		RMSE	R Squared
CARPET VALUE				
Exponential Carpet	-3.918663348186325	0.0003624022446393382	0.01960712346455304	0.7866537673654433
Polynomial	[0.00000000e+00 4.69008693e-06	-6.07368172e-09 1.50563032e-12]	0.018956361781946	0.8716962090304008

Fig. 11. Assessment Metrics and Regression Coefficients in Training Data

The graph in Fig. 12 compares the estimated RUL from polynomial regression, which is visualized in green, to the actual RUL, which is represented by the diagonal black line. The time at which the fitted carpet value exceeded the defined threshold as determined by PELT was then used to extrapolate the expected failure time. Considering only the time the signal entered the degradation phase until it reached the failure threshold (at 8092 h or 337 days), the actual RUL of the signal is calculated to be 2979 h. As a result, the signal has 2979 h until it fails as soon as it enters the degradation phase. Meanwhile, extrapolating the estimated RUL yields 7928 h or 330 days, implying that the signal has 2812 h left when it enters the degradation phase. The difference between the actual life and the estimated time left for the bearing to function properly is 168 h, or 7 days. The green line in Fig. 12 regressing the estimated life time underestimates the signal's life by a few hours; however, some time intervals between 1000 and 1500 h are comparable to the true RUL. The prediction error, mean square error (MSE) is the distance between estimated line and the actual line. Since the estimated values can be less or greater than actual values, a simple sum of differences can be zero and this lead to the incorrect conclusion that the forecast is correct. As we square and use RMSE, all errors are positive, and the mean is positive, indicating that there is some difference between the estimates and the actual. The calculated RMSE is 210. While no RMSE value is universally correct, a lower mean indicates a more accurate forecast.

5.1 Threats to Validity

As any other experimental work, also this paper needs to take into consideration threats to validity [31]. Internal and construct validity have to deal with the set-up of the experiments and the potential bias of the involved researchers. In this respect, the developed techniques use standard data cleaning and analysis techniques and no refinement procedure, e.g. for outliers and thresholds, has been adopted in accordance with (railway) domain experts. When it comes to conclusion validity, the availability of bearing data is limited to a single failure case. This limitation does not allow us to make conclusions about the precision of the estimation algorithm with an adequate level of confidence. Nonetheless, the approach is generic into distinguishing between healthy and unhealthy states by utilizing domain knowledge about signal characteristics. While the approach accurately detects the states, it is worth mentioning that by integrating more data depicting failure bearing patterns, the precision of the predictions can be improved.

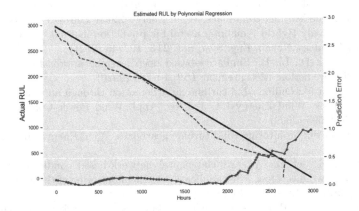

Fig. 12. Regression Model for Predicting RUL (Color figure online)

6   Conclusion

A RUL prediction method has been developed by leveraging real-world data from gearbox bearings. Initially, the data was analyzed to identify increasing trends, and the one-class SVM was used to eliminate any outliers. Moreover, the PELT algorithm identified changes in signal properties, allowing the construction of valid degradation thresholds without prior knowledge of them. Two regression models were trained and compared, with polynomial regression achieving a higher R2 value of 0.87 compared to exponential regression. RUL prediction utilized the polynomial function and anticipated the failure with 7 days in advance to the real failure. Furthermore, it was observed that adding data filtering techniques to our model, such as a low pass filter, significantly improves the performance and helps to smooth out the fluctuations in the gearbox degradation trend. The method, however, is dependent on a certain known degradation trend, resulting in restricted data for defining the thresholds. More data on similar behaviors will allow for the construction of more rigorous degradation criteria.

References

1. Macchi, M., et al.: Maintenance management of railway infrastructures based on reliability analysis. Reliab. Eng. Syst. Saf. **104**, 71–83 (2012)
2. Yao, D., et al.: Remaining useful life prediction of roller bearings based on improved 1D-CNN and simple recurrent unit. Measurement **175**, 109166 (2021)
3. Cao, M., et al.: Study of wind turbine fault diagnosis based on unscented Kalman filter and SCADA data. Energies **9**(10), 847 (2016)
4. Qiu, Y., et al.: Applying thermophysics for wind turbine drivetrain fault diagnosis using SCADA data. IET Renew. Power Gener. **10**(5), 661–668 (2016)
5. Carroll, J., et al.: Wind turbine gearbox failure and remaining useful life prediction using machine learning techniques. Wind Energy **22**(3), 360–375 (2019)
6. Zang, Y., et al.: Hybrid remaining useful life prediction method. A case study on railway D-cables. Reliab. Eng. Syst. Saf. **213**, 107746 (2021)
7. Hou, M., Pi, D., Li, B.: Similarity-based deep learning approach for remaining useful life prediction. Measurement **159**, 107788 (2020)
8. Zaher, A., et al.: Online wind turbine fault detection through automated SCADA data analysis. Wind Energy Int. J. Prog. Appl. Wind Power Convers. Technol. **12**(6), 574–593 (2009)
9. Feng, Y., et al.: Monitoring wind turbine gearboxes. Wind Energy **16**(5), 728–740 (2013)
10. Bangalore, P., et al.: An artificial neural network-based condition monitoring method for wind turbines, with application to the monitoring of the gearbox. Wind Energy **20**(8), 1421–1438 (2017)
11. Elasha, F., et al.: Prognosis of a wind turbine gearbox bearing using supervised machine learning. Sensors **19**(14), 3092 (2019)
12. Shao, W., Hao, Y., et al.: Study on preventive maintenance strategies of filling equipment based on reliability-cantered maintenance. Tehnički vjesnik **28**(2), 689–697 (2021)
13. Susto, G.A., et al.: Machine learning for predictive maintenance: a multiple classifier approach. IEEE Trans. Ind. Inform. **11**(3), 812–820 (2014)
14. Xie, J., et al.: Systematic literature review on data-driven models for predictive maintenance of railway track: implications in geotechnical engineering. Geosciences **10**(11), 425 (2020)

15. Sadeghi, F., et al.: A review of rolling contact fatigue. J. Tribol. **131**(4), 041403 (2009)
16. Peng, H., et al.: A review of research on wind turbine bearings' failure analysis and fault diagnosis. Lubricants **11**(1), 14 (2022)
17. Rezamand, M., et al.: An integrated feature-based failure prognosis method for wind turbine bearings. IEEE/ASME Trans. Mechatron. **25**(3), 1468–1478 (2020)
18. Teng, W., et al.: Prognosis of the remaining useful life of bearings in a wind turbine gearbox. Energies **10**(1), 32 (2016)
19. Elforjani, M., Shanbr, S.: Prognosis of bearing acoustic emission signals using supervised machine learning. IEEE Trans. Ind. Electron. **65**(7), 5864–5871 (2017)
20. Carvalho, T.P., et al.: A systematic literature review of machine learning methods applied to predictive maintenance. Comput. Ind. Eng. **137**, 106024 (2019)
21. Amruthnath, N., Gupta, T.: A research study on unsupervised machine learning algorithms for early fault detection in predictive maintenance. In: 2018 5th International Conference on Industrial Engineering and Applications (ICIEA), pp. 355–361. IEEE (2018)
22. Amruthnath, N., Gupta, T.: Fault class prediction in unsupervised learning using model-based clustering approach. In: 2018 International Conference on Information and Computer Technologies (ICICT). IEEE (2018)
23. Kundu, P., Chopra, S., Lad, B.K.: Multiple failure behaviors identification and remaining useful life prediction of ball bearings. J. Intell. Manuf. **30**, 1795–1807 (2019)
24. Hong, S., et al.: Bearing remaining life prediction using gaussian process regression with composite Kernel functions. J. Vibroengineering **17**(2), 695–704 (2015)
25. Li, N., et al.: An improved exponential model for predicting remaining useful life of rolling element bearings. IEEE Trans. Ind. Electron. **62**(12), 7762–7773 (2015)
26. Ahmad, W., et al.: A reliable technique for remaining useful life estimation of rolling element bearings using dynamic regression models. Reliab. Eng. Syst. Saf. **184**, 67–76 (2019)
27. Hashemian, H.M.: State-of-the-art predictive maintenance techniques. IEEE Trans. Instrum. Meas. **60**(1), 226–236 (2010)
28. Butte, S., Prashanth, A.R., Patil, S.: Machine learning based predictive maintenance strategy: a super learning approach with deep neural networks. In: 2018 IEEE Workshop on Microelectronics and Electron Devices (WMED), pp. 1–5. IEEE (2018)
29. Wambui, G.D., Waititu, G.A., Wanjoya, A.: The power of the pruned exact linear time (PELT) test in multiple changepoint detection. Am. J. Theor. Appl. Stat. **4**(6), 581–586 (2015)
30. Mortada, M.-A., Yacout, S., Lakis, A.: Diagnosis of rotor bearings using logical analysis of data. J. Qual. Maintenance Eng. **17**(4), 371–397 (2011)
31. Wohlin, C., et al.: Experimentation in Software Engineering. Springer, Cham (2012). https://doi.org/10.1007/978-3-642-29044-2

Towards Scenario-Based Certification of Highly Automated Railway Systems

Michael Wild$^{(\boxtimes)}$ (iD), Jan Steffen Becker (iD), Günter Ehmen,
and Eike Möhlmann (iD)

DLR Institute for Systems Engineering for Future Mobility (DLR-SE), Oldenburg,
Germany
{michael.wild,jan.becker,guenter.ehmen,eike.moehlmann}@dlr.de

Abstract. In the future, fully automated trains can play a vital role
in improving performance of the railway system. Although technologies
exist that make driverless train operation already possible, certification of
new technology is an open issue. Building on experiences from the automotive domain, we expect that development and certification of future
railway technology will be based on a scenario-driven process supported
by simulation technology. This work identifies a preliminary list of relevant scenario aspects and phenomena that simulators must be able to
virtually recreate in order to completely support this process.

Keywords: Simulation · Scenario-based · Certification · GoA3 · GoA4

1 Introduction

Due to characteristics of the railway domain, operations are safeguarded at various levels: On a macroscopic level through the planning of operational processes,
where dispatchers coordinate these processes on the basis of established rules and
regulations. Classically, collisions of trains are avoided at this level by releas-
ing lines centrally (from the regionally responsible interlocking) for individual
train movements. This is supported by a range of technical equipment, generally referred to as control and safety technology. These include signaling, techniques for locating trains (or detecting occupied track sections), and train control
systems (intermittent automatic train running control (German: *Punktförmige
Zugbeeinflussung*, PZB), continuous train control (*Linienzugbeeinflussung*, LZB),
European Train Control System (ETCS)). For GoA-1 (Grade of Automation)
the latter serve as a fallback level, e.g. by automatically triggering emergency
stops when passing stop signals, as well as for communicating information and
instructions (e.g. maximum speed) to the train driver. The train is operated by
the driver, who has a central role in ensuring safe operation, since he or she
must recognize immediate hazards along the route and act accordingly. For this
reason, the driver's activity is considered as the intermediate level between the
macroscopic and the technical level (see Fig. 1).

B. Milius et al. (Eds.): RSSRail 2023, LNCS 14198, pp. 78–97, 2023.
https://doi.org/10.1007/978-3-031-43366-5_5

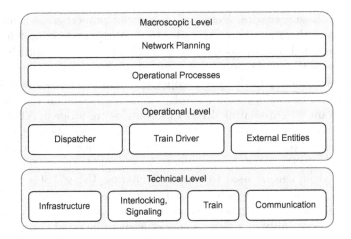

Fig. 1. Safeguarding of operations at different hierarchical levels

Currently, GoA-2 can be achieved via automated train operation (ATO) over ETCS (AoE). Here, ATO is not considered being a safety-critical system[1], because any unsafe action initiated by the ATO will be overridden by ETCS, which can be seen as a safety envelope [1]. However, a majority of safety related tasks[2] are still in the responsibility of the driver or other railway staff. Examples include operation of the doors and supervision of passenger change, as well as observing the track for obstacles and other anomalies. For GoA-3 and GoA-4 these tasks need to be executed by an automated system, with (GoA-3) or without (GoA-4) human supervision. Studies on the potential for automation in the railway domain see the greatest challenges at precisely this intermediate level [2,3].

Whereas the AoE itself is no critical system in the full supervision mode, once the driver no longer exists as a fallback, the system can be characterized as "high risk", according to the European AI Act [4, Title III, Chap. 1, Article 6]. This means, specific attention needs to be given to the training, validation and testing data sets. They "[...] should be sufficiently relevant, representative and free of errors and complete in view of the intended purpose of the system" [4]. In the automotive domain this key research topic was lately addressed by scenario-based development processes [5,6]. Structuring the space of all possible (railway) scenarios and making sure all properties are covered in the concrete derived test cases is one of the main motivations to use a scenario-based safety assessment approach. These methods require support from high-quality simulation frameworks (this is an observation from automotive domain). Our contribution lies in identifying the characteristic properties of the railway domain, that need to be

---

[1] Note, that ATO can be safety critical in some ETCS modes, e.g. "Shunting" or "On Sight".

[2] A task is understood (in the current, not highly automated state) as a requirement for railroad employees based on the regulations.

addressed in those scenarios. Here, we understand properties as concepts and their relations, where a concept is understood as the underlying "thing" that shall be represented by a symbol. Those symbols are used for capturing scenarios, where scenario is understood as a sequence of situations (cf. [7]).

Because automation in the macroscopic and technical levels are widely covered by existing technology such as AoE, we thereby focus on the phenomena that are relevant for automating driver tasks outside the scope of ATO. At some point in the process of deriving concrete test cases, a more abstract representation of a scenario (e.g. functional or logical scenario, using the terminology in [8]), needs to be instantiated. In an outlook, we give an idea how Traffic Sequence Charts (TSCs) [9] can be used to capture scenarios. Using TSCs immediately allows to use an ontology (which shall contain our list of concepts) and specify constraints of allowed and prohibited behavior including how to measure the criticality. The criticality of a given scenario needs to be rated in order to select and evaluate appropriate test cases. Therefore, we also give a short overview on applicable criticality metrics from the automotive domain and how they apply to the railway domain.

The remainder of this paper is structured as follows. In Sect. 2, the use of scenario-based processes in railway are motivated in more detail. Section 3 provides an overview of related research work, including an introduction to scenario-based methods in the automotive domain. The applied methodology and solution to get the characteristic properties of railway scenarios are detailed in Sect. 4. In Sect. 5 we outline planned future work. The final section presents conclusions.

2   A Motivation for Scenario-Based Approaches

The technical systems required for automated operation range from sensor and data processing systems for environment perception to maneuver planning and fail-safe communication between trains and control centers. At this level, the main task is to identify and avert a wide variety of local risks, some of which are difficult to predict and which, by their very nature, have a very low probability of occurrence. For example, a statistically sound safety argument for a system that implements fully automated railway travel (GoA-4), with railway facilities that are accessible to the public, would require an unrealistically large number of kilometers traveled in order to observe critical events in sufficient quantity. In the automotive domain, this problem is well known. Statistically, 440 million test kilometers are necessary to prove with a confidence level of 95% that a self-driving car causes less fatalities than a human driver [10]. In the automotive domain, a scenario-driven development approach is therefore pursued. The above number of test kilometers results from a statistical argument that assumes 1 fatality per 150 million kilometers (in the USA in the year 2013 [10]). Compared to that, Evans et al. give an average of 1 fatality per every 79 million train-km on Europe's railways, averaging over the years 2000 to 2009, counting fatalities in collisions and derailments and fatalities in serious level crossing accidents [11,

Table 5]. So, around 237 million test kilometers would be necessary to prove safety of an autonomous train[3].

With the scenario-based approach [5], one has a tool to generate critical situations in a targeted manner and thus validate the behavior of the system. Other factors that make simulations useful are that they can be executed faster than real-time, and be played out without any risk of harm. There are also challenges to this approach. Hauer et al. address the question if all scenario types were tested by applying the coupon collector problem [12]. The second question is then, if enough instances of those scenario types were tested. This challenge is not solved yet.

We assume that certification of future autonomous railway systems will happen in a (scenario-based) simulation-supported safety process, but the open challenges need to be addressed. Traditionally railway systems are certified based on the norms DIN EN 50126, 50128, 50129, which are not sufficient for certifying GoA4 functions. In this paper we argue, that in order to allow for certification of an autonomous system, we first need to gather evidence for its abilities and performance, i.e. allowing for assessment of the system. Based on the assessment results a certification may happen.

It can be assumed that in the railway domain the scenarios are less complex and fewer in number than in the automotive domain, but the scope of automation is larger. In the former, one can also automate the dispatching, the configuration of the railway network, the interaction with the passengers, as well as recommendations to intermodal travel chains, whereas in the latter only the pure driving task of the ego vehicle is to be automated. At this point it should be mentioned that in the automotive domain there is an overall set of rules (road traffic regulations), but compliance with these rules is the responsibility of individual road users. A deviation from these rules can often be observed, especially in urban environments. Such a deviation is not possible on rail, which leads to a different safety concept. These and other differences are discussed in detail by Jäger et al. [13].

3 Background and Related Work

There are three major areas of background work related to this paper: State of practice and related research on certification of highly automated railway systems, state of practice in railway simulators, and state of the art in the automotive domain related to verification and validation of autonomous driving systems.

3.1 Autonomous Train Operation and Certification

Scenario-based methods per-se are not new to the railway domain. For example, the ETCS specification contains a large set of standardized test sequences that

---

[3] Using the formula from [10], the number of required test kilometers is $n = \frac{\ln(1-C)}{\ln(1-F)}$ with confidence $C = 0.95$ and failure rate $F = 1.3 \cdot 10^{-8}$ (fatalities per kilometer).

are based on typical operational scenarios, called *mission profiles* (including a reference infrastructure) [14].

On the road towards autonomous driving, AoE has been specified and also certified for use in restricted areas. For example, the tram line S21 in Hamburg, Germany, drives with AoE and allows driverless operation (without passengers) between the final station and the depot [15]. The development of AoE has been scenario-driven in the sense that common operation scenarios have been systematically analyzed [16]. However, AoE (when in ETCS mode "Full Supervision") is deemed not safety critical because it is assumed that ETCS will enforce all necessary emergency actions (i.e. safe distances and speed limits) to ensure safe operation. This is a valid safety argument as long as a train driver is present who can recognize and handle all (manageable) safety critical situations that are not in the scope of ETCS.

For driverless train operation, the drivers tasks have to be automated as well. Recent research by Tagiew et al. is concerned with identifying sensor needs for enabling environment perception that is adequate for safe driving of passenger trains [17]. Their assumption was, that the perception functionalities of the AoE system shall be at least as good as the human senses. SIEMENS already provides vehicles equipped with the necessary sensors for automatic driving that are similar to the measuring system identified by Tagiew et al. [18].

Albeit train protection systems and infrastructure are highly standardized, there is no domain-specific normative standard for certifying the sensor systems and software required for environment perception in the railway domain. One domain-agnostic safety standard for those systems is the new ANSI/UL 4600 [19]. Peleska et al. evaluated the application of this standard for certification of a fictive ATO system implementation [20].

Grossmann et al. describe how synthetic images and videos for testing of artificial intelligence (AI) components are generated from random scenarios using a 3D simulation and rendering engine [21]. The scenarios are sampled with help of a railway domain ontology that follows principles (i.e. [22]) from the automotive domain. The focus is clearly on generating image/video data. In contrast, our method and results presented in Sect. 4 aim at a more abstract view on relevant phenomena, that go beyond object detection.

RailML [23] is an XML-based format for the description of railway systems. It focuses on the macroscopic level and allows for example to describe rolling stock, timetables and track schematics.

3.2 Existing Railway Simulators

In the railway domain, commercial simulation platforms are used for training and educational purposes, similar to the maritime domain. The structure is essentially quite the similar. There is the driver's cab, which consists of a visualization that is as realistic as possible with the corresponding control elements and is ideally provided with a true-to-the-original enclosure. Am image of reality is created in which the driver performs his tasks.

The railway simulators we considered include *ZUSI Railway Simulator* [24], *Simsphere Train* [25], *MST Traction Simulator* [26], *DLR RailSiTe* [27], *Open-Rails* [28], *TrainSim* [29], and *KI-LOK* [21] which uses the Air-Sim extension from Microsoft. In general, however, it can already be stated that none of the simulation environments mentioned can be used directly in the area of scenario-based verification and validation, since the original application is different and not all characteristic properties are covered. For example the subset of the tasks of the driver (in one man operation) that is concerned with monitoring and controlling passenger movement is not included. For our future work (see Sect. 5), among the simulators we reviewed, TrainSim is the most promising option, since it allows for an easy manipulation of scenarios and creates the environment in a straight-forward way based on a sequence of 3D waypoints [29]. Their main applications include providing datasets for Visual Odometry and LiDAR Odometry. The authors note, that future work contains "[t]he generation of datasets for tasks like 2D and 3D object detection". We see the focus of *DLR RailSiTe* [27] in the technical level (see Fig. 1), e.g. covering the test sequences specified in ETCS Subset-076. Further, human factors studies can be conducted using the RailSET environment.

3.3 Scenario-Based Methods in the Automotive Domain

The automotive domain is faced with the problem that traditional methods are not sufficient for the verification and validation of autonomous driving systems. Especially, basing a safety argument solely on physical testing is infeasible. Therefore, the use of simulation-based methods in addition to physical proto-typing and testing is pursued. Simulations are usually driven by scenario specifications [7]. Together with an increased need for simulations, scenarios have been identified as a driver in the development and certification process. Menzel et al. identified benefits of scenario-based methods in various phases of a V-development process [30]. In a series of research projects, different methods have been developed that utilize scenario specifications and simulations. In the ENABLE-S3 project, many of these have been placed into a scenario-based development process [6]. The core idea followed in ENABLE-S3 is to gather relevant critical scenarios from real world observations, and use them for risk assessment, requirement specification and testing.

Neurohr et al. worked out fundamental considerations around scenario-based testing, and show how it can be used to contribute to a safety case [31]. Extensive scenario specifications form the basis of both system design and validation [32]. One of the fundamental ideas of this approach is to represent relevant phenomena (critical events, operational sequences, driving maneuvers, etc.) through a collection of abstract scenarios [32]. An abstract scenario is a "formalized, declarative description of a traffic scenario focusing on complex relations [...]" [32]. These can then be used to automatically derive a large set of *concrete scenarios*, which are ultimately used for validation (e.g., testing and quantification of risks) [30]. Through the use of simulation tools, a much higher coverage can be achieved than in pure field and laboratory tests [33].

Traffic Sequence Charts [9] are a specification language for abstract scenarios that combine the advantages of graphical specification and formal methods: The used graphical representations convey an intuitive idea about the described scenario without requiring deep knowledge in formal methods, while its formal semantics mathematically tell whether a given concrete scenario is covered by the TSC. Becker et al. describe how concrete scenarios can be sampled from TSCs using their formal semantics [34].

Using scenario specifications in a larger scope such as in a development, standardization or certification process requires a common understanding of the relevant concepts and relations (e.g. types of traffic participants and how they interact) [35]. Therefore, ASAM has started the OpenXOntology [36] project, where a formalization of relevant concepts of the automotive domain has been developed. Similarly, the new/upcoming family of ISO standards ISO/DIS 34501 to 34504 [37–40] define relevant scenario attributes of test scenarios and an autonomous vehicle's operational design domain (ODD) specification. Earlier work organizes environment descriptions for automotive traffic scenarios into six concept layers being *street layer*, *road infrastructure*, *temporal modifications* to streets and infrastructure, *movable objects* (e.g. traffic participants and their maneuvers), *environment conditions* (e.g. weather), and *digital information* (e.g. vehicle communication) [22].

4   Characteristic Properties of Railway Scenarios

Existing standards do not provide a complete basis for certification of GoA-4. Thinking about possible approaches and capabilities of future highly automated systems, we orient ourselves on the current operational procedures in Germany. As hinted at in Sect. 1, the tasks of the train driver are of special interest. We assume that these tasks will have to be executed one way or another in highly automated railway systems as well. Therefore, and because the technology, concepts, and regulations necessary for GoA3/4 are subject to continuous change, we will list, but not consider some of the current approaches in Sect. 4.3. We assume that the derived concepts will still be valid in large parts. In this section, we present the main results of our research so far, which is a list of characteristic properties of railway scenarios shown to be relevant for automation. This also includes an initial list of concepts which should be part of a railway domain ontology used in simulators.

4.1   Method Description

In order to conclude the characteristic known properties of railroad scenarios, we start with an analysis of the operational processes as they are currently realized in Germany. It is worth mentioning that we are in the process of automating rail traffic all over Europe (GoA-2 has already been achieved in large parts), but we are still in a transitional state. We fall back on the currently valid regulations for train drivers (RiL 408) [41] and the signal book (RiL 301) [42]. Since these sources are also the basis for the *initial list of concepts*, the latter also reflects the current (not highly automated) state and the train driver is prominently represented.

In addition to the operational procedures, we consider characteristic generic features of the railway domain. Our main source for documented dangerous events in the railway domain are the extensive investigation reports (German: "Un-ter-su-chungs-be-rich-te") from the federal authority for railway accident investigation (*Bundesstelle für Eisenbahnunfalluntersuchung*, BEU) [43], as well as the open dataset [44], also published by BEU. To a lesser extent, the published Austrian investigation reports were considered [45]. This approach is similar to the analysis of the German In-Depth Accident Study (GIDAS) database in the automotive domain [46]. These sources yield the characteristic known phenomena of the railway domain, which in turn are a source for the characteristic properties of the rail scenarios, and the initial list of concepts. We emphasize that these are known phenomena. In the "scenario discovery process" [47] which is based on TSCs and a world model WM it is envisaged that experts may discover that a WM does not reflect all relevant phenomena, and needs to be extended.

Our approach is outlined in Fig. 2. During our research, also RailML has been considered. However, RailML focuses on the macroscopic level and covers the operational level only to a small extend (external entities are completely out of scope), so it is more an addendum to our list of concepts than a source of information.

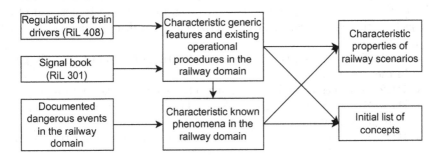

Fig. 2. Process to derive the characteristic properties of railway scenarios and the initial list of concepts

The operational processes change with the particular GoA under consideration. Currently, in Germany, mostly GoA-1 or GoA-2 is implemented. Trackside safety functions (securing the route and train sequence), as well as monitoring compliance with speed and signaling are already handled by the system. However, the operational driving task is not yet fully performed. In GoA-3, the human is still needed as a fallback level, which will no longer be the case in GoA-4. It is worth noting that a fundamental consideration in implementing ATO is the overall view of the train-side (ATO-OB (on board)) component, the track-side (ATO-TS) component, and the air interface between the two [48]. For the dispatcher, the tasks and responsibilities also change with the GoA level. For example, for a long time the technical securing of a level crossing had to be done by hand with a crank by a barrier guard. This type of safeguarding is still found very sporadically and in some cases still plays a role in documented dangerous events that have occurred recently.

4.2 Results

Based on the existing operational procedures, characteristic known phenomena, and documented dangerous events, we derived a list of characteristic properties of the railway domain, that scenarios need to be able to address. As stated above, this list is an initial collection, yet covering only the listed procedures and regulations. It needs to be extended to also cover concepts in Sect. 4.3, future developments, and potentially regulations from other countries.

The process is shown in Fig. 2. In order to derive the tasks of the driver, we oriented ourselves on the main phases of a train journey, which are "preparing train", "drive", "stop", and "park train". Note, that we left out "shunting", where different regulations apply. Since the tasks of the driver are of special interest here, they are listed in Fig. 3.

Now we list the derived characteristic properties (P) of the railway domain in no particular order.

- **P1:** The spatial, relative arrangement of objects is relevant in rail scenarios. Here, the rail network can be viewed as a graph, where the position of an object in this graph can be characterized by the distance along an edge. Furthermore:
  - **P1.1:** The position, velocity and acceleration of a train is usually given in the direction of travel.
  - **P1.2:** Branches (switches, crossings, etc.) shall be taken into account.
  - **P1.3:** For non-rail objects (e.g. external traffic participants), the distance, or relative position, to the track is also relevant.
  - **P1.3a:** A non-rail object can also be located at or behind the end of a track.
  - **P1.4:** For dynamic rail-bound objects, the affiliation to a sequence of track section must be unique[4].
  - **P1.5:** For static track-side equipment, the affiliation to a track section must be unique.
- **P2:** Properties and states of the track system are relevant. These include:
  - **P2.1:** Physical states and properties (e.g., setting of railroad switches).
  - **P2.2:** Logical states and properties (e.g., route).
  - **P2.3:** Links of trains and their route (occupation of which track section at which time).

---

[4] They can change their sections and can be present in more than one sections at the same time.

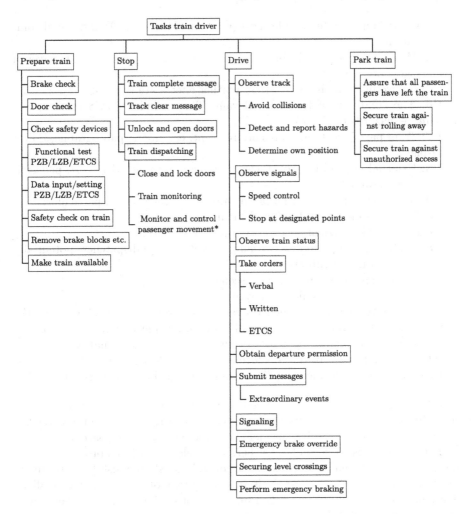

Fig. 3. Tasks of the train driver. A task is understood as a requirement for railroad employees based on the regulations. Tasks marked with (*) are only relevant in one-person operation, i.e. when no train conductor is on board.

Notably, these are not constant, but can change dynamically over the course of a scenario.

- **P3:** Signals and other infrastructure (platforms, level crossing, trackside train control equipment, etc.) are relevant, including:
  - **P3.1:** their logical affiliation to a track.
  - **P3.2:** their logical and physical properties, as well as dynamic states (e.g., shown signals or disturbances).

  Signals include in particular:
  - **P3.3:** Audible signals and hand signals.

- **P3.4:** Markings (e.g., pole signs (German "Mastschild")) and signal combinations.
- **P4:** Message exchanges (including type, time, content, sender and receiver of messages) are relevant.
- **P5:** Environmental characteristics/weather effects are relevant.
- **P6:** The condition of trains is relevant. This includes ETCS level, speed, damage/hazards (e.g. fire).
- **P7:** Train parts and their states are relevant, e.g. doors, pantographs, ETCS displays.
- **P8:** External objects (e.g. obstacles, animals) and road users (e.g. pedestrians) are relevant.
- **P9:** Staff members of the railroad operation are relevant, in particular:
  - **P9.1:** the mental state of staff members.
  - **P9.2:** their physical position (within the scenario).
  - **P9.3:** including remotely working operators (e.g. dispatcher, potentially remote train operator).
- **P10:** The timetable is relevant for scenarios.
- **P11:** The clearance profile is relevant.
- **P12:** Deviations from planned operations are relevant. In addition to the representation of the occurred, actual, situation, it must therefore be possible to represent the planned (but not occurred) situation in scenarios.
- **P13:** (Virtually) coupled train formations are relevant. In particular, such formations can be formed, modified, and disbanded during a scenario.

Other relevant objects, environmental phenomena, and communication relationships are listed in the initial list of concepts in Fig. 4. Despite the extensive research, this is also not to be considered complete (also due to space limitations, a complete listing is not feasible). Rather, other relevant objects, properties, environmental phenomena, and communication relationships must be determined separately as part of a risk analysis in the context of a system that shall be developed and/or secured and taken into account during scenario-driven development (see also [32]).

4.3   Potential Adaptions of Concepts

Technologies, regulations, and specifications are in constant flux. Since our analysis was mainly based on the current operational procedures and standards in Germany, the concepts will need to be extended and adapted. We give some examples for this.

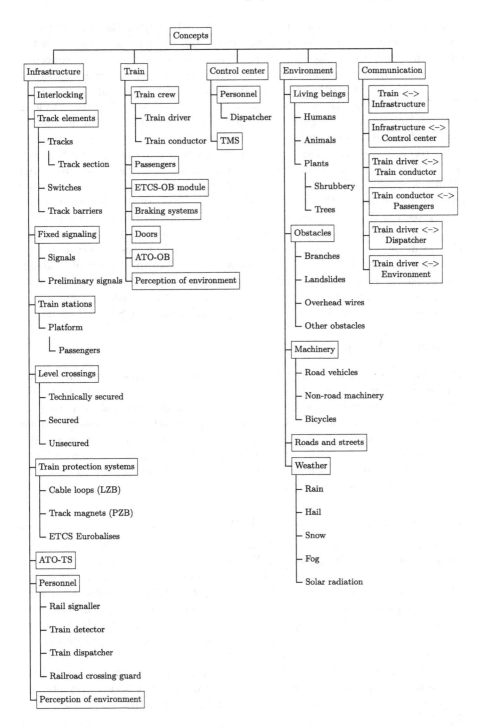

Fig. 4. Initial list of concepts

As part of the Next Generation Train 3 (NGT3) project, the conceptualization of a remote control workstation has been advanced [49]. This would make the role of the train driver obsolete[5], thus requiring an adaptation of the concepts. This view roughly coincides with that of ERA's Automatic Train Operation (ATO) framework, as outlined e.g. in [48]. Trackside signaling can be omitted, if all trains running on the line are equipped with a train control system. As long as this is not the case (as currently), the fixed signals must remain in place to ensure safe mixed operation [51].

In the ETCS driver's handbook it is stated that automated (Full Supervision (FS)), partially automated (Limited Supervision (LS)), and non-automated (Staff Responsible (SR)) modes can be alternated during a journey [52]. Other relevant modes include the On Sight (OS) mode, which allows the train to enter a track section that may already be occupied by another train. In this mode it is the responsibility of the driver to keep the speed limit and to drive on sight. The OS mode is exited when the front end of the train leaves the OS area.

There are plans for a new concept that would substitute the traditional signaling system. This moving block concept does not rely on fixed track sections. It requires a continuous two-way digital communication between trains and a trackside control center [53]. This will be possible from ETCS level 3 onward.

5   Future Work

In the previous section, an initial set of concepts has been derived that shows what needs to be simulated to support the development of autonomous trains, with focus on the needed perception chain. The long-term goal is to transfer and evaluate the simulation and scenario-based methods to the railway domain that have been studied so far mostly from the automotive perspective. Besides setting up railway simulators being able to validly incorporate aforementioned concepts in a virtual environment, other building blocks are needed as well. Two of them are highlighted in the following.

5.1   Extending TSCs to the Railway Domain

Building on the introduction in Sect. 3.3, future research includes extending TSCs for use in the railway domain. Figure 5 shows a TSC for a simple test scenario which is relevant, when irregularities are encountered at a level crossings [41]. We consider the case when the "level crossing (LX) not protected symbol (LX01)" [52] is displayed on the Driver Machine Interface (DMI). The TSC is to be read as follows: The rectangular boxes are so called *invariant nodes* depicting traffic situations. They may be equipped with mathematical predicate expressions such as distance measures along and perpendicular to the track, or speed limits. The rounded rectangle is the *bulletin board* naming special symbols, here for the main track, the ego train, and a level crossing. A TSC is interpreted by mapping invariant nodes to time intervals and symbols to objects.

---

[5] Some of the train driver tasks would be taken over by the newly created position of a train operator (TO), who would not ride on the train [50].

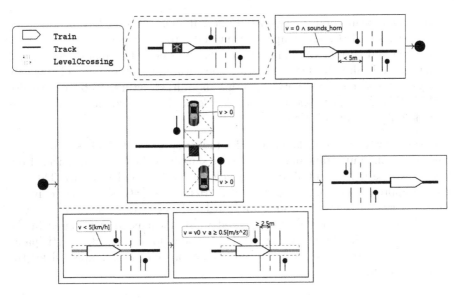

Fig. 5. Example railway TSC that shows intended behavior at unprotected level crossings

The said scenario is a seamless sequence of the situations depicted in the invariant nodes. A train driver needs to come to a complete stop, warn potential entities by giving the signal ZP 1 [42] (sounding the horn) before continuing the journey over the crossing and vacating the crossing as quickly as possible. Parallel to that, the driver needs to observe the crossing and make sure that there are no obstacles on the tracks. Note, that this scenario is also relevant when reactivating old tracks in areas with little traffic, in an economical way without technically securing existing level crossings.

Although showing a railway scenario, Fig. 5 does not require any extensions beyond what has been specified for the automotive domain (TSCs are intentionally open with respect to the design domain, so they allow to define the used symbols in the bulletin board as needed). However, taking the whole list of relevant aspects given in Sect. 4 into account, we see that at least the following modifications will be necessary.

- So far, used symbols (for vehicles, roads, etc.) in TSCs have not been standardized. At least in Germany, a wide set of railway concept symbols has already been standardized by Deutsche Bahn in RiL 819. The symbols for track and train in Fig. 5 have been adopted from that standard. The defined symbols are intended to be used in track schematics and are widely known by domain experts. Therefore, we propose to use these symbols whenever possible.
- In the automotive domain, scenarios are mostly restricted to a single road segment or crossing. In railway, especially when targeting scenarios at the macroscopic level (see Fig. 1), the track layout is more important and a sce-

nario may span complex layouts. Hence, it must be possible to add track schematics to TSCs and map invariant nodes to parts of it.

– Reliable and correct communication is key in safe autonomous train operation, as AoE already shows. Existing and future approaches for ATO widely rely on message passing between trains and infrastructure. To be able to also cover this in scenario specifications, TSCs need to be extended with means to describe communication.

Together with the TSC language, also tool support for TSCs has to be developed. Here, one important building block is sampling of concrete scenarios from TSCs, because it is essential for being able to simulate and test with TSCs. A feasible approach has been shown in [34]. Here, the TSC is translated into a constraint system whose solutions are translated to concrete scenarios. Because trains have only 1D movements (opposed to 2D movements considered in the automotive domain), and no exact dynamics models for other traffic participants are needed, an even better scalability of the approach can be expected for the railway domain.

5.2   Testcase Evaluation

Other future work includes setting up a railway simulator that is capable of executing concrete scenarios sampled from TSCs. The validity of this simulator shall also be addressed. Out of the existing simulation frameworks that were reviewed in Sect. 3.2, none is able to cover all characteristic properties.

Concrete test cases for a specific system under test (SUT), e.g. a perception system or a system that executes other tasks previously allocated to the train driver, can be derived. A threshold on criticality metrics (CM) as used in the automotive domain could serve as pass/fail criteria. CM are used to quantify the criticality of a specific scenario. We give some examples of CM adapted from the survey by Westhofen et al. that might be applicable in the railway domain [54].

Time to Collision (TTC) [55]. This commonly used CM provides the minimum time until two entities E_1 and E_2 collide, if their respective motion model is taken as given. Since there is no lateral steering for trains, this motion model is simpler than for cars.

Proportion of Stopping Distance (PSD) [56]. Since a train cannot swerve, it must come to a complete stop at an obstacle. The Minimal Stopping Distance (MSD) can be calculated from the maximum negative acceleration a. $MSD = \frac{v^2}{2a}$, where v is the current speed. If RD (remaining distance) is the distance to the obstacle, one can calculate PSD according to $PSD = RD/MSD$. One needs a PSD value of 1 or greater to stop safely.

Brake Threat Number (BTN) [57]. This CM is defined as the necessary acceleration that is imposed on E_1 as a consequence of a movement of another entity E_2, divided by the maximum possible acceleration $a_{1,max}$ of E_1.

$$\text{BTN}(A_1, A_2, t) = \frac{a_{\text{req}}(A_1, A_2, t)}{a_{1,\max}(t)}$$

A BTN value of ≥ 1 means that E_1 cannot brake safely. This CM seems to be particularly relevant for train sequences.

Post Encroachment Time (PET) [56]. This CM calculates the time between leaving a conflict area (CA) of E_1 and entering the same CA of E_2. This CM is particularly relevant at level crossings.

$$\text{PET}(E_1, E_2, CA) = t_{\text{entry}}(A_2, CA) - t_{\text{exit}}(A_1, CA)$$

The CMs listed so far have in common that they can be computed without involving a central coordinating instance. Analyses of descriptions of dangerous events in the railroad domain show that in many such events the dispatcher was involved, e.g. when a route was resolved too early, or a barrier was not lowered in time to give a long truck enough time to maneuver across an overpass. To account for these situation as well, novel CMs need to be developed.

6   Conclusion

In this paper we gave a summary, how a simulation-based approach fits in an safety argument which could be used in the future to virtually certify highly automated railway systems. We legitimized the approach and gave an overview of the way it is conducted in the automotive domain. Our main contribution to this topic is a list of 13 characteristic properties of the railway domain that scenario specifications shall be able to address. As described in Sect. 4.1, this list is based on existing regulations for train drivers and railway accident reports, and therefore can only represent the current state of practice and is not yet complete.

Since scenarios have the ambition to be able to represent all possible situations [8], this list can serve as a necessary subset of phenomena to be covered. However, the collections of properties and concepts are a starting point for building critical railway scenarios, which may be specified as TSCs [9]. This helps to fulfill the requirements on systems with AI components, especially those related to completeness and representativeness. Further, the derived list of concepts, which shall be included in an ontology, can be used to instantiate concrete tests that shall be simulated. We also give some examples of criticality metrics, which can serve as pass/fail criteria in those tests, once a target value is given, that shall not be exceeded.

References

1. Koopman, P., Wagner, M.: Toward a framework for highly automated vehicle safety validation. In: SAE Technical Paper Series. SAE Technical Paper Series, SAE International400 Commonwealth Drive, Warrendale, PA, United States (2018). https://doi.org/10.4271/2018-01-1071.
2. Flamm, L., Meirich, C., Meyer zu Hörste, M., Hagemeyer, F.W., Preuss, M.: Regulatorischer anpassungsbedarf für das automatische fahren im bahnbetrieb (01) (2019)
3. Hagemeyer, F., Preuß, M., Meyer zu Hörste, M., Meirich, C., Flamm, L.: Automatisiertes Fahren auf der Schiene. Springer Fachmedien Wiesbaden (2021). https://doi.org/10.1007/978-3-658-32328-8
4. European Commission: Proposal for a regulation of the European parliament and of the council laying down harmonised rules on artificial intelligence (artificial intelligence act) and amending certain union legislative acts (2021)
5. Riedmaier, S., Ponn, T., Ludwig, D., Schick, B., Diermeyer, F.: Survey on scenario-based safety assessment of automated vehicles **8**, 87456–87477 (2020). https://doi.org/10.1109/ACCESS.2020.2993730
6. Leitner, A.: Enable-s3: Project introduction. In: Leitner, A., Watzenig, D., Ibanez-Guzman, J. (eds.) Validation and Verification of Automated Systems. Springer, Cham(2020)
7. Ulbrich, S., Menzel, T., Reschka, A., Schuldt, F., Maurer, M.: Defining and substantiating the terms scene, situation, and scenario for automated driving. In: 2015 IEEE 18th International Conference on Intelligent Transportation Systems, pp. 982–988. IEEE (2015). https://doi.org/10.1109/ITSC.2015.164
8. Kalisvaart, S., Slavik, Z., Op den Camp, O.: Using scenarios in safety validation of automated systems. In: Leitner, A., Watzenig, D., Ibanez-Guzman, J. (eds.) Validation and Verification of Automated Systems, pp. 27–44. Springer, Cham (2020). https://doi.org/10.1007/978-3-030-14628-3_5
9. Damm, W., Möhlmann, E., Rakow, A.: Traffic sequence charts for the ENABLE-S$_3$ test architecture. In: Leitner, A., Watzenig, D., Ibanez-Guzman, J. (eds.) Validation and Verification of Automated Systems, pp. 45–60. Springer, Cham (2020). https://doi.org/10.1007/978-3-030-14628-3_6
10. Kalra, N., Paddock, S.M.: Driving to safety: how many miles of driving would it take to demonstrate autonomous vehicle reliability? Transp. Res. Part A Policy Pract. **94**, 182–193 (2016). https://doi.org/10.1016/j.tra.2016.09.010
11. Evans, A.W.: Fatal train accidents on europe's railways: 1980–2009 **43**(1), 391–401 (2011). https://doi.org/10.1016/j.aap.2010.09.009. comparative Study Journal Article
12. Hauer, F., Schmidt, T., Holzmuller, B., Pretschner, A.: Did we test all scenarios for automated and autonomous driving systems? (2019). https://doi.org/10.1109/ITSC.2019.8917326
13. Jäger, B., Meyer zu Hörste, M., Hesse, T., Köster, F.: Automated driving - can rail traffic learn from road traffic? (140) (2016)
14. ERTMS/ETCS: Safety requirements for the technical interoperability of etcs in levels 1 & 2
15. Schröder, J., Gonçalves, C.A., Dickgießer, B., Knollmann, V.: Digital s-bahn hamburg - germany's first implementation of ato over etcs, May 2021
16. ERTMS Users Group: Ertms/ato operational scenarios. Document version **1**, 11 (2022)

17. Tagiew, R., Leinhos, D., von der Haar, H., Klotz, C., Sprute, D., Ziehn, J., Schmelter, A., Witte, S., Klasek, P.: Onboard sensor systems for automatic train operation. In: Marrone, S., de Sanctis, M., Kocsis, I., Adler, R., Hawkins, R., Schleiß, P., Nardone, R., Flammini, F., Vittorini, V. (eds.) Dependable Computing - EDCC 2022 Workshops, Communications in Computer and Information Science, vol. 1656, pp. 139–150. Springer International Publishing (2022). DOI: https://doi.org/10.1007/978-3-031-16245-9_11

18. Wolf, R., Langer, H.G.: Goa4-readiness - challanges for future rail vehicles 146 (2022)

19. Underwriters Laboratories: ANSI/UL 4600: Evaluation of autonomous products (2022)

20. Peleska, J., Haxthausen, A.E., Lecomte, T.: Standardisation considerations for autonomous train control. In: Margaria, T., Steffen, B. (eds.) Leveraging Applications of Formal Methods, Verification and Validation. Practice. LNCS, vol. 13704, pp. 286–307. Springer, Cham (2022). https://doi.org/10.1007/978-3-031-19762-8_22

21. Grossmann, J., Grube, N., Kharma, S., Knoblauch, D., Krajewski, R., Kucheiko, M., Wiesbrock, H.W.: Test and training data generation for object recognition in the railway domain. In: Masci, P., Bernardeschi, C., Graziani, P., Koddenbrock, M., Palmieri, M. (eds.) Software Engineering and Formal Methods. SEFM 2022 Collocated Workshops. LNCS, vol. 13765, pp. 5–16. Springer, Cham (2023). https://doi.org/10.1007/978-3-031-26236-4_1

22. Scholtes, M., et al.: 6-layer model for a structured description and categorization of urban traffic and environment 9, 59131–59147 (2021). https://doi.org/10.1109/ACCESS.2021.3072739

23. Nash, A., Huerlimann, D., Schuette, J., Krauss, V.P.: Railml - a standard data interface for railroad applications. In: Vorticity and Turbulence Effects in Fluid Structure Interactions, WIT Transactions on State of the Art in Science and Engineering, vol. 1, pp. 3–10. WIT Press (2010). https://doi.org/10.2495/978-1-84564-500-7/01

24. Hölscher, C.: Zusi bahnsimulatoren (2023). https://www.zusi.de. Accessed 11 Apr 2023

25. HENSOLDT: Simsphere train (2023). https://www.hensoldt.net/stories/training-train-drivers-etcs-app-by-hensoldt/. Accessed 11 Apr 2023

26. Müller Systemtechnik: Mst triebfahrzeug simulator (2023). https://muellersystemtechnik.de/mst-triebfahrzeug-simulator. Accessed 11 Apr 2023

27. Deutsches Zentrum für Luft- und Raumfahrt e.V.: Railsite (rail simulation and testing) 2(A88) (2016). https://doi.org/10.17815/jlsrf-2-144

28. Open Rails (2023). https://www.openrails.org/. Accessed 11 Apr 2023

29. D'Amico, G., et al.: Trainsim: A railway simulation framework for lidar and camera dataset generation (28022023), under review

30. Menzel, T., Bagschik, G., Maurer, M.: Scenarios for development, test and validation of automated vehicles. In: 2018 IEEE Intelligent Vehicles Symposium (IV), pp. 1821–1827. IEEE (2018). https://doi.org/10.1109/IVS.2018.8500406

31. Neurohr, C., Westhofen, L., Henning, T., de Graaff, T., Mohlmann, E., Bode, E.: Fundamental considerations around scenario-based testing for automated driving. In: 2020 IEEE Intelligent Vehicles Symposium (IV), pp. 121–127. IEEE (2020). https://doi.org/10.1109/IV47402.2020.9304823

32. Neurohr, C., Westhofen, L., Butz, M., Bollmann, M.H., Eberle, U., Galbas, R.: Criticality analysis for the verification and validation of automated vehicles 9, 18016–18041 (2021). https://doi.org/10.1109/ACCESS.2021.3053159

33. Wachenfeld, W., Winner, H.: Die freigabe des autonomen fahrens. In: (ed.) Autonomes Fahren, pp. 439–464. Springer, Heidelberg (2015)
34. Becker, J.S.: Simulation of abstract scenarios: towards automated tooling in criticality analysis (2022). https://elib.dlr.de/186897/, februar
35. Westhofen, L., Stierand, I., Becker, J.S., Möhlmann, E., Hagemann, W.: Towards a congruent interpretation of traffic rules for automated driving: Experiences and challenges. In: Borges, G., Satoh, K., Schweighofer, E. (eds.) Proceedings of the International Workshop on Methodologies for Translating Legal Norms into Formal Representations (LN2FR 2022) in association with 35th International Conference on Legal Knowledge and Information Systems (JURIX 2022) (2022)
36. ASAM: Openx ontology (2023), accessed Mai 02, 2023. https://www.asam.net/standards/asam-openxontology
37. International Organization for Standardization: ISO/DIS 34501:2022: Road vehicles - test scenarios for automated driving systems - vocabulary (2022)
38. International Organization for Standardization: ISO/DIS 34502:2022: Road vehicles - test scenarios for automated driving systems - scenario based safety evaluation framework (2022)
39. International Organization for Standardization: ISO/DIS 34503: Road vehicles - test scenarios for automated driving systems - taxonomy for operational design domain (2023), under development
40. International Organization for Standardization: ISO/DIS 34504: Road vehicles - test scenarios for automated driving systems - scenario categorization (2023), under development
41. Deutsche Bahn AG: Fahrdienstvorschrift richtlinie 408.21-27: Züge fahren (2015)
42. Deutsche Bahn AG: Fahrdienstvorschrift richtlinie 301: Signalbuch (2019)
43. Bundesstelle für Eisenbahnunfalluntersuchung: Untersuchungsberichte. https://www.eisenbahn-unfalluntersuchung.de. Accessed Mai 02, 2023
44. Bundesstelle für Eisenbahnunfalluntersuchung: Daten zu abschließend untersuchten gefährlichen ereignissen im eisenbahnbetrieb. https://www.eisenbahn-unfalluntersuchung.de/EUB/DE/Publikationen/Open_Data/Open_Data_node.html. Accessed Mai 02, 2023
45. des Bundes (SUB), S.: Untersuchungsberichte. https://www.bmk.gv.at/ministerium/sub/schiene/berichte.html. Accessed Mai 02, 2023
46. Babisch, S., Neurohr, C., Westhofen, L., Schoenawa, S., Liers, H.: Leveraging the gidas database for the criticality analysis of automated driving systems **2023**, 1–25 (2023). https://doi.org/10.1155/2023/1349269
47. Damm, W., Möhlmann, E., Rakow, A.: A scenario discovery process based on traffic sequence charts. In: Leitner, A., Watzenig, D., Ibanez-Guzman, J. (eds.) Validation and Verification of Automated Systems, pp. 61–73. Springer, Cham (2020). https://doi.org/10.1007/978-3-030-14628-3_7
48. Gerd Tasler, V.K.: Einführung des hochautomatisierten fahrens - auf dem weg zum vollautomatischen bahnbetrieb, June 2018
49. Brandenburger, N., Hörmann, H.J., Stelling, D., Naumann, A.: Tasks, skills, and competencies of future high-speed train drivers **231**(10), 1115–1122 (2017). https://doi.org/10.1177/0954409716676509
50. Brandenburger, N., Naumann, A., Grippenkoven, J., Jipp, M.: Der train operator (2017)
51. Fendrich, L., Fengler, W.: Handbuch Eisenbahninfrastruktur. Springer, Berlin Heidelberg (2019). https://doi.org/10.1007/978-3-662-56062-4

52. European Union Agency for Railways: Etcs driver's handbook (2019). https://www.era.europa.eu/system/files/2022-11/Generic%20ETCS%20Drivers%20Handbook.docx
53. Bonetto, E.: D2.1 modelling of the moving block signalling system (2019)
54. Westhofen, L., et al.: Criticality metrics for automated driving: a review and suitability analysis of the state of the art (2022). https://doi.org/10.1007/s11831-022-09788-7, pII: 9788
55. Hayward, J.C.: Near-miss determination through use of a scale of danger. Highway Research Record (1972)
56. Allen, B.L., Shin, B.T., Cooper, P.J.: Analysis of traffic conflicts and collisions. Transportation Research Record (1978)
57. Jansson, J.: Collision avoidance theory: With application to automotive collision mitigation. Ph.D. thesis, Linköping University (2005)

Dependability Analysis of UPS Architectures for the Italian Railway Signaling System

Giulio Masetti[1,2(✉)], Felicita Di Giandomenico[1], and Silvano Chiaradonna[1]

[1] Istituto di Scienza e Tecnologia "A. Faedo", Consiglio Nazionale delle Ricerche, Pisa, Italy
{giulio.masetti,felicita.digiandomenico,silvano.chiaradonna}@isti.cnr.it
[2] Istituto Comprensivo di Anghiari e Monterchi, Anghiari, Italy

Abstract. Continuous power supply in railway systems is vital to guarantee dependable accomplishment of energy-supported critical operations. With reference to the Italian railway infrastructure, this paper focuses on the railroad signaling system, used to control the movement of railway traffic, where Uninterruptable Power Supply systems (UPS) for Safety and Signalling are employed. Fault tolerant UPS architectures are adopted to cope with unpredictable fault events occurring at UPS level, potentially resulting in safety/availability violations. This paper proposes a stochastic model-based analysis to support the comparison between different UPS redundant architectures in terms of dependability attributes, primarily reliability and availability indicators. The analysis results can be fruitfully exploited by a designer to set up the most effective UPS configuration, able to satisfy dependability requirements, while also accounting for possible saving in energy consumption.

Keywords: Dependability · Uninterruptable Power Supply system · Stochastic model · Railroad Signaling System

1 Acronyms and Symbols

AC	Alternate Current
DC	Direct Current
MTBF	Mean Time Between Failures
MTTF	Mean Time To Failure
UPS	Uninterruptable Power Supply
A_∞	Steady state availability
$\mathcal{I}_{MTBF}$	Percentage of improvement in MTBF of UPS_{CR} with respect to UPS_{SR}
λ_B	Battery failure rate
λ_I	Inverter failure rate
λ_R	Rectifier failure rate
λ_T	Transformer failure rate
L	Load

B. Milius et al. (Eds.): RSSRail 2023, LNCS 14198, pp. 98–114, 2023.
https://doi.org/10.1007/978-3-031-43366-5_6

μ Recovery rate of components

r Ratio between lambdas of UPS_{CR} and UPS_{SR}

UPS_{CR} Component redundancy architecture

UPS_{SR} System redundancy architecture

$\mathcal{C}$ Critical operation condition

$\mathcal{N}$ Normal operation condition

l_m UPS_{CR}: load per module

m UPS_{CR}: number of components of a given kind in hot standby

n UPS_{CR}: number of components of a given kind required to serve the load

2 Introduction

Railroad signaling systems are highly critical components within the railway infrastructure, being used to control the movement of railway traffic. Reliable signaling systems and accurate transit management are key factors in the profitability of a railway system. Therefore, railway operators afford significant investment in control and signaling systems to maximize the use of rail networks, and lower the cost of new infrastructure and railway lines. To properly satisfy the requested uptime capacity, Uninterruptable Power Supply (UPS) systems[1] are employed, to ensure that rail networks deliver efficient and reliable services. UPS is typically organized in a modular structure to be customizable in accordance with the specific railway segment. Moreover, redundancy at level of different granularity of components is adopted for promoting the ability to cope with unpredictable faults which could affect the UPS, potentially resulting in safety/availability violations of the signalling system.

In particular, the offered contribution is a study to model and analyze different redundant configurations of UPS, targeting quantitative dependability assessment. Moving from the currently adopted redundant UPS configuration in the Italian railway system, where redundancy is applied at level of the whole system (referred to as UPS_{SR}), the study aims at comparing its dependability attributes with those of an alternative fault tolerant organization where redundancy is exploited at level of individual UPS components (referred to as UPS_{CR}). Actually, UPS_{CR} is going to supersede the currently adopted UPS_{SR}, so this study provides a useful support to sustain this decision or otherwise raise substantiated criticisms.

The developed evaluation resorts to stochastic model-based analysis, which is widely recognized as an effective support to system design, being applicable since the early stage of system design and thus providing prompt and useful feedback to the system designer in performing optimal design choices. Indicators representative of dependability-related attributes (namely, availability, Mean Time To Failure (MTTF) and Mean Time Between Failures (MTBF)) are considered, for which markovian models are built, under specified fault assumptions. Numerical

---

[1] In the railway sector UPS is often referred as Integrated Power Supply (IPS). In this paper we adhere to the most general terminology.

experiments are then conducted in different scenarios; the obtained results allow to discuss strengths and weaknesses of the UPS_{CR} and UPS_{SR} architectures, also taking into account energy consumption aspects.

The paper is structured as follows: Sect. 3 briefly recall the system architecture and its evolution; Sect. 4 describes UPS_{SR}, the UPS architecture currently in use, and presents UPS_{CR}, the new proposal; Sect. 5 discusses related work, focusing in particular on UPS architectures that are close to UPS_{CR}; Sect. 6 illustrates the stochastic models employed in the analysis; Sect. 7 shows numerically the improvements in switching from UPS_{SR} to UPS_{CR} in terms of MTBF, considering a couple of scenarios, where different parameters' settings are investigated; Sect. 8 draws conclusions and discusses future work.

3   Context

Many rail applications, such as traffic management systems and automatic train protection systems, require uninterrupted power of appropriate quality, as they cannot tolerate even minimal interruption or disturbances in power flow. In fact, in these critical contexts power disruptions are not just inconvenient; they are also serious threats to correct operation, being potentially responsible of major safety violations. Therefore, they are electrical loads that need protection from any type of input power interruption or power quality disturbance.

This work makes reference to the Italian railway system, where measures to guarantee uninterruptable power supply for safety and signalling systems have been introduced since the early eighties of the last century. In particular, the apparatus to protect safety and signalling systems we focus on is called SIAP-Sistema Integrato di Alimentazione e Protezione, conforming to the RFI Specifications, dated 2010 [9] and currently adopted, and its forthcoming evolution SMAP-Sistema Modulare di Alimentazione e Protezione, conforming to the RFI (the Italian railway infrastructure manager) Specifications, dated 2015 [10]. To keep the terminology simple, the SIAP related architecture will be referred in the following as UPS_{SR}, while the SMAP related one as UPS_{CR}. Although the focus is on the Italian railways, for which documents needed for the analysis study were made available, similar uniterruptable power supply systems are adopted by railways operators in other Countries, which could likewise get benefit from the outcomes and considerations made on the SIAP/SMAP architectural solutions.

From an abstract high level point of view, Fig. 1 depicts the overall organization around the considered UPS system. Electrical power to UPS (AC source) is provided by either Utility or Diesel Generator, this last being activated upon problems experienced by the former. In normal ($\mathcal{N}$) operation mode, where either Utility or the Diesel Generator are working and provide AC source, UPS ensures that IT devices (AC and DC loads) receive clean, reliable electricity. Instead, if the AC input supply is interrupted, UPS enters a critical ($\mathcal{C}$) operation mode, where it uses the battery it is equipped with to keep supported loads up and running, and continues to utilize battery power until the AC input returns back or the battery runs out of power. Finally, should UPS fail, it is disconnected from the loads and the switch Bypass path is turned on quickly, to support the output loads. This paper addresses the reliability and availability analysis of the UPS architectures in Fig. 1, which are presented in the next Sect. 4.

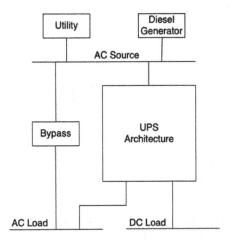

Fig. 1. Abstract, high-level view of the equipment involved in the energy supply for safety and signalling systems. The box "UPS architecture" is the object targeted by the conducted analyses.

4 Redundant UPS Architectures

Two redundant UPS architectures based on modular and redundant components are considered in this paper: a) the system redundancy-based architecture UPS$_{SR}$, that is the currently adopted solution in the Italian railway system[2], where redundancy is applied at level of the whole system as shown in Fig. 2a; b) the component redundancy-based architecture UPS$_{CR}$, that is a new proposal[3], where redundancy is exploited at level of individual UPS components as shown in Fig. 2b.

UPS$_{SR}$ comprises two units in a $1+1$ configuration: the primary and hot standby unit. Each unit can cover the entire load and includes a transformer, a cabinet that encloses a rectifier and an inverter, and a battery bank.

UPS$_{CR}$ exploits higher modularity by considering each individual component, i.e., the rectifier, the inverter and the battery bank (excluding the transformer), as a modular and redundant unit deployed in $n+m$ configuration: n primary units and m hot standby units, for a total of $3(n+m)$ units (or modules). For each component, modular and redundant units are deployed in layers and each is connected to all those in the next one through smart (synchronus) switches. Each set of n primary units can cover the entire load. If one fails then the switch

---

[2] SIAP, RFI IS732 - Ed. 1999.
[3] SMAP [10].

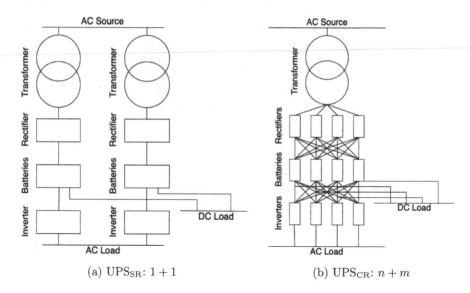

(a) UPS$_{SR}$: $1+1$ (b) UPS$_{CR}$: $n+m$

Fig. 2. Logical architectures of UPS under investigation: UPS$_{SR}$ (a) in a $1+1$ redundancy configuration with primary and hot standby UPS unit, and UPS$_{CR}$ (b) in $n+m$ redundancy configuration for each individual component (excluding the transformer), with $n=3$ and $m=1$, where n and m are the number of primary and hot standby units, respectively.

isolates it and closes the circuits with another one; in normal operating condition, usage is balanced among primary components.

The rectifier (which converts the input utility power from AC to DC and recharges the batteries) is operational only when the Alternate Current (AC) source is working, i.e. in the $\mathcal{N}$ mode. The inverter converts DC power from batteries back into AC power for load use. So, considering only DC loads, inverters can be omitted from the diagram of Fig. 2.

In both UPS$_{CR}$ and UPS$_{SR}$ architectures, hot spare units are standing by until a primary unit fails. A hot spare unit, if any, is then switched into service to replace the failed primary unit. The UPS fails when there are no redundant hot spare units left to replace the failed primary units (*UPS failure*), that is when there are no longer enough units to cover the loads. When the UPS fails, then the railroad signaling systems fails, whatever the current operation mode $\mathcal{N}$ or $\mathcal{C}$ (both outages and low quality service are considered a failure).

In the case of the UPS system under consideration, n primary units in the UPS$_{CR}$ perform the same function overall as the corresponding single primary component in the UPS$_{SR}$, i.e., they cover the same loads. So a unit in the UPS$_{CR}$, e.g., the rectifier, has different characteristics, in terms of failure rate, power consumption, etc., than the corresponding unit in the UPS$_{SR}$.

Usually, in a railway station there is a maintenance team that, whenever an alert is raised by the UPS monitoring system, substitutes or repairs failed components. In the following maintenance is modeled but is highly simplified.

Considering that in UPS_{CR} only one transformer is employed, it is immediate to observe that switching from UPS_{SR} to UPS_{CR} halves the number of transformers, that are the main source of power waste[4]. A more accurate computation of the energy consumption incurred by the two architectures would require to account for detailed consumption by the individual components, which is beyond the scope of this paper and postponed as future work.

In general, the two architectures present different trade-offs among availability, energy efficiency, maintainability and capabilities of dynamic reconfiguration. The analysis results proposed in this paper can be fruitfully exploited by a designer to set up the most effective UPS architecture configuration in order to support innovative design of the station power systems, especially in terms of: 1) identification of critical components (transformers, rectifiers, batteries and inverters) of the existing configuration; 2) identification of the degree of redundancy of particularly critical components.

5 Related Work

In the literature, several studies have addressed dependability and architectural solutions for UPS systems, either without reference to specific application contexts (e.g., [6,7,11]), or targeting specific areas (e.g., [5,13] where the focus is on data centers). As already discussed, in this paper the emphasis is on the modular, redundant architectures adopted for the signalling system by the Italian railways, presented in Sect. 4. Although similar solutions are implemented also in other Countries (for example, the architecture in [8] with reference to the Indian railways), to the best of the authors' knowledge a dependability analysis targeting the addressed UPS organizations is not available. The analysis developed in this paper provides a contribution in the direction to fill this gap. The obtained results could then be helpful to understand trend behaviours, from the reliability and availability perspective, of such similar schemes.

To better position the considered UPS_{SR} and UPS_{CR} architectures with respect to alternative, but rather compatible, solutions already investigated, in the following a few considerations are drawn with the two generic modular UPS systems presented and analyzed in [2,3], respectively, and depicted in Fig. 3.

The improvement in availability, MTTF and MTBF switching from the architecture depicted in Fig. 2a (or very close ones) to the one[5] depicted in Fig. 3a is analyzed in [2]. As in this paper, cabinets structure, connections, operation control and management electronics are not included in the analysis. Differently from the analyses performed in this paper, in [2] only the failure of the Direct

---

[4] A typical transformer employed in the considered context can waste about 4% of the transformed power in heat.

[5] Notice that the mentioned standard is EN 62040 VFI, that is not specific for railway applications.

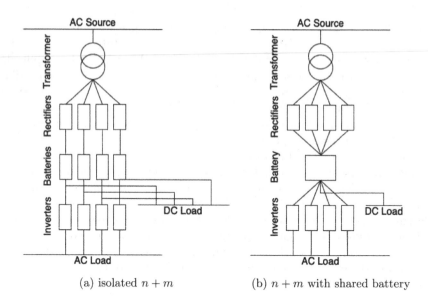

(a) isolated $n + m$ (b) $n + m$ with shared battery

Fig. 3. Other UPS logical architectures studied in the literature: (a) is close to UPS$_{\text{CR}}$ depicted in Fig. 2b ($n = 3$ and $m = 1$) but each unit is connected only to the corresponding unit of the next layer, while (b) is close to (a) but there is only one large shared battery.

Current (DC) bus, including the connection with the battery, is considered, not the failure of the batteries themselves. Two variants of the components switching mechanism are mentioned for the modular architecture: each unit has a (decentralized) switch vs there is only one (centralized) switch.

In [3] all the units have a (decentralized) bypass switch and four architecture are investigated: those depicted in Figs. 3a and 3b with $m = 0$ or $m = 1$.

The differences, both at architectural level and at modeling assumptions level, make the dependability analysis conducted in [2,3] different from that performed in this paper. Among major distinctive aspects characterizing this work from referred previous studies there are: i) the level of miniaturization and redundancy. UPS$_{\text{CR}}$ is designed considering 10 as a typical value of n, i.e., a much greater value than in [2,3], and also m can span a larger range of values. This has also consequences on how to parametrize failure rates, as detailed in Sect. 6; ii) the analysis performed here explicitly accounts for the failure of the AC source (utility and diesel generator) through distinguishing the two UPS operational modes (i.e., $\mathcal{N}$ and $\mathcal{C}$), while this distinction is not addressed in [2,3].

6   Dependability Models

In this Section Markovian stochastic models [12] are defined to support the analysis and comparison of the UPS architectures UPS_{SR} and UPS_{CR} in terms of dependability attributes.

6.1   Assumptions and Measures of Interest

Both UPS_{SR} and UPS_{CR} architectures are modeled and analyzed separately for each operation mode $\mathcal{N}$ (when rectifiers can fail) or $\mathcal{C}$ (when rectifiers are not used and therefore cannot fail).

The failure time of rectifiers, inverters, battery banks and transformers is an exponentially distributed random variable with rates λ_R, λ_I, λ_B and λ_T, respectively.

Maintenance after a component failure is modeled for both UPS_{SR} and UPS_{CR} as an atomic action performed by a single maintenance team that is memoryless, i.e., the recovery time of failed components is an exponentially distributed random variable with rate μ. In support of this assumption, it needs to be considered that typically in critical applications there are orders of magnitude between components' time to failure and recovery time, meaning that the probability distribution shape of the recovery time has a relatively small impact on the availability measure of interest. In the conducted experiments, μ has been selected in accordance with the white papers and previous analyses reported in Sect. 5.

The failure model is based on the following assumptions:

- The failure rate of the transformer is negligible, so it is not considered in the models.
- The failure rate of each considered component (rectifier, inverter, battery bank) includes both hardware failures and control software failures (as reported in the technical reference document[6]).
- The failure rate of components does not depend on load and is statistically independent of each other, as typically assumed for hardware components.
- The UPS fails both when it cannot cover the entire load or the quality of service of the load is not meet (e.g., while the rectifier performs poorly so that the current is no longer stable).
- The recovery time is the same regardless of the number of failed components, since it depends substantially on the random availability of the maintenance team, while the actual maintenance interventions take a negligible time.

Although (some) the above assumptions may appear rather simplistic, it is reminded that the study has a comparative purpose between two architectures and, as long as the modeled aspects have the same impact on both of them, adopting simplifications do not impair validity of the obtained results. Of course, enhancing accuracy of the analysis is desirable and postponed as future work.

---

[6] SMAP [10].

For each combination of UPS architecture and operation mode (UPS$_{\text{SR}}$-$\mathcal{N}$, (UPS$_{\text{SR}}$-$\mathcal{C}$, (UPS$_{\text{CR}}$-$\mathcal{N}$ and (UPS$_{\text{CR}}$-$\mathcal{C}$) two Markovian stochastic models have been defined: a reliability model, with absorbing states representing the UPS failure, and an availability model, with all states positive recurrent [12]. Notice that whereas in the availability model each failed component is always recovered, in the reliability model each failed component is only recovered if it does not cause the UPS failure, when the model enters an absorbing state.

Using these models, the following metrics representative of reliability and availability have been analyzed:

MTTF: the mean time to failure of the UPS, defined as the average amount of time the UPS operates before it fails; it is computed by solving the reliability model in which recovery from UPS failure is not considered.

A_∞: the steady state UPS availability, defined as the limit of the probability that the UPS will be operational at a specific time, as time tends to infinity; it is computed by solving the availability model in which recovery of UPS takes place after failure.

MTBF: the expected operating time between two consecutive failures of the UPS, given by

$$\text{MTBF} = \frac{\text{MTTF}}{A_\infty}. \tag{1}$$

$\mathcal{I}_{MTBF}$: percentage of improvement in MTBF of UPS$_{\text{CR}}$ (MTBF$^{\text{UPS}_{\text{CR}}}$) with respect to UPS$_{\text{SR}}$ (MTBF$^{\text{UPS}_{\text{SR}}}$), given by

$$\mathcal{I}_{\text{MTBF}} = 100\frac{\text{MTBF}^{\text{UPS}_{\text{CR}}} - \text{MTBF}^{\text{UPS}_{\text{SR}}}}{\text{MTBF}^{\text{UPS}_{\text{SR}}}}. \tag{2}$$

Based on the study reported in [12] for "system vs component redundancy", it can be mathematically demonstrated that for the same failure rates, UPS$_{\text{CR}}$ has a better reliability profile than UPS$_{\text{SR}}$. However, as already observed in Sect. 4, components used to perform the same function have different characteristics when used in UPS$_{\text{SR}}$ architecture rather than in UPS$_{\text{CR}}$. To account for these specificities, different combinations of failure rates for each component in the two UPS$_{\text{SR}}$ and UPS$_{\text{CR}}$ architectures were used in the analysis. For example, the failure rate $\lambda_R^{\text{UPS}_{\text{CR}}}$ of the rectifier in UPS$_{\text{CR}}$ is defined in terms the failure rate $\lambda_R^{\text{UPS}_{\text{SR}}}$ of the rectifier in UPS$_{\text{SR}}$ through a multiplier r, i.e.,

$$\lambda_R^{\text{UPS}_{\text{CR}}} = r \cdot \lambda_R^{\text{UPS}_{\text{SR}}}. \tag{3}$$

Notice that, as the number of components and complexity of a modular architecture increases, the switches that handle interactions among components in turn can also become quite complex. In that case, as shown in [12], it becomes important to model the (failures of the) components switching mechanism. Because of the complexity of this aspect, in this paper, we have chosen not to explicitly model the failure of such switch mechanisms, but to account for it through adopting increased failure rates for components in the UPS$_{\text{CR}}$ architecture with respect to those of the UPS$_{\text{SR}}$ ones (see discussion in Sect. 7).

In the following only models limited to DC loads are described (where inverters are not considered), being relatively easy to address AC loads: for UPS$_{SR}$ just adding λ_I to $\lambda_R + \lambda_B$ in UPS$_{SR}$-$\mathcal{N}$ and λ_B in UPS$_{SR}$-$\mathcal{C}$; for UPS$_{CR}$ considering three Kronecker sums instead of two, as will be detailed in Sect. 6.3.

6.2 UPS$_{SR}$ Model

As depicted in Fig. 4a, the model for UPS$_{SR}$-$\mathcal{N}$ is in state 1 when all the components (2 batteries and 2 rectifiers) are correctly working and can switch to state 2 if either one of the batteries or one of rectifiers fails. Only state 3, reachable from state 2 when another battery or rectifier fails, is the system failure state. From state 2 the system can recover without affecting the service quality; to study the system availability also the recovery from state 3 is considered.

The model for UPS$_{SR}$-$\mathcal{C}$, depicted in Fig. 4b, is similar to the model for UPS$_{SR}$-$\mathcal{N}$. The only difference is the absence of rectifiers' failure rate λ_R.

6.3 UPS$_{CR}$ Model

The model for UPS$_{CR}$-$\mathcal{C}$, depicted in Fig. 4d, comprises only the batteries layer of Fig. 2 (since the rectifier is not operational in $\mathcal{C}$ mode, as observed in Sect. 4), for $n = 6$ and $m = 3$. In state 1 all the $n + m$ batteries are working, in state 2 all but 1 are working, and so on, until state $m + 1$ (state 4 in Fig. 4d) where there are only n working batteries (i.e., just enough to cover the dc loads). All the remaining combinations (i.e., where there are less than n working batteries) are collapsed into the final state, that is the system failure state. In general, in state i there are $n + m - i + 1$ working batteries. So, the transition rate from state i to $i + 1$ is $(n + m - i + 1)\lambda_B$ (e.g., $8\lambda_B$ in state 2). Overall, there are $m + 2$ states, among which $m + 1$ states where the service is correctly delivered and 1 state of system failure. From all the states the system can recover with rate μ. Notice that recovering from the last state (the system failure state) is only considered in the availability model.

The model for UPS$_{CR}$-$\mathcal{N}$, depicted in Fig. 4c, comprises first and second layers of Fig. 2b, where each rectifier can provide power to each battery (i.e., each box within the first layer of Fig. 2b is connected to each box of the second layer). In order to represent all the relevant dependencies, the Kronecker algebra [1,4] has been employed: each layer comprises $m+2$ states and is modeled through a transition rate matrix R_i similar to the one of UPS$_{CR}$-$\mathcal{C}$, where i labels the layer in Fig. 2b; the overall model is defined by the transition rate matrix

$$R^{\text{UPS}_{CR}-\mathcal{N}} = R_1 \oplus R_2 = R_1 \otimes I_{m+2} + I_{m+2} \otimes R_2,$$

where I_{m+2} is the identity matrix with $m + 2$ rows and columns. Thus, the overall model comprises $(m+2)^2$ states. The association among states in Fig. 4c and number of working/failed rectifiers and batteries is not reported to improve the figure readability, but can be easily derived: in R_i the number of failed components increases at increasing of the state number (state 1 denotes 0 failed

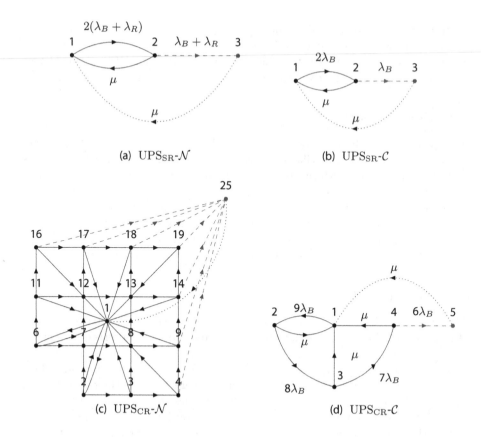

Fig. 4. Reliability and availability models of UPS$_\text{SR}$-$\mathcal{N}$ (a), UPS$_\text{SR}$-$\mathcal{C}$ (b), UPS$_\text{CR}$-$\mathcal{N}$ (c) and UPS$_\text{CR}$-$\mathcal{C}$ (d) to address DC loads only (for AC loads the models are easily derived starting from the shown ones), with $n = 6$ and $m = 3$ for UPS$_\text{CR}$. Black dotted arcs, denoting recovery from UPS failure, are only considered for the availability models. Blue nodes represent working states and blue full arcs represent failure or recovery events between them. Red nodes represent UPS failure states, and red dashed arcs failure events. In (c) the failure state 5, 10, 15 20, 21, 22, 23, 24 and 25 are collapsed into the single failure state 25, and rates are not reported for sake of clarity.

components), and the lexicographic ordering is enforced by the Kronecker products in $R^{\text{UPS}_\text{CR}-\mathcal{N}}$. All the combinations of system failure are collapsed into one state and recovering from that state is only considered in the availability model (as for UPS$_\text{CR}$-$\mathcal{C}$).

7   Numerical Evaluation

In this Section a numerical comparison[7] between UPS_{SR} and UPS_{CR} architectures is presented in terms of $\mathcal{I}_{MTBF}$ and MTBF for both $\mathcal{N}$ and $\mathcal{C}$ operation modes, considering a couple of scenarios, where different parameters settings are investigated. The setting for the model parameters considered in the performed analyses for both scenarios is the following.

Assuming $l_m = 10$ kW as a typical load per module, $n = 10$ modules are required to cover 100 kW of load, $n = 11$ for 110 kW, and so on. In general, n is given by

$$n = \lceil \mathcal{L}/l_m \rceil, \tag{4}$$

where $\mathcal{L}$ is the DC load, that is assumed constant over the time. The DC load has been fixed to 100 kW, so that $n = 10$, unless otherwise specified.

Several algorithms for choosing m can be considered. In the presented studies, a fixed value of $m = 3$ has been considered. The recovery rate has been fixed at $\mu = 0.5\,h^{-1}$, i.e., half an hour.

Realistic values of failure rates for each component in the two UPS_{SR} and UPS_{CR} architectures, denoted by adding a superscript UPS_{SR} and UPS_{CR} to the rate symbol, respectively, were used in the analysis. While the values of $\lambda_B^{\text{UPS}_{\text{SR}}}$ and $\lambda_R^{\text{UPS}_{\text{SR}}}$ are known from field investigation, currently there are no available estimates for $\lambda_B^{\text{UPS}_{\text{CR}}}$ and $\lambda_R^{\text{UPS}_{\text{CR}}}$. However, it can be observed that UPS_{CR} shows a higher degree of complexity compared to UPS_{SR}, with negative impact on the failure rate of its components, mainly due to:

- miniaturization of components, meaning reduced physical size of delicate circuits such as rectifiers or inverters;
- increasing the number of components also the connections among them, and the related switching mechanisms to isolate/activate components as needed, become more complex and their failures cannot be neglected.

Therefore, to account for the combined effect of the above aspects resulting in a more complex UPS_{CR} whose components are characterized by a higher failure rate than the corresponding ones of UPS_{SR}, a multiplicative factor r has been introduced:

$$\lambda_B^{\text{UPS}_{\text{SR}}} = 11.76 \cdot 10^{-6}\,h^{-1}, \qquad \lambda_R^{\text{UPS}_{\text{SR}}} = 16.6 \cdot 10^{-6}\,h^{-1},$$
$$\lambda_B^{\text{UPS}_{\text{CR}}} = r \cdot \lambda_B^{\text{UPS}_{\text{SR}}}, \qquad \lambda_R^{\text{UPS}_{\text{CR}}} = r \cdot \lambda_R^{\text{UPS}_{\text{SR}}}, \tag{5}$$

where $r \geq 1$. At growing of r, the failure rate of UPS_{CR} components increases; in the conducted analyses, a rather high value has been adopted being r fixed to 17, unless otherwise specified.

---

[7] https://gitea-s2i2s.isti.cnr.it/gmasetti/CompareSRandCRinRailwaySignalingUPS. git: free code written in MATLAB, but with small changes can also be executed with Octave. No special programming skills are required.

7.1   Study 1: MTBF at Increasing of Load

In this study, the DC load $\mathcal{L}$ increases from 40 to 140 kW and the scaling factor r is set to 17. Results are reported in Figs. 5a and 5b for $\mathcal{N}$ operation mode, and in Figs. 5c and 5d for $\mathcal{C}$ operation mode. In UPS$_{SR}$, the only primary unit covers the entire load for all load values considered, so that the same configuration is considered for different values of $\mathcal{L}$. As a result, MTBF for UPS$_{SR}$ is constant as $\mathcal{L}$ changes. In UPS$_{CR}$, the number n of primary units increases as $\mathcal{L}$ increases, as derived from (4). As a result, $\mathcal{I}_{MTBF}$ and MTBF for UPS$_{CR}$ decrease as $\mathcal{L}$ increases due to the larger number n of primary units that can fail, the number m of hot standby units being constant. It is interesting to observe that, as $\mathcal{L}$ increases, the measure $\mathcal{I}_{MTBF}$ varies from values greater than 0, for which MTBF for UPS$_{CR}$ is greater than MTBF for UPS$_{SR}$, to values lower than 0, for which MTBF for UPS$_{CR}$ is less than MTBF for UPS$_{SR}$.

Figures 5b and 5d show that the MTBF for both UPS$_{CR}$ and UPS$_{SR}$ in the $\mathcal{C}$ mode is approximately half and one-third, respectively, of the corresponding MTBF in the $\mathcal{N}$ mode. Figures 5a and 5c show that the $\mathcal{I}_{MTBF}$ in the $\mathcal{C}$ mode is approximately 1.8 the value of the corresponding in the $\mathcal{N}$ mode. This is because in $\mathcal{C}$ mode the rectifier component is not operational, thus reducing the number of units that can fail in UPS$_{SR}$ and UPS$_{CR}$ by 2 and by $n + m$, respectively.

7.2   Study 2: MTBF at Increasing of r

In this study, the DC load $\mathcal{L}$ has been fixed to 100 ($n = 10$) or 160 kW ($n = 16$), and the scaling factor r increases from 1 to 20. Results are reported in Figs. 6a and 6b for $\mathcal{L} = 100$ kW, and in Figs. 6c and 6d for $\mathcal{L} = 160$ kW.

The UPS$_{SR}$ architecture does not depend on r or $\mathcal{L}$, so MTBF for UPS$_{SR}$ remains constant as r or $\mathcal{L}$ varies.

In the UPS$_{CR}$ architecture, the failure rate of the units (batteries and rectifiers) increases as r increases, as derived from (5). As a result, $\mathcal{I}_{MTBF}$ and MTBF for UPS$_{CR}$ decrease as r increases due to the larger failure rate of the primary and hot standby units that can fail.

Figures 6a and 6b show that, for $r < 19$, UPS$_{CR}$ has a better reliability profile than UPS$_{SR}$, being MTTF for UPS$_{CR}$ greater than MTBF for UPS$_{SR}$, corresponding to $\mathcal{I}_{MTBF} > 0$. It is interesting to observe that MTBF is very sensitive to changes in r with a difference between the minimum and maximum value of about 5 orders of magnitude.

Figures 6b and 6d show that the MTBF for UPS$_{CR}$ in the $\mathcal{C}$ mode is approximately one order of magnitude less than the corresponding MTBF in the $\mathcal{N}$ mode, so that the interval of r in which UPS$_{CR}$ has a better reliability profile than UPS$_{SR}$ is reduced by almost half ($r < 12$). This is because with $\mathcal{L} = 160$ the configuration of UPS$_{CR}$ becomes $n = 16$, thus increasing the number of primary units that can fail, while the UPS$_{SR}$ configuration does not change.

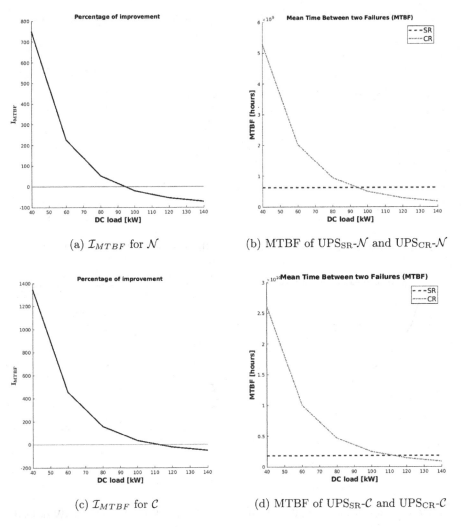

(a) $\mathcal{I}_{MTBF}$ for $\mathcal{N}$

(b) MTBF of UPS$_{SR}$-$\mathcal{N}$ and UPS$_{CR}$-$\mathcal{N}$

(c) $\mathcal{I}_{MTBF}$ for $\mathcal{C}$

(d) MTBF of UPS$_{SR}$-$\mathcal{C}$ and UPS$_{CR}$-$\mathcal{C}$

Fig. 5. Study 1: percentage of improvement in MTBF of UPS$_{CR}$ with respect to UPS$_{SR}$ at increasing of DC loads for normal operation condition in (a) and critical condition in (c). The corresponding MTBF is reported in (b) and (d), respectively. Here $r = 17$.

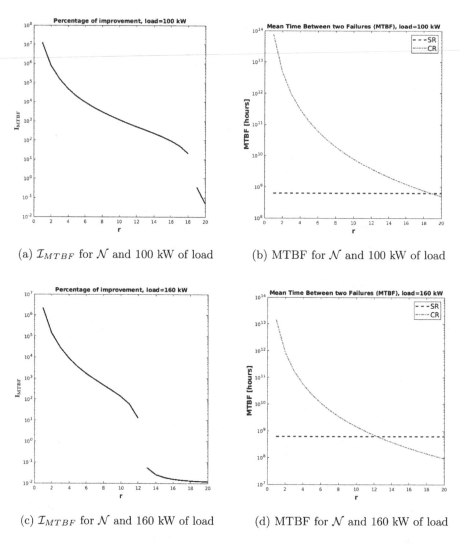

(a) $\mathcal{I}_{MTBF}$ for $\mathcal{N}$ and 100 kW of load   (b) MTBF for $\mathcal{N}$ and 100 kW of load

(c) $\mathcal{I}_{MTBF}$ for $\mathcal{N}$ and 160 kW of load   (d) MTBF for $\mathcal{N}$ and 160 kW of load

Fig. 6. Study 2: percentage of improvement in MTBF of UPS_{CR} with respect to UPS_{SR} for normal operation condition at increasing of r for 100 kW DC load in (a) and 160 kW in (c), respectively. The corresponding MTBF is reported in (b) w and (d), respectively.

8   Conclusion and Future Work

This paper presented a dependability analysis of UPS_{SR} and UPS_{CR}, two alternative architectures for uninterruptable power supply equipment for safety and signalling systems in the railway sector, where redundancy is exploited at system level and at component level, respectively. The analysis goal was to understand the advantages and limitations of the two solutions, in terms of reliability and availability, also with an eye to energy consumption. Stochastic models have been developed to represent the two UPS architectures at a level of abstraction and under failure mode assumptions adequate for conducting comparative analysis. The obtained results, although limited to the adopted parameter setting, suggest that redundancy at component level brings better dependability levels than the alternative approach where replication is operated at system level. Although based on rather simplistic assumptions, also the considerations from the energy consumption perspective are more favourable to UPS_{CR} than to UPS_{SR}. These results positively support the planned replacement of the currently adopted UPS_{SR} with UPS_{CR} in the Italian railway system.

Extensions of the presented study are possible in several directions. Among them, developing corresponding analyses for AC loads would make the comparison more complete, although indications on how to extend the presented models for DC loads to also account for AC loads have been already briefly discussed. Moreover, in the current study loads have been kept constant. However, depending on the specific application, variable loads are possible and the impact of such variability, especially for the UPS_{CR} architecture, is expected to be significant.

Going deeper in the analysis of energy consumption is another aspect that would make the comparison between the two UPS approaches more solid.

Of course, investigating comparison with other UPS architectural configurations, within the context of railways or other critical application sectors, as inspired by related work proposals, is another promising direction.

Finally, extending the models to include also the components and phenomena around the analysed UPS system (as shown in Fig. 1), as well as considering costs aspects would allow to better understand the effectiveness of the two energy supply solutions for safety and signalling systems in the railway sector.

Acknowledgements. This study was partially carried out within MOST - Sustainable Mobility National Research Center and received funding from the European Union Next-GenerationEU (PIANO NAZIONALE DI RIPRESA E RESILIENZA (PNRR)-MISSIONE 4 COMPONENTE 2, INVESTIMENTO 1.4-D.D. 1033 17/06/2022, CN00000023), and SmaRIERS, POR FESR Toscana 2014–2020 Asse 1 - Azione 1.1.5 sub a1. This paper reflects only the authors' views and opinions, neither the European Union nor the European Commission can be considered responsible for them.

References

1. Buchholz, P., Kemper, P.: Kronecker based matrix representations for large Markov models. In: Baier, C., Haverkort, B.R., Hermanns, H., Katoen, J.P., Siegle, M. (eds.) Validation of Stochastic Systems: A Guide to Current Research, LNCS, vol. 2925, pp. 256–295. Springer, Berlin Heidelberg, Berlin, Heidelberg (2004). https://doi.org/10.1007/978-3-540-24611-4_8
2. Ciurans, R.: White paper: are modular ups systems really more reliable? Tech. Rep. JN003A01, SALICRU R&D (2016)
3. Colombi, S., Garcia, D.: White paper: Reliability computation of modular uninterruptible power supply (UPS) with decentralized parallel architecture (DPA). Tech. rep., ABB (2021)

4. Donatelli, S.: Superposed stochastic automata: a class of stochastic Petri nets with parallel solution and distributed state space. Perform. Eval. **18**(1), 21–36 (1993)

5. Qi, S., Sun, W., Wu, Y.: Comparative analysis on different architectures of power supply system for data center and telecom center. In: 2017 IEEE International Telecommunications Energy Conference (INTELEC), pp. 26–29 (2017). https://doi.org/10.1109/INTLEC.2017.8211672

6. Rahmat, M.K., Sani, M.N.: Fault tree analysis in UPS reliability estimation. In: 2014 4th International Conference on Engineering Technology and Technopreneurship (ICE2T), pp. 240–245 (2014). https://doi.org/10.1109/ICE2T.2014.7006255

7. Rahmat, M.K., Zaki Abdul Karim, A., Salleh, M.N.: Uninterruptible power supply system configurations: reliability & cost-benefit analysis. In: 2018 IEEE 7th International Conference on Power and Energy (PECon), pp. 252–256 (2018). https://doi.org/10.1109/PECON.2018.8684147

8. Research Designs & Standards Organization: SMPS based integrated power supply. Tech. rep., RDSO/SPN/165/2023 (2016). https://rdso.indianrailways.gov.in

9. RFI: Sistema integrato di alimentazione e protezione per impianti di sicurezza e segnalamento. Tech. rep., SF 732 D (2010). https://epodweb.rfi.it

10. RFI: Sistema modulare di alimentazione e protezione no-break per impianti di sicurezza e segnalamento. Tech. rep., SF 771 A (2015). https://epodweb.rfi.it

11. Saro, L., Zanettin, C.: The impact of a single module's MTBF value in modular UPS systems: Technique for its assessment, improvement and final validation. In: 2016 IEEE International Telecommunications Energy Conference (INTELEC). pp. 1–8 (2016). DOI: https://doi.org/10.1109/INTLEC.2016.7749148

12. Trivedi, K.S., Bobbio, A.: Reliability and Availability Engineering: Modeling, Analysis, and Applications. Cambridge University Press, Cambridge (2017)

13. Varnavskiy, K., Nepsha, F., Chen, Q., Ermakov, A., Zhironkin, S.: Reliability assessment of the configuration of dynamic uninterruptible power sources: a case of data centers. Energies 16(3) (2023). https://doi.org/10.3390/en16031419, https://www.mdpi.com/1996-1073/16/3/1419

Formal Methods for Safety Assessment

The SafeCap Trajectory: Industry-Driven Improvement of an Interlocking Verification Tool

Alexei Iliasov[1], Dominic Taylor[2], Linas Laibinis[3],
and Alexander Romanovsky[1,4(✉)]

[1] The Formal Route, London, UK
alexander.romanovsky@ncl.ac.uk
[2] Systra Scott Lister, London, UK
[3] Institute of Computer Science, Vilnius University, Vilnius, Lithuania
[4] School of Computing, Newcastle University, Newcastle upon Tyne, UK

Abstract. This paper reports on the industrial use of our formal-method based interlocking verification tool, called SafeCap, and on what we needed to change in SafeCap as a result of our experience in applying it to a large number of commercial signalling projects. The substantial efforts dedicated to tool improvement are caused by the novelty of the technology and by a substantial gap to be bridged between the academic prototype, developed initially, and the industry-strength tool SafeCap has become now. It is our belief that when such innovative tools and technologies are developed for industrial use it is often impossible to fully understand and correctly elicit the complete set of requirements for their development. The paper describes the extensions added and the modifications made to the functionality of SafeCap after it was demonstrated to be successful in a number of real signalling projects and, as a result of this, was formally approved for use in the UK railway. We believe this experience will be useful for the developers of formal verification methods, tools and technologies to be deployed in industry.

Keywords: Safety verification · Railway · Automated theorem proving · Scalability · Industrial deployment · Solid State Interlocking

1 Introduction

Effective signalling is fundamental to the safe and efficient operation of railway networks. At the heart of any signalling system there are one or more interlockings. These devices constrain authorisation of train movements as well as movements of the infrastructure to prevent unsafe situations arising. One of the earliest forms of computer-based interlocking was the Solid State Interlocking (SSI) [1,4], developed in the UK in the 1980s. Currently, SSI is the predominant interlocking technology used on UK mainline railways. It also has applications overseas, including in Australia, New Zealand, France, India and Belgium. Running on bespoke hardware, SSI software consists of a generic application

© The Author(s), under exclusive license to Springer Nature Switzerland AG 2023
B. Milius et al. (Eds.): RSSRail 2023, LNCS 14198, pp. 117–127, 2023.
https://doi.org/10.1007/978-3-031-43366-5_7

(common to all signalling schemes) and site specific geographic data. The latter configures a signalling area by defining site specific rules, concerning the control of the signalling equipment as well as internal latches and timers, that the interlocking must obey. Despite being referred to as data, a configuration resembles a program in a procedural programming language and is iteratively executed in a typical loop controlling the signalling equipment.

This paper discusses the SafeCap tool used for formal verification of geographical data of SSI and derived (Smartlock and Westlock) interlockings [6,8,9]. It provides scalable and fully-automated verification by mathematical proof. The tool is now actively used for safety verification of mainline interlockings by several UK signalling companies. SafeCap is deployed at different phases of SSI preparation to check the designs and to provide signalling engineers with the diagnostics to help them to enhance (and, where necessary, to correct) the design data. It has proven to be successful in improving the safety of the signalling systems and reducing the rework cycle. SafeCap is extremely efficient, it takes but few minutes to verify the safety of any UK interlocking on a fairly standard desktop computer.

The development of SafeCap started in 2013 in a series of public projects led by Newcastle University. It was originally conceived as an experimental extendable Eclipse-based tool for railway simulation and verification.

From 2017 we have focused our work exclusively on developing a fully-reworked version of SafeCap targeting SSI verification (described in [6][1]). Two main decisions leading to the industrial adoption of the tool were made during this period, namely,

- to focus on fully-automated scalable verification by mathematical proof;
- to ensure that the tool inputs the data developed by signalling engineers and outputs the diagnostics reports exclusively presented in terms of these data.

These decisions in effect allowed us to successfully address the majority of the factors limiting the acceptance of formal methods by industry (see, for example, Sect. 5.5 of paper [5]).

Since 2019 we have been conducting commercial projects and making substantial improvements to SafeCap. This has been a period of extensive use, during which we have verified over 60 interlockings in England, Wales and Scotland, including those controlling the most complex layouts in London and Birmingham. We have worked with a mixture of SSI-derived interlocking technologies and layout complexities, written at different times by different design offices. In particular, during this time it has been demonstrated that SafeCap is now fully equipped for conducting formal, scalable and automated verification of SSI/Smartlock/Westlock interlockings developed for ETCS (European Train Control System). This has been an important period during which we have been using the experience gained in the commercial projects to enhance the tool and to make it more useful and attractive for our customers.

This industrial paper focuses on the changes made to improve SafeCap during the latter phase of its development and on the industry-driven research that

---

[1] The paper was prepared in 2020 and submitted to the journal in early 2021.

formed the foundations for these improvements. The experience from commercial SafeCap applications gained during this phase has been a key for meeting the needs of the signalling companies that use SafeCap.

The rest of the paper is structured as follows. The next section discussed the three main categories of SafeCap improvements, providing inside information about each improvement implemented. Section 3 reports on the comparative statistics from the live commercial projects delivered before the improvement phase and after the improvements were implemented. The last section discusses some conclusions and future directions of our work on SafeCap.

2   Tool Improvements

SafeCap is a novel technology for which it was not possible to define a full set of requirements at the time when we started its development. During this development, there has been a continuous process of eliciting new requirements and modifying many of the initial ones. The main improvements have necessarily been based on learning from experience.

SafeCap is a unique tool, based on substantial advances in formal methods and supporting verification tools, which is actively used by industry. This means that all its improvements are driven by the industrial needs, and that all research advances supporting these improvements are driven by these needs.

The three main categories of tool improvements discussed in this paper are improvements of safety properties (i.e., how SafeCap understands safety), of the employed proof systems (i.e., how SafeCap verifies safety), and of the produced diagnostics and reporting (i.e., how SafeCap reports the verification results).

2.1   Improvements of Safety Properties

Safety properties assert the safe behaviour of the interlocking system that Safe-Cap verifies. When the system is demonstrated to satisfy all these properties, it is considered to be safe. The properties play a critical role in SafeCap formal verification, which is why we put substantial efforts in ensuring they are correct, unambiguous and relevant for signalling engineers.

During the improvement period we have finalised and started using a systematic process for property engineering. The process we are applying now guides us during property identification, modification, documentation, testing and correction, and allows us to document all these steps to make the property development accountable.

In the railway signalling domain, opportunities to specify a complete set of safety properties from scratch are rare and typically only occur on newly built, stand-alone metro lines. In other cases, interlockings are usually constrained by legacy considerations.

As SafeCap targets the safety verification of UK mainline interlockings, safety properties had to be inferred from the railway standards. This required a thorough review of standards catalogues to identify relevant standards followed by a review of those standards to elicit the specific properties within the scope of

SafeCap verification. The scope of SafeCap verification, and hence the standards clauses from which safety properties are derived, is continually expanding: initially it covered only functionality for which automated verification was explicitly required in standards; it was then expanded to cover the majority of functionality related to internal states within signalling interlockings; it now also covers processing of inputs and generation of outputs by the interlocking. Nonetheless, many clauses in standards are likely to remain permanently outside the scope of SafeCap verification, for example:

– safety integrity of interlocking hardware and generic software;
– accuracy of signalling plans used as inputs into SafeCap;
– correct wiring of physical equipment to the interlocking;
– seldom-used and site-specific functionality for which manual verification is more cost effective than automated verification.

The argument for the correctness and completeness of these safety properties (in terms of the scope of SafeCap verification) stems from their traceability to the standards and the pedigree of those standards, which have evolved over many decades through design, risk assessment, operational experience and lessons learnt from accidents.

When defining safety properties, consideration needs to be given not only to the safety requirements contained in railway standards, but how those are actually implemented in data. Failure to do this correctly results in many false positives. The SSI data is effectively a computer program that determines site-specific functionality of the interlocking system. It includes files defining interlocking identities (files of the following types: FLG, PTS, QST, ROU, SIG, TCS) which define the names of various variables corresponding to trackside equipment, and files which define functionality in terms of those identities (FOP, IPT, MAP, OPT, PFM, PRR). During the improvement phase, in addition to identifying the new safety properties from the textual standards, we added a substantial number of new properties by importing new types of files (including, IPT/OPT files) which allowed us to formulate new properties in terms on newly added types of identities from these files and their functionalities.

In the last three years we have increased the number of safety properties SafeCap verifies from 40 to 136, which substantially improved the coverage and the quality of SafeCap verification.

Dealing with false positives has became an important part of safety property development due to the complexity of safety requirements described in standards, which often allow for many exceptions to general rules and how the properties are implemented in data. The false positives encountered during the SafeCap verification process arise for various reasons: over-simplification of the property expressed in the textual standard; failure to recognise and exclude scenarios that cannot plausibly happen in the railway domain; the effect of safety over-approximation in the formal representation of a property due to limited scope of a mathematical model of railway; and, lastly, due to limitations inherent to theorem proving in application to inductive safety invariant verification. The first three types of false positives are dealt with by improving the properties (which sometimes can increase their complexity and affect the verification time) and extending railway model. Dealing with false positives of the last kind is explained in more detail in Sect. 2.2, which also provides more information about how the SafeCap prover works.

Another aspect of property engineering is the need to have robust change management procedures. To this end, SafeCap uses regression testing to check that previously found, and manually confirmed, violations are still present and that no new violations appear after a property is revised. To achieve this, SafeCap reproduces the effect of a source code error seeding by directly manipulating proof conjectures, generated from interlocking code (without any seeded errors) and the safety property itself. More details about that are given in Sect. 2.2.

In addition, due to the critical importance of the safety properties for Safe-Cap verification, traceability to the referred standards of all new and revised properties are now manually checked by an independent checker from our team.

2.2   Improvements of the Proof System

As its primary means of mathematical proof, SafeCap employs a custom rewriting-based prover for a language based on first-order logic and set theory. Since set theory is the preferred modelling mechanism, there is a quite a large number of predefined simplification rules for it. The prover also relies on decision procedures for rule selection and hypotheses filtering, which were produced by analysing a large number of historic proofs and building a SVM-based predictor.

A symbolic transition system, built via symbolic execution of input signalling data, is used to generated, by instantiation of a schematic axiom of inductive safety invariant, conjectures called *proof obligations*. Each such proof obligation attempts to establish that a particular state transition maintains safety invariant. A conjecture is a logical sequent, consisting of a list of hypotheses (derived from state transition pre-conditions) and a goal (derived safety invariant).

Proofs are computations over the conjectures that aim to find a chain of predefined rewrite steps resulting in a copy of a current goal in hypotheses or demonstration of falsity of hypotheses. The prover is completely automatic – it has a procedure for selecting a next rewrite step as well as for ignoring currently irrelevant hypotheses. In some cases, the prover employs a rule translating conjecture into a SAT problem to be disproved via a SAT solver.

In addition to a verdict on whether a given conjecture is correct (i.e., a theorem), the prover also constructs the complete proof script detailing all computations carried out during the proof. It is not designed as a small kernel prover – we can freely add new rewrite steps without having to prove their correctness. Instead we rely on a generated proof script and an independent proof checker to demonstrate proof soundness.

The first-order logic underpinning the SafeCap mathematical notation is both semi-decidable and undecidable. A general proving procedure exists (thus semi-decidable), however there is no guarantee that the prover can deliver definite result within any fixed time (thus still undecidable) It is very rare that the prover can positively demonstrate that a conjecture is not a theorem; in most cases we simply let the prover exhaust all possible venues of proof and, if the proof is still not completed, declare the conjecture to be unproven. It is also possible to keep rewriting for an impractically long time because of, e.g., rewrite cycles emerging during the proof or when the number of options presented to the prover is simply too large to be explored. One typical case is the presence of disjunctive clauses with many composite parts (in the region of hundreds).

Proof complexity ranges from a few steps for very simple cases to millions of steps for a few extreme situations. The median number, measured on a random sample of five projects, is 802 proof steps with 37 sub goals. The mean, however, is 2802 proof steps and 386 sub goals; hence, there is a relatively small population of much harder-to-prove conjectures.

The vast majority of proof conjectures we deal with are shown to be theorems. For the same sample of five projects, 99.7% of all the generated conjectures are shown to theorems. Thus, from the efficiency viewpoint, we aim to discharge simpler cases of provable conjectures in fewer steps and then spend more time on harder cases. Luckily, proofs of the same safety predicates tend to be very similar across different projects and this enables us to construct macro-steps that narrowly target certain patterns reappearing in the generated conjectures. Here a macro-step is a proof script that computes a sequence of rewrite rules for a given set of hypotheses and a goal. For most situations, the script simply encodes pattern matching on conjecture elements to detect certain recurring situations.

In the end, we are able to discharge thousands of proof obligations within seconds. As a comparison, it takes the Why3 framework [3] (with the Alt-Ergo backend) around twenty seconds to discharge some simpler proof obligations.

Attempting to prove a conjecture is only the first step in the process of finding safety violations. A failed conjecture on its own only tells us that a certain safety property does not hold for given interlocking data. This is not useful to railway engineers, who expect to see a link to a specific line in the interlocking data as well as identification of relevant signalling plan elements. There is a world of difference between saying that one or more points are not deadlocked correctly somewhere in the data and a statement naming a specific set of points and giving the precise location in the interlocking data where the violation occurs.

To present a failed conjecture in the manner that is useful to railway engineers, SafeCap uses two techniques: (i) undoing some proof steps (without altering the overall verdict) to reach a state that is easier to analyse and explain, and (ii) extracting the context information from a conjecture goal and its hypotheses. The first technique undoes the proof steps in which variables or identifiers linking the proof to the signalling plan are renamed or removed. The second technique uses the source code provided by the data parser to locate relevant data and extract a human-readable summary of a failed proof state from the conjecture hypotheses (e.g. occupied tracks, locked sub routes, etc.).

The extracted proof state and source code tracing information are combined to generate a human readable summary of a found safety violation. This is formatted using the predefined templates to describe the purported violation. The summary contains, among other things, the location, in interlocking data, of the original source code of an offending state transition, highlights of relevant elements on the signalling plan, and the proof context summarising, in human readable terms, a set of signalling system states in which the violation occurs.

One common approach to identifying and reporting a property violation is positing any one example for which the given property does not hold. Our experience clearly shows that this is not sufficient for industrial scale verification. The first reason is that the engineers need to have all the contexts, in which the property does not hold, reported and corrected. The second one is that in large and complex systems, like railways, there are often a few exceptional cases where the engineers intentionally violate a general property for operational reasons; for example, allowing a train to shunt backwards and forwards at low speed on a non-passenger line without the signaller setting routes for each move. This renders possible situation where a benign case of a violation is reported and while serious cases that need corrective actions are not. At the core of our solution developed during the improvement period and presented earlier [7], lies an approach to name all possible violations in the terms of a unique combination of signalling assets plus atomic section of signalling code. This makes it impossible to wrongly combine several distinct violations.

2.3   Improvement of Reporting

The SafeCap diagnostics report is the only information we provide to clients. For each safety property, it identifies whether the interlocking data complies with that property and, if not, where violations were found. The improvements in the properties and proof system, described above, have enabled a step change improvement in the precision with which violations are reported.

Previously it was only possible to group apparently similar violations based on where they occurred in the code and the pre-conditions (context) under which they occurred. This led to occasional misgrouping of distinctly different errors as well as repetitive reporting of the same error, both of which made reports difficult and time-consuming to analyse. With the new approach [7], what constitutes an individual property violation is now clearly defined and thus instances of the same violation are grouped accordingly. Each individual violation is separately reported making reports longer than they were, but much easier to analyse. The approach also makes the reports consistent in the labelling of individual violations, facilitating comparisons between reports on different versions of the same interlocking data. This enables enumeration of all potential errors in a given interlocking data independently from proof obligation generation. This in turn enables us to detect missing (or extraneous) proof obligations.

Further improvements have been made in the diagnostics information provided for property violations. The SafeCap philosophy has always been to present findings in terms understood by signalling designers with no reference to intermediate formal notations or generated prover outputs. Instead property violations are presented as textual descriptions accompanied by the section of code and graphical layout to which the violation applies and the failed proof states (contexts) that led to the violation. This has been further improved upon by additionally presenting all sub routines called by the applicable section of code and using coloured highlighting to identify the path through the code for which the violation was found. Illustrations of signal aspects have also been added to facilitate diagnosis of violations of new safety properties pertaining to signals.

3 Statistics from Live Projects

The following tables summarise the scale and verification effort for a random sample of industrial projects. Table 1 shows the projects sampled from the period from 2020 to the first half of 2022. These projects were verified for 59 predicates defining safety properties. At that time we did not formulate any conditions for SSI logic covering output telegrams (procedures computing messages sent to various trackside equipment) and thus verification coverage was only partial.

The *Routes, Signals, Points, LOC* columns characterise a project in terms of the total number of routes, signals, points and the total number of lines of codes (LOC) in signalling data (all types of files included).

The *POs, total* column gives the overall number of non-trivial proof conjectures generated for a project. Simple instantiation of safety property templates yields many more conjectures, many of which are trivial ones that have a copy of a goal in their hypotheses. Such trivial cases are detected and dropped during the generation phase and not included in this figure.

The *POs, unf* column is the number of conjectures for which proof was forcibly stopped due to an overrun in the number of generated proof branches or a predefined time limit rather than simply running out of any applicable rewrite rules (what we regard as a proper termination). Logically, these are no different from failed, but properly terminated conjectures. In practice, their presence indicates a weakness in the prover or domain axiomatisation as the automated proof process is tuned to deadlock where successful proof is unlikely (empirically and drawing from the experience in this particular domain). They are also often indicative a computationally expensive runaway situation stemming from generation of proof sub branches, derivation of new hypotheses and possibly cyclical behaviour of rewrite rules. Finally *Proof time, s* gives the overall proof time in seconds. All time measurements are given for an AMD 5950X PC with 128GB memory using 16 cores; it excludes extra time needed for the construction of a state transition system from source SSI translation (typically under 5 s).

Table 1. SafeCap statistics from 2020 to mid 2022

Id	Routes	Signals	Points	LOC	POs, total	POs, unf	Time, s
P1	164	71	48	13244	12172	108	96
P2	92	45	36	9320	8098	0	60
P3	62	31	28	11002	11711	14	203
P4	47	28	23	8750	6003	0	22
P5	59	30	24	8573	17241	2	129

Table 2. SafeCap statistics from mid 2022 to 2023

Id	Routes	Signals	Points	LOC	POs, total	POs, unf	Time, s
P6	170	56	59	18917	48992	0	72
P7	46	67	25	16200	24002	0	8
P8	164	63	73	16027	172404	0	130
P9	42	48	22	16288	24566	0	2
P10	122	68	60	18745	344072	6	602

One conclusion to draw from Table 1 is that there is no simple correlation between the size of a railway interlocking and the required proof effort. However, we can notice that the projects P3 and P5 had complex swinging overlaps with complex control logic which, in its turn, leads to a higher number of state transitions. There is also a small number of cases where proof depends on detecting a contradiction, e.g., in timing conditions expressed as simultaneous inequalities in hypotheses. Such proofs first exhaust all venues of rewriting and only then translate a subset of relevant hypotheses into an external SAT solver for a contradiction check. The higher number of proof obligations does normally lead to longer verification although this is not completely clear cut: much of the proof time is often spent discharging a small proportion of harder proof obligations.

Table 2 covers the period from the second half of 2022 to the first quarter of 2023, using the current version of SafeCap with all major improvements implemented. It verifies 136 safety properties with nearly all extra predicates addressing output telegrams.

One relevant trait of output telegrams associated with signals is that they are rarely small and simple – it is unusual to have signal output telegram with fewer than 600 state transitions and some have up to 9000. This means that the output telegram part of SSI completely dominates the rest in terms of number of state transitions. Hence, there was a marked increase in the number of generated proof conjectures when SSI output telegrams were included in the scope of verification.

These required efficiency improvements to the prover were achieved mainly via addition of macro rewriting steps combining several existing rewrite rules.

4   Discussion and Conclusions

The paper discusses our experience in improving the SafeCap tool since it was approved by Network Rail for the use by the UK railway industry and started to be used commercially. Before this, we have used real data of several (developed earlier) SSI interlockings for demonstrating the tool's usefulness to signalling companies in the UK and to prepare for its official approval. Since the approval, the real work on the live commercial projects with our industrial customers has led us to conducting substantial targeted improvements of the tool.

Our strong belief is that the improvement phase is now coming to an end as our substantial and diverse experience in verifying interlockings developed by different companies and design offices clearly shows that the SafeCap tool is sufficiently flexible and scalable.

In the course of this intensive, 3-year long period of interlocking project verification we have also drawn several lessons about how SSI data could be developed to make the verification process simpler and to reduce the risk of errors. It is interesting to note here that our recommendations for achieving these two goals are very much overlapping, and that following them will make understanding and maintenance of the SSI code easier as well. We are now working on summarising this experience and these recommendations.

Our ongoing and future work on SafeCap focuses on a full tool re-development to streamline its architecture after the period of improvements and to make the tool more extendable to other verification applications and resilient to obsolescence. This future work additionally includes the following:

- the development of the safety assurance case for use of SafeCap as an alternative to established manual checking processes, including:
  - re-development of the software for T2 qualification in accordance with the CENELEC EN 50128 standard [2];
  - ensuring traceability and independent verification of safety properties;
  - bug reporting, tracking and fixing.
- the adaption of SafeCap to other technologies, including:
  - development of a front end to import data in the ladder logic or structured text formats;
  - prototyping using machine readable representations of GB relay signalling circuits, to which the existing safety properties could be applied;
  - future extensions to cover ladder logic interlockings and PLCs in railway signalling and other industries.

References

1. Solid State Interlocking. Code of practice for the testing and commissioning of SSI signalling schemes, SSI 8501, Issue 1. British Railways Board (1989)
2. EN 50128: Railway applications - Communication, signalling and processing systems - Software for railway control and protection systems. CENELEC (2020)
3. Bobot, F., Filliâtre, J.C., Marché, C., Paskevich, A.: Why3: shepherd your herd of provers. In: Proceedings of Boogie 2011, pp. 53–64 (2011)
4. Cribbens, A.H.: Solid state interlocking (SSI): an integrated electronic signalling system for mainline railways. Proc. IEE **134**(3), 148–158 (1987)
5. Garavel, H., Beek, M.H., Pol, J.: The 2020 expert survey on formal methods. In: ter Beek, M.H., Ničković, D. (eds.) FMICS 2020. LNCS, vol. 12327, pp. 3–69. Springer, Cham (2020). https://doi.org/10.1007/978-3-030-58298-2_1
6. Iliasov, A., Taylor, D., Laibinis, L., Romanovsky, A.: Practical verification of railway signalling programs. IEEE Trans. Dependable Secure Comput. **20**(Jan–Feb), 695–707 (2023)
7. Iliasov, A., Laibinis, L., Taylor, D., Lopatkin, I., Romanovsky, A.: Safety invariant verification that meets engineers' expectations. In: Collart-Dutilleul, S., Haxthausen, A.E., Lecomte, T. (eds.) RSSRail 2022. LNCS, vol. 13294, pp. 20–31. Springer, Cham (2022). https://doi.org/10.1007/978-3-031-05814-1_2

8. Iliasov, A., Taylor, D., Laibinis, L., Romanovsky, A.: Formal verification of signalling programs with SafeCap. In: Gallina, B., Skavhaug, A., Bitsch, F. (eds.) SAFECOMP 2018. LNCS, vol. 11093, pp. 91–106. Springer, Cham (2018). https://doi.org/10.1007/978-3-319-99130-6_7
9. Iliasov, A., Taylor, D., Romanovsky, A.: Automated testing of SSI data. IRSE (Institution of Railway Signal Engineers) News 241 (2018)

A Formal Model of Train Control with AI-Based Obstacle Detection

Jan Gruteser, David Geleßus⊙, Michael Leuschel$^{(\boxtimes)}$ ⊙, Jan Roßbach, and Fabian Vu⊙

Institut für Informatik, Universität Düsseldorf, Universitätsstr. 1, 40225 Düsseldorf, Germany
{jan.gruteser,dagel101,leuschel,jan.rossbach,
fabian.vu}@uni-duesseldorf.de

Abstract. The research project KI-LOK aims to develop a certification methodology for incorporating AI components into rail vehicles. In this work, we study how to safely incorporate an AI for obstacle detection into an ATO (automatic train operation) system for shunting movements. To analyse the safety of our system we present a formal B model comprising the steering and AI perceptions subsystems as well as the shunting yard environment. Classical model checking is applied to ensure that the complete system is safe under certain assumptions. We use SimB to simulate various scenarios and estimate the likelihood of certain errors when the AI makes mistakes.

Keywords: Railway System · AI · B method · Validation · Verification

1 Introduction and Motivation

Artificial Intelligence (AI) is increasingly being used in safety-critical application fields, such as automotive [8,17,29], aerospace [21], and medicine. This article is part of the KI-LOK research project[1] which is working on certification strategies for AI-based railway systems.

Formal methods are of high interest in the railway sector and are recommended by the norm EN50128 for SIL3 and SIL4 systems. About 30% of the Communication-Based Train Control (CBTC) systems worldwide contain software developed using the B formal method. Formal methods also play a role in safety cases and certification at the system level [4,5,25,26]. For autonomous systems, however, classical certification approaches have reached a major obstacle [6]. The challenge of certifying AI systems is the focus of many research activities, and new standards are starting to appear [22].

---

[1] https://ki-lok.itpower.de.

This research is part of the KI-LOK project funded by the "Bundesministerium für Wirtschaft und Energie"; grant # 19/21007E.

The KI-LOK research project addresses this challenge for railway applications. The project provides a variety of measures to ensure safety, and hopefully enable certification of fully autonomous AI-based railway systems in the future. These measures include

1. ensuring that the AI training and validation data covers all relevant situations while avoiding model overfitting [7] and brittleness [30]
2. performing robustness checks of the AI system, both during validation and at runtime,
3. detecting "out-of-distribution" uses of the AI system, to detect when the AI system is being used outside of its intended scope,
4. using certificate checking [15] for runtime verification,
5. process the AI output in the scope of a rule-based system that can detect and correct certain errors made by the AI.

Figure 1 shows these measures in the context of one case study, an obstacle detection system using an AI-based perception system and a rule-based steering system.

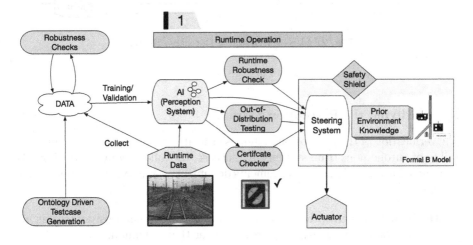

Fig. 1. Various measures towards certification of AI-based obstacle detection

This article mainly focuses on the last two points for this case study, where we develop a formal B model of an AI-based system which contains the steering system and components of the perception system. The purpose of the model is to study the impact of failures of the AI system and to establish effective countermeasures of the steering system. We aim to achieve stronger guarantees of the perception system by using certified control [15]. The study ensures that the complete KI-LOK system is safe under certain assumptions about the perception system. Simulation techniques are used to estimate the likelihood of certain errors.

2   Case Study: AI-Based Obstacle and Sign Detection

For this project, we consider a case study of an obstacle detection system for locomotives during shunting movements. It came with a set of requirements and mission orders devised by Thales (now Ground Transportation Systems).

The system includes an AI-based perception system and a deterministic steering system (see Fig. 2). The role of the perception system is to detect and classify obstacles (persons, animals, vehicles, ...) and railway infrastructure elements. The steering system then makes appropriate decisions about moving the locomotive based on that information.

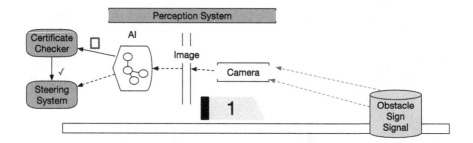

Fig. 2. AI-based Obstacle Detection System

2.1   Verifying the Perception System

The verification of the perception system is crucial in ensuring the safety and reliability of autonomous train systems. In our case, the following property (**REC1-5** extracted from the Thales requirements document) is relevant to the perception system:

- **REC1-5:** The perception system must recognise point positioning, signal status, derailers, wagons, and persons better than a human.

This is a challenging task. Current standardisation attempts [22] focus on making a safety case for AI-based perception systems by showing good performance metrics, comprehensive training data, good test coverage and robustness against common pitfalls like overfitting. We want to explore the extent to which more formal approaches can add value to this approach.

While there have also been considerable efforts to formally verify neural networks [10,12,13,16,24,27], to our knowledge, none can scale to large networks or complex high-level properties yet.

Another formal approach to the verification of such systems is the certified control architecture [15]. The core idea is that, in addition to its regular output, the AI component generates a *certificate* that provides a case for the correctness of its output. This certificate can then be checked by a trusted monitor component, that is formally verified and guarantees the safety requirements. This makes it possible to leave the AI component unverified, while still providing confidence in the accuracy of the result.

In its simplest form, our case study only accounts for a single camera sensor.[2] In the context of modern multi-sensor perception system architectures, this may seem limited. However, the focus of this research is not on the complexity or comprehensiveness of the perception system, but rather on the application of certified control to verify the perception system's ability to classify and detect obstacles. In the first instance, we have also focused on the detection of shunting signs, as opposed to geometrically more challenging obstacles like humans or animals.

While the efficacy of the certified control architecture was shown for two tasks in [15], it is unclear if the approach can be extended to tasks such as obstacle detection in general or shunting sign classification in particular.

In this context, we provide the following proof-of-concept approach for implementing a certified controller in the perception system for sign classification.

1. For the perception system, we fine-tuned a YOLO model [23] [3], for object-detection on a small dataset of train signs[4] that contains shunting yard signs from the case study. (Note that YOLO models are actually used in practice in the automotive and railway industries for object detection.)
2. The YOLO model outputs the bounding box as its certificate (see Fig. 3a),
3. We then implemented a Python program that applies classical feature detection on the image inside the resulting bounding box (see Fig. 3b; the green check mark in the bounding box in Fig. 3c shows that the certificate was successfully checked).

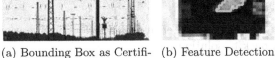

(a) Bounding Box as Certificate   (b) Feature Detection   (c) Successful Certificate Check

Fig. 3. Yolov8 Object-Detection and Subsequent Certificate Checking via Feature Detection

For 3) we used OpenCV [14] contour-detection [31] to find the half-circles of Sh0 and Sh1 signs, which are shunting ground signs like in Figure 3 with

---

[2] But we are also investigating systems with two cameras or with LiDAR sensors.

[3] https://github.com/ultralytics/ultralytics.

[4] https://universe.roboflow.com/kilok/sign-detection-4oqe4/dataset/2.

different angles of half-circle (e.g. horizontal, diagonal). They represent Stop and Go signals for the locomotive. With the contours, we then used principal component analysis (PCA) [9] and some basic trigonometry[5] to find the angles of the semi-circles. That makes it possible to differentiate the two classes in the image by their respective angle values, and thus validate the class assigned from the model. If the angles do not match the assigned class or the half-circles can not be detected, the detection is rejected. If they do match our expectations, this provides additional confidence in the detection.

Figure 3 illustrates the process on an example from the data set. The bounding box found by the YOLO model is put through the angle analysis, to verify the detection of an Sh1 sign. Using this method, we can likely eliminate most, if not all, false positive detections, while hopefully not decreasing the accuracy too much. Preliminary results on the mentioned dataset show the software successfully eliminating *all* false positive detections, i.e., the certificate checker eliminates all false sign detections of the AI. On the negative side, the certificate checker unfortunately also flags a significant number of true positive reductions as erroneous (17 % for Sh0 and 39 % for Sh1 signs). This is due to the small size of many signs in the dataset, which are unrecognizable even to the human eye. This shows the importance of image quality for this method and should be considered in future research. But, to some extent, it is unavoidable that true positives are flagged by a certificate checker.

In conclusion, we have presented a prototype of certificate checking. It is promising for sign detection, but it seems unlikely we can extend this to all classes of objects (such as persons). Also, we can check the certificates in case a sign was detected, but currently not when no sign is detected by the AI. In addition, there is a possibility of signs being vandalized, leading to situations where a sign is misread or even not detected. Our solution is twofold:

1. provide a deterministic steering system which knows the location of signals, and signs and can thus go into a safe mode when no sign is at positions which expect one,
2. or accept that the AI can make errors and conduct a probabilistic analysis, rather than a deductive black-and-white verification.

Note that if solution 1 is not realistic, e.g., because no topology information is available, we can always fall back to solution 2.

In Sect. 3 we present the formal B model of the system, which enables one to formalize and verify mitigating measures (solution 1), but also study the impact of undetected errors of the AI to be able to conduct solution 2 (which we tackle in Sect. 4). Therefore, we decide to use the formal B method [1] which was also used for other railway systems [4,5,25,26]. While this work focuses mostly on formally modelling and verifying the steering system and environment, we plan to address direct verification of the perception system in future work.

---

[5] https://automaticaddison.com/how-to-determine-the-orientation-of-an-object-using-opencv/.

3   B Model of Shunting

To help certification of our AI-based system, we are developing a formal system-wide model of shunting movements and possible error sources to determine their impact. The formal B model describes the environment, field elements, object detection, and the deterministic processing of the output of AI within the steering system.

Usually, formal models must not contain invariant violations, otherwise, undesired behaviour has occurred which should be avoided. Our model allows invariant violation as the AI can identify objects incorrectly or even ignore them which could lead to accidents. This is necessary to reason about the impact of the AI's wrong decisions. However, later during the validation process, we will check that under certain circumstances these errors must not occur.

There are some similarities to the interlocking model as presented by Abrial in Chap. 17 of [2], but our model has considerably more detail. We are modelling the system under consideration and the environment. The machine hierarchy of our formal model is shown in Fig. 4.

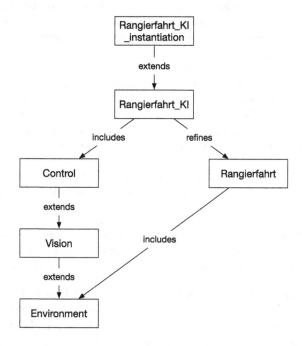

Fig. 4. Machine Hierarchy

Environment. Within Environment, we model the general properties of a track topology. At a later refinement, those environment elements are instantiated with a concrete environment which must fulfil those properties. In particular, the environment contains a train, derailers, signals, points, the track topology, and positions of objects and obstacles. Furthermore, `Environment` includes operations to change the track occupancy, activate/deactivate derailers, switch signals, and move points.

Vision contains the perception system which works in an environment. In particular, `Vision` contains variables and events for the recognition of signals, points, and obstacles (within its visual range). For simplicity, those elements are always recognised either correctly or incorrectly. For example, `Vision` might detect a signal which is visible in front of the train. Its application corresponds to the assumption that the signal sign has been correctly detected by the perception system. `Vision` might also detect wrong signal signs at any position. This means that the perception system has recognised an existing signal sign incorrectly or one that does not exist. The design of the detection operations for other objects and obstacles follows the same principle.

Control models decisions of a basic steering system based on the perception system's vision. More precisely, `Control` computes how far the train is allowed to move (forwards and backwards). The allowed distance for moving forwards and backwards is computed by respective operations, and stored by respective variables in the model.

Rangierfahrt (shunting movement in English) models the train movement in an environment. Therefore, operations are introduced to move the train forwards and backwards. `Rangierfahrt` does not yet take any safety restrictions into account, meaning that both operations do not use the perception system. Thus, the train movement is only restricted by the environment physically.

Rangierfahrt_KI (KI is the German abbreviation of AI) refines `Rangierfahrt` by considering the decisions of `Control` for movement with safety constraints.
    The safety requirement to be considered here is:

- **SAF1-5:** When point positions, stop signals, derailers, and obstacles are recognised correctly, the train must not enter a safety-critical state (train derailing, train entering a blocked session, or collision with an obstacle).

We model the steering system logic to behave safely based on how the AI recognises the environment (assuming that the detection is correct). An AI might recognise an obstacle or decide to continue moving. However, the steering system must not decide to continue driving when an obstacle is detected ahead in the direction of the train's movement. This is modelled by additional conditions for the train's movements: The train is only allowed to move by a distance smaller than the maximum allowed distance given by `Control`. As mentioned before, the latter depends on the recognition of the perception system. Note that we are modelling and verifying the steering logic in terms of its perception, and not the perception itself.

Rangierfahrt_ KI_ instantiation. For the case study, we received a specific track topology with a mission order to achieve which is as follows:

Drive from the current position on track 347 to position B on track 855. Position B is defined as wagon C55's position (QR code). Approach the wagon to the clutch position. Recognise all field elements and people. The task for the system: Recognise the described field elements (points, derailers, brake shoes) and signals reliably.

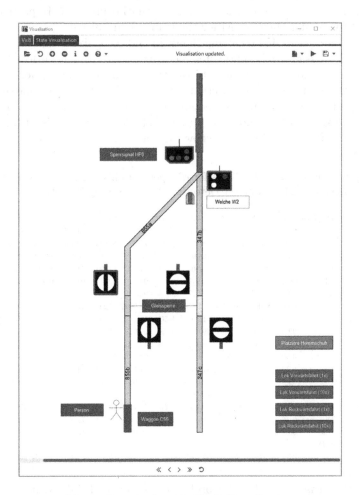

Fig. 5. Domain-Specific VISB Visualisation

Therefore, `Rangierfahrt_KI_instantiation` extends `Rangierfahrt_KI` by creating the concrete instantiation of the environment corresponding to the track topology. In principle, the model is currently intended to support freely chosen topologies. Technically, all constants in the *Environment* are instantiated with concrete values which fulfil the properties. We use VISB [33] to create a domain-specific visualisation that corresponds to the visualisation in the case study document which is shown in Fig. 5. VISB is a visualisation component of PROB [20].

4   Simulation with SimB

SIMB [32] is a simulation tool which is built on top of PROB. Using SIMB, a modeller can formulate simulations with probabilistic and timing behaviour on a formal model, trying to capture realistic scenarios precisely. In particular, we use SIMB to simulate how an AI for the train could behave.

We simulate KI-LOK by moving the train and recognizing signals and obstacles. Here, we assign probabilities for recognizing an obstacle (in)correctly and ignoring them, taking the distance to the obstacle into account. More precisely, the probabilities for correct detection increase when the train approaches the obstacle, while those for wrong detection and ignoring decrease. We also assume that the AI would rather ignore the signal/obstacle than recognise it incorrectly. An overview of all probabilities is shown in Table 1.

Table 1. Overview of all probabilities for AI's perception system with distances to field element or obstacle, CD = Correct Detection, WD = Wrong Detection, I = Ignore

Signal	Distance	0-10	11-20	21-30	31-40	41-50	51-60	61-70	71-80	81-90	91-100	101-110
	CD	99.9%	99.9%	64.9%	49.9%	39.9%	29.9%	19.9%	14.9%	9.9%	4.9%	0.0%
	WD	0.01%	0.01%	3.51%	5.01%	6.01%	7.01%	8.01%	8.51%	9.01%	9.51%	0.0%
	I	0.09%	0.09%	31.59%	45.09%	54.09%	63.09%	72.09%	76.59%	81.09%	85.59%	100.00%
Point Positioning	Distance	0-10	11-20	21-30	31-40	41-50	51-60	61-70	71-80	81-90	91-100	101-110
	CD	99.9%	99.9%	54.9%	34.9%	19.9%	9.9%	4.9%	0.0%	0.0%	0.0%	0.0%
	WD	0.01%	0.01%	4.51%	6.51%	8.01%	9.01%	9.41%	0.0%	0.0%	0.0%	0.0%
	I	0.09%	0.09%	40.59%	58.59%	72.09%	81.09%	85.59%	100.0%	100.0%	100.0%	100.0%
Derailer	Distance	0-10	11-20	21-30	31-40	41-50	51-60	61-70	71-80	81-90	91-100	101-110
	CD	99.9%	99.9%	64.9%	49.9%	39.9%	29.9%	19.9%	14.9%	9.9%	4.9%	0.0%
	WD	0.01%	0.01%	3.51%	5.01%	6.01%	7.01%	8.01%	8.51%	9.01%	9.51%	0.0%
	I	0.09%	0.09%	31.59%	45.09%	54.09%	63.09%	72.09%	76.59%	81.09%	85.59%	100.00%
Wagon	Distance	0-10	11-20	21-30	31-40	41-50	51-60	61-70	71-80	81-90	91-100	101-110
	CD	99.9%	99.9%	64.9%	49.9%	39.9%	29.9%	24.9%	19.9%	14.9%	9.9%	4.9%
	WD	-	-	-	-	-	-	-	-	-	-	-
	I	0.1%	0.1%	35.1%	50.1%	60.1%	70.1%	75.1%	80.1%	85.1%	90.1%	95.1%
Person	Distance	0-10	11-20	21-30	31-40	41-50	51-60	61-70	71-80	81-90	91-100	101-110
	CD	99.9%	99.9%	64.9%	49.9%	39.9%	29.9%	24.9%	19.9%	14.9%	9.9%	4.9%
	WD	-	-	-	-	-	-	-	-	-	-	-
	I	0.1%	0.1%	35.1%	50.1%	60.1%	70.1%	75.1%	80.1%	85.1%	90.1%	95.1%

Note that the values for the probabilities are artificial. Although we can provide probabilities for possible AI behaviour, we do not know whether those values are realistic/precise wrt. to the actual AI behaviour.[6] Ideally, we would receive these values from the evaluation of the AI. However, we have decided to use those artificial values to receive an impression regarding the probability

---

[6] We hope to obtain such precise figures from industrial partners in our project.

of a safety-critical situation. So, the simulated scenarios can be used to gain knowledge about possible behaviours, and to communicate with domain experts.

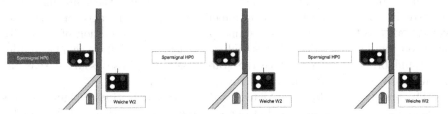

(a) Train Approaches Signal and Point Positioning   (b) AI recognises Train correctly   (c) Train moves forwards

Fig. 6. Example: Simulation in SimB

Figure 6 shows parts from a simulation in SIMB. Here, one can see that the train approaches the signal and the point position at **347a**. In this simulation, the AI recognises the signal correctly and continues moving forwards.

In Sect. 6, we will also present a Monte Carlo simulation with hypothesis testing and estimation of probability based on the SIMB simulation. In particular, we will compute the probability of accidents when KI-LOK's detection fails. There are two (probabilistic) requirements to validate in this context: the first one is about the probability of a safe drive along the complete track (see **PROP1**), and the second one is about the probability of achieving the **Mission Order** (see **PROP2**).

- **PROP1:** When driving along the route from 347a to 855b, safety-critical situations (train derailing, train entering a blocked section, collision with wagon or person) must occur less frequently with KI-LOK than with humans[7].
- **PROP2:** The probability of achieving the mission order by KI-LOK must be as good as humans[8].

5   Verification

The complete model has various operations that lead to a significant blow-up of the state space. For example, in the current model, there are up to 200 possibilities to move a train in any direction from each position as the distance is provided as a parameter. Furthermore, the brake shoes can be placed anywhere on the track which also enlarges the state space. For this reason, a complete verification of the model with model checking is infeasible. To address this issue, we explored

---

[7] For now, we define that the probability of a safe drive from 347a to 855b must be $\geq$ 99.9%.

[8] For now, we define that the probability of achieving the mission order must be $\geq$ 99.9%.

the state space for some reduced models with additional constraints. These models can be used to verify certain properties under reasonable constraints, where we focused on obstacle detection and signal aspects.

The reduced models[9] exclude the backward movement of the train and specify a fixed distance for the forward movement. Fixing the distance of movement corresponds to travelling at a constant speed in a fixed direction of travel. To focus on the detection of obstacles and signal aspects, we also excluded border signs and brake shoes to reduce the state space. It is also assumed that the positions of signals and points are known to the train.

The first model (CD) is restricted to the correct detection of signal aspects and point positions, provided that one of these objects is detected. Except for the placement of brake shoes, the modelling of the environmental behaviour is the same as that of the complete model, which includes the activation of derailers and the switching of points. Note that "correct" only refers to the correctness of the detected signal aspect or point position and does not guarantee the detection of all signals and points. This means that the train could pass a closed signal because it did not recognise it at all. The assumption that all signals are correctly recognised before passing them can be implemented using temporal properties as described in Sect. 6.

The CD model is then extended to detect wrong signal aspects (+WS), leaving the other properties unchanged. In the next step, the wrong detection of point positions (+WP) is added. There are two cases to be distinguished here. The +WP model only considers the detected point positions to determine if they cannot be passed over because the point is not in an end position. As a further extension, the train in the +WP_DT model also updates its detected track based on the incorrectly detected switch position.

Table 2. Model Checking Results for Selected Reduced Models

Model	Operations	Variables/ Constants	States	Transitions	Time (min)	Memory (GB)
CD	13	34	269 153	2 240 046	6.8	1.3
+ WS	14	34	480 409	5 403 158	12.3	2.6
+ WP	15	34	807 001	10 733 462	23.4	4.8
+ WP_DT	15	34	>16 785 959	>185 250 252	>530	>80
complete	22	46	n/a	n/a	n/a	n/a

We used the PROB model checker[10] [19] in combination with operation caching and state compression [18] (`-p COMPRESSION true -p OPERATION`

---

[9] The models can be found at https://github.com/hhu-stups/kilok_shunting_model/tree/14c2ecdb6e32ba593cac64e5868c94773139b391.

[10] Version: 1.12.0-final (`fef4b935b59d76e353ab67230f6206b15f903f4b`, 05.04.2023).

_REUSE full). All benchmarks are executed on the high-performance cluster "HILBERT" at the University of Düsseldorf. The results are shown in Table 2.

The first three models (CD, WS, WP) can be model checked with reasonable performance (time and memory). We stopped model checking WP_DT after it exceeded a memory limit of 80 GB when about three-quarters of the current queue had been explored. This shows that the slight changes from WP to WP_DT lead to a considerable increase in the state space, which also indicates that the state space of the complete model must be even larger.

These experiments have shown that model checking is feasible for some reduced models with reasonable restrictions, so that further properties such as LTL formulas can be checked on these models, which is described in the following Sect. 6. Since the capabilities of the reduced models are limited, the validation of the entire model will focus on simulations using SIMB as described in Sects. 4 and 6.

In the future, we plan to invest more effort to make the B model easier to verify. Here, we would like to evaluate whether abstraction techniques, e.g., as presented by Stock et al. [28] can help us to tackle the state space explosion problem. Currently, the model is not designed for mathematical proofs; but in the future, we aim to rewrite/refactor the model to make provers such as AtelierB [3] feasible. This could also enable verifying the model's behaviour across various topologies, and not only a specific case study.

6   Validation

This section describes the validation of the requirements for the AI-based steering system. (The requirements and the mission orders were set out by Thales for the case study.) Here, we make use of various validation techniques including animation/trace replay, (LTL) model checking and simulation.

Scenario: Mission Order. For easier reasoning about the environment, the steering system and the perception system, we have split the **Mission Order** into a high-level scenario with six steps as shown below:

- **Mission Order (Scenario):**
    1. Drive from the current position on track 347a to the stop signal and point
    2. Recognise stop signal and point position
    3. Enter 855a and drive to the derailer
    4. Recognise derailer
    5. Enter 855b and approach the wagon to the clutch position
    6. Recognise the person and the waggon

    Steps (2), (4) and (6) must recognise field elements or people correctly, otherwise, the Mission Order might not be achieved.

However, the mission order might not be accomplished if steps (2), (4), and (6) fail. To validate the mission order, we animated 24 traces[11] with different variations of steps (2), (4), and (6).

The correct execution of the mission order (as desired in the description) is validated by a single trace. The other 23 traces represent variations of steps (2), (4), and (6), and cover scenarios where signals and objects may be ignored or recognised incorrectly. In particular, these traces were used to test potential consequences in safety-critical or dangerous situations that could arise:

- Neither wagon nor person recognised correctly — leads to collision with both
- Person recognised correctly, but not wagon — leads to collision with wagon
- Active derailer not recognised correctly — leads to the train entering a section where collision is possible
- Neither stop signal nor moving point position recognised correctly — leads to the train derailing
- Point position recognised correctly, but not stop signal — leads to the train entering a section where collision is possible

If the AI detects the stop signal but not the point position, then there is no dangerous situation. This is caused by the fact that when the point is moving, then the stop signal is always active.

Temporal Properties: SAF1-SAF5. As analysed in Sect. 5, model checking is feasible for application on reduced models, but not on the complete model due to the state space explosion problem. On the reduced models, we were able to check the safety properties **SAF1-SAF5** with LTL model checking. Since they assume correct detection, it follows that the train must not derail or collide with other objects. One of the temporal properties we checked assumes that whenever the train moves, the control unit must have updated its decision for the allowed movement range, and all signals, points, and objects must have been correctly detected before. The high-level formulation of the LTL formula is as follows:

G({"train moves forwards" ⇒
    Y ("control unit updates decision to move train forwards" ∧
       "train detected all signals correctly" ∧
       "train detected points correctly" ∧
       "train detected obstacles correctly" ∧
       "train detected track correctly"})
  ⇒ G({"train does not reach safety-critical situation"})

The formula could be successfully verified for the first three models in Table 2. Since the assumptions of this formula are very strict and probably not realizable by an AI system, we investigate other formulas with less stringent assumptions.

---

[11] Some of the traces can be accessed as an interactive HTML document at
https://stups.hhu-hosting.de/models/kilok/HTML_Traces.

Probabilistic Properties: PROP1, PROP2. Based on the simulation in Sect. 4, we compute the probability of a safe drive along the complete route. Referring to **PROP1**, it is desired that the safety-critical situation occurs less often than with a human driver. For now, we define the occurrence of an accident at 1 out of 1000 runs. More precisely, we apply a hypothesis test to check that the probability of a safe drive is $\geq 99.9\%$ with a significance level of 0.1%. In particular, we define the end condition of the simulation as follows: the train has either reached the end of the route, or a safety-critical has occurred (see **ending**). Furthermore, it is desired that a safety-critical situation never occurs so that a drive is safe (see **prop**). As a result, the formulated hypothesis test is accepted.

> SIM(ending: "train reaches the end of 855b" ∨
> "train reaches the end of 347c" ∨
> "train reaches a safety-critical situation"
> prop: "train never reaches a safety-critical situation"
> check: **HYPOTHESIS**
> procedure: **LEFT_TAILED**
> probability: **0.999**
> α: **0.001**)

To check **PROP2**, we formulate another hypothesis test with the same ending condition for the simulation. Here, we check that the Mission Order is achieved with a probability of $\geq 99.9\%$. This hypothesis is accepted as well.

> SIM(ending: "train reaches the end of 855b" ∨
> "train reaches the end of 347c" ∨
> "train reaches a safety-critical situation"
> prop: "train reaches the end of 855b safely"
> check: **HYPOTHESIS**
> procedure: **LEFT_TAILED**
> probability: **0.999**
> α: **0.001**)

7   More Related Work, Conclusion, and Future Work

In the following, we compare this work with other related work including standardisation approaches, the verification of AI systems, and other railway systems.

Standardisation. Peleska et al. propose a method of making a safety case according to the UL4600 standard [22]. It relies on the statistical independence of different input channels to make a case for the reliability of identified hazard mitigation pipelines.

In the future, the project could attempt to apply this procedure to the case study. This would require the implementation of a full multi-sensor perception system with a multi-channel plus voting design and subsequent training and evaluation of AI models on a multi-channel dataset like the Open Sensor Data for Rail[12].

Formal Verification of AI Systems. Ensuring the safety of AI systems with machine learning is challenging. Several approaches have been presented to formally verify AI systems with neural networks [10,12,13,16,24,27], but to our knowledge, they do not scale to the kind of properties and kind of neural network model we require here.

Railway Systems. Formal methods, especially the B method have been used to model several railway systems such as Abrial's interlocking system [2], CBTC systems [4,5,25,26], and the Hybrid Level 3 system [11]. Similar to our approach, the main goal is to formally describe all behaviours in the railway system, and to verify/validate certain properties. However, we also incorporate the AI perceptions system which relies on the visual recognition of objects and elements to make decisions. Here, we checked that all safety properties are fulfilled under the condition of correct recognition. Additionally, we also evaluated the impact when the AI makes mistakes.

Conclusion. In this work, we aim to study how to certify railway systems using AI components. We illustrated this in a case study ensuring the safety of an AI which controls train movements in a shunting yard.

Therefore, we first implemented a prototype for a certificate checker of the perception system. Although certificate checking seems promising for signs, it seems unlikely that it can be used to classify all classes of objects. In our preliminary results, we were able to reduce most false positives detections at the cost of reduced true positives. On the other hand, false negatives can be tackled if the positions of signs are known. In particular, KI-LOK activates safe mode when no signs are detected where one is expected.

Using the formal B method, we encode the shunting movements and possible behaviours of the AI. Based on the model, we can check certain safety requirements provided the AI's detection is done correctly. Due to the complexity of the complete model, it was necessary to reduce/abstract some details in the model to make model checking feasible in a reasonable time. Applying techniques like trace replay and simulation, we can study the impact of certain errors of the AI. In particular, we utilize SIMB to estimate the likelihood of accidents. Still, more work is required so that simulation captures the AI's trained behaviour with precision.

Future Work. Although we have made progress towards certification, our work is not yet ready for certification. To achieve this goal, it is necessary to further verify the system to ensure stronger safety guarantees. This may also require rewriting the model to make it feasible for mathematical proof. In the end, we

---

[12] https://data.fid-move.de/dataset/osdar23.

hope that we can obtain a proof that the system is safe under certain conditions, e.g., when the location of signals and points is known and when some of the AI's perception decisions can be cross-checked by the certifying control technique.

Runtime monitoring and verification approaches, e.g., safety shielding is also an important aspect in the future. Furthermore, one could implement a virtual environment for KI-LOK to link the simulation with the AI more actively, similar to [17] for autonomous cars. This could make it possible for the AI to run simulations directly instead of trying to capture the AI's behaviour in a SIMB simulation. Finally, the resulting traces could then still be validated by SIMB's validation techniques.

Acknowledgements. Infrastructure for model checking benchmarks was provided by the "Centre for Information and Media Technology" (ZIM) at the University of Düsseldorf (Germany). We thank anonymous reviewers for their very helpful comments and links to related work.

References

1. Abrial, J., Hoare, A.: The B-Book: Assigning Programs to Meanings. Cambridge University Press (2005)
2. Abrial, J.-R.: Modeling in Event-B: System and Software Engineering. Cambridge University Press (2010)
3. ClearSy. Atelier B, User and Reference Manuals. Aix-en-Provence, France (2016). https://www.atelierb.eu/
4. Comptier, M., Déharbe, D., Perez, J.M., Mussat, L., Thibaut, P., Sabatier, D.: Safety analysis of a CBTC system: a rigorous approach with Event-B. In Proceedings RSSRail, LNCS, vol. 10598, pp. 148–159 (2017)
5. Comptier, M., Leuschel, M., Mejia, L., Perez, J.M., Mutz, M.: Property-based modelling and validation of a CBTC zone controller in Event-B. In: Proceedings RSSRail. LNCS, vol. 11495, pp. 202–212 (2019)
6. Cummings, M.L.: Rethinking the maturity of artificial intelligence in safety-critical settings. AI Mag. **42**(1), 6–15 (2021)
7. dos Santos, C.F.G., Papa, J.P.: Avoiding overfitting: a survey on regularization methods for convolutional neural networks. CoRR, abs/2201.03299 (2022)
8. A. R. Fayjie, S. Hossain, D. Oualid, and D.-J. Lee. Driverless car: Autonomous driving using deep reinforcement learning in urban environment. In 2018 15th international conference on ubiquitous robots (ur), pages 896–901. IEEE, 2018
9. K. P. F.R.S. LIII. On lines and planes of closest fit to systems of points in space. The London, Edinburgh, and Dublin Philosophical Magazine and Journal of Science **2**(11), 559–572 (1901)
10. Gehr, T., Mirman, M., Drachsler-Cohen, D., Tsankov, P., Chaudhuri, S., Vechev, M.: Ai2: safety and robustness certification of neural networks with abstract interpretation. In: 2018 IEEE Symposium on Security and Privacy (SP), pp. 3–18. IEEE (2018)
11. Hansen, D., Leuschel, M., Schneider, D., Krings, S., Körner, P., Naulin, T., Nayeri, N., Skowron, F.: Using a formal B model at runtime in a demonstration of the ETCS hybrid level 3 concept with real trains. In: Butler, M., Raschke, A., Hoang, T.S., Reichl, K. (eds.) ABZ 2018. LNCS, vol. 10817, pp. 292–306. Springer, Cham (2018). https://doi.org/10.1007/978-3-319-91271-4_20

12. Huang, X., Kwiatkowska, M., Wang, S., Wu, M.: Safety verification of deep neural networks. In: Majumdar, R., Kunčak, V. (eds.) CAV 2017. LNCS, vol. 10426, pp. 3–29. Springer, Cham (2017). https://doi.org/10.1007/978-3-319-63387-9_1

13. Huang, X., Ruan, W., Tang, Q., Zhao, X.: Bridging formal methods and machine learning with global optimisation. In: Riesco, A., Zhang, M. (eds) ICFEM 2022. LNCS, vol. 13478, pp. 1–19. Springer, Cham (2022)

14. Itseez. Open source computer vision library (2015). https://github.com/itseez/opencv

15. Jackson, D., et al.: Certified control: An architecture for verifiable safety of autonomous vehicles. CoRR, abs/2104.06178 (2021)

16. Katz, G., Barrett, C., Dill, D.L., Julian, K., Kochenderfer, M.J.: Reluplex: an efficient SMT solver for verifying deep neural networks. In: Proceedings CAV, LNCS, vol. 10426, pp. 97–117 (2017)

17. Leurent, E.: An environment for autonomous driving decision-making (2018). https://github.com/eleurent/highway-env

18. Leuschel, M.: Operation caching and state compression for model checking of high-level models - how to have your cake and eat it. In: Proceedings iFM. LNCS, vol. 13274, pp. 129–145 (2022)

19. Leuschel, M., Butler, M.: ProB: a model checker for B. In: Proceedings FME, LNCS, vol. 2805, pp. 855–874 (2003)

20. Leuschel, M., Butler, M.J.: ProB: an automated analysis toolset for the B method. STTT **10**(2), 185–203 (2008)

21. Nonami, K., Kendoul, F., Suzuki, S., Wang, W., Nakazawa, D.: Autonomous flying robots: unmanned aerial vehicles and micro aerial vehicles. Springer Science & Business Media (2010)

22. Peleska, J., Haxthausen, A.E., Lecomte, T.: Standardisation considerations for autonomous train control. In: Proceedings ISoLA. LNCS, vol. 13704, pp. 286–307 (2022)

23. Redmon, J., Divvala, S.K., Girshick, R.B., Farhadi, A.: You Only Look Once: Unified, Real-Time Object Detection. In: 2016 IEEE Conference on Computer Vision and Pattern Recognition (CVPR), pp. 779–788, Los Alamitos, CA, USA, June 2016. IEEE Computer Society

24. Ruan, W., Huang, X., Kwiatkowska, M.: Reachability analysis of deep neural networks with provable guarantees. In: Proceedings IJCAI International Joint Conferences on Artificial Intelligence Organization, pp. 2651–2659, 7 2018

25. Sabatier, D.: Using formal proof and B method at system level for industrial projects. In: Lecomte, T., Pinger, R., Romanovsky, A. (eds.) RSSRail 2016. LNCS, vol. 9707, pp. 20–31. Springer, Cham (2016). https://doi.org/10.1007/978-3-319-33951-1_2

26. Sabatier, D., Burdy, L., Requet, A., Guéry, J.: Formal proofs for the NYCT line 7 (flushing) modernization project. In: Derrick, J., Fitzgerald, J., Gnesi, S., Khurshid, S., Leuschel, M., Reeves, S., Riccobene, E. (eds.) ABZ 2012. LNCS, vol. 7316, pp. 369–372. Springer, Heidelberg (2012). https://doi.org/10.1007/978-3-642-30885-7_34

27. Seshia, S.A., Sadigh, D., Sastry, S.S.: Toward verified artificial intelligence. Commun. ACM **65**(7), 46–55 (2022)

28. Stock, S., Vu, F., Gelexsus, D., Leuschel, M., Mashkoor, A., Egyed, A.: Validation by abstraction and refinement. In: Proceedings ABZ. LNCS, vol. 14010, pp. 160–178 (2023.) https://doi.org/10.1007/978-3-031-33163-3_12

29. Sun, P., et al.: Scalability in perception for autonomous driving: Waymo open dataset. In: Proceedings of the IEEE/CVF Conference on Computer Vision and Pattern Recognition, pp. 2446–2454 (2020)
30. Sun, Y., Wu, M., Ruan, W., Huang, X., Kwiatkowska, M., Kroening, D.: Concolic testing for deep neural networks. CoRR, abs/1805.00089 (2018)
31. Suzuki, S., Abe, K.: Topological structural analysis of digitized binary images by border following. Comput. Vis. Graph. Image Process. **30**(1), 32–46 (1985)
32. Vu, F., Leuschel, M., Mashkoor, A.: Validation of formal models by timed probabilistic simulation. In: Raschke, A., Méry, D. (eds.) ABZ 2021. LNCS, vol. 12709, pp. 81–96. Springer, Cham (2021). https://doi.org/10.1007/978-3-030-77543-8_6
33. Werth, M., Leuschel, M.: VisB: a lightweight tool to visualize formal models with SVG graphics. In: Raschke, A., Méry, D., Houdek, F. (eds.) ABZ 2020. LNCS, vol. 12071, pp. 260–265. Springer, Cham (2020). https://doi.org/10.1007/978-3-030-48077-6_21

Automated Compositional Verification
of Interlocking Systems

Anne E. Haxthausen[1]([✉]) [ID], Alessandro Fantechi[2] [ID], Gloria Gori[2] [ID],
Óli Kárason Mikkelsen[1], and Sofie-Amalie Petersen[1]

[1] DTU Compute, Technical University of Denmark, Lyngby, Denmark
aeha@dtu.dk
[2] University of Florence, Firenze, Italy
{alessandro.fantechi,gloria.gori}@unifi.it

Abstract. Model checking techniques have often been applied to the
verification of railway interlocking systems. However, these techniques
may fail to scale to interlockings controlling large railway networks, com-
posed by hundreds of controlled entities, due to the state space explosion
problem. We have previously proposed a compositional method to reduce
the size of networks to be model checked: the idea is to divide the network of the system to be verified into two sub-networks and then model
check the model instances for these sub-networks instead of that for the
full network. If given well-formedness conditions are satisfied by the network and the kind of division performed, it is proved that model checking
safety properties of all such sub-networks guarantees safety properties of
the full network. In this paper we observe that such a network division
can be repeated, so that in the end, the full network has been divided
into a number of sub-networks of minimal size, each being an instance
of one of a limited set of "elementary networks", for which safety proofs
have easily been given by model checking once for all. The paper defines
a division algorithm, and shows how, applying it to some examples of
different complexity, a network can be automatically decomposed into a
set of elementary networks, hence proving its safety. The execution time
for such a verification turns out to be a very small fraction of the time
needed for a model checker to verify safety of the full network.

Keywords: Formal Methods · Model Checking · Compositional
Verification · Interlocking Systems

1 Introduction

Formal methods have successfully been applied to development and verification
of railway systems [3,5,6]. In particular, model checking techniques have often
been applied to the verification of railway interlocking systems. However, model
checking is subject to *state space explosion*, which limits scalability of the approach, so that automatic verification of interlocking systems for large networks
is demanding in terms of computing resources, and may even fail [4].

© The Author(s), under exclusive license to Springer Nature Switzerland AG 2023
B. Milius et al. (Eds.): RSSRail 2023, LNCS 14198, pp. 146–164, 2023.
https://doi.org/10.1007/978-3-031-43366-5_9

Abstraction techniques have typically been adopted to limit state space explosion in model checking. Abstraction should preserve the desired properties and the adopted abstraction technique should be defined specifically for the kind of system and properties under examination. For interlocking systems, a convenient abstraction can be based on the *locality* principle [9,21]: properties concerning the safe allocation of a route to a train are typically not influenced by other train movements over networks elements that are distant from, and not interfering with, the considered route. Locality of a safety property can be used to limit the state space by abstracting away such "distant movements".

In our previous work, the locality principle is at the base of a *compositional* approach to the verification of interlockings for large networks: the network is divided into two (or more) sub-networks, to which model checking is applied, with a substantial reduction of state space explosion [2,8,13,14]. The soundness result for compositional safety verification given in [8] guarantees that, when properly cutting a network, proving safety for the sub-networks suffices to prove safety for the full network. In this way, the task of proving safety for a large network can be reduced to the task of verifying safety for sub-networks of a size manageable by the model checker.

We have based our compositional approach on the RobustRailS verification framework [20], that exploits the powerful SMT-based RT-Tester bounded model checker[1], although it can be adapted to other verification frameworks: the idea of compositional verification is also shared by the approach described in [10–12]. The two approaches are compared in [1], where it turns out that the latter is grounded on pragmatic domain-related criteria for the definition of how and where to perform the cut into two sub-networks.

The discussion about criteria for localisation of cuts has actually triggered the contribution of this paper, in which a novel iterative decomposition strategy is proposed, to achieve a fine granularity decomposition of a network into a number of small sub-networks, that under certain conditions belong to a library of pre-verified elementary networks. The soundness result for compositional safety verification guarantees that safety for the full network is given by the pre-verified safety of sub-networks. Therefore, to verify a network, it is in principle no more needed to run a model checker, independently of the size of the network, if specific network conditions are met. To the best of our knowledge, we are the first to propose and explore this idea.

The paper formally specifies and implements a division algorithm, and reports on some experiments in which the executable specification as well as the implementation have been applied to some networks of different complexity. In all these experiments, the considered networks were automatically divided into a set of elementary sub-networks, hence proving their safety. In each experiment, the execution time for the algorithm turned out to be a very small fraction of the time needed for a model checker to verify safety of the full network.

After a short description of the RobustRailS verification method in Sect. 2 and a summary of the compositional verification method in Sect. 3, Sect. 4

---

[1] https://www.verified.de/products/rt-tester/.

introduces the possible types of elementary networks, and describes the proposed strategy for performing decomposition into elementary networks. The strategy had been preliminarily sketched in [7]: we now fully formalise it using RSL in Sect. 5, and the executable RSL specification of the division algorithm and its C++ implementation are then applied to some case studies, for which the gains in verification time are shown (Sect. 6). Section 7 draws conclusions and states ideas for future work.

2   The RobustRailS Verification Method and Tools

In the RobustRailS research project[2] that was accompanying the Danish re-signalling programme on a scientific level in 2012–2017, a formal method with tools support for automated, formal verification of railway interlocking systems was developed [17–20].

About the Considered Interlocking Systems. An *interlocking system* is a signalling system component that is responsible for safe routing of trains through (a fraction of) a railway network under its control.

In Fig. 1 an example of a railway network layout for a small station is given. As it can be seen, it consists of (1) train detection sections that are either linear sections (like t10) or switchable points (like t11) having a stem side and two branching sides (e.g. t11 has its stem next to t10 and its branches next to t20 and t12, respectively); (2) markerboards[3] (like mb10) placed at the ends of linear sections and only visible in one direction (e.g. mb10 is visible in direction UP). As general rules for the networks considered in this paper, (1) there is at most one markerboard in each end of a linear section, that can only be seen when leaving the section; (2) at the borders of a network, there are always two linear sections (like b10 and t10) with a signal configuration having an *entry signal* on the border section and an *exit signal* on the section next to the border section. Furthermore, networks are assumed to be *loop-free*[4].

About the Tool. The RobustRailS tool, *RR-T*, can be used to verify that an interlocking system instance controlling a certain railway network is safe by giving the tool the following as input: (1) a generic, formal, behavioural model of the interlocking system and generic safety properties, as well as (2) a specification of the network under its control[5]. The tool then checks that the input is wellformed,

---

[2] http://robustrails.man.dtu.dk.

[3] We are considering modern ERTMS level 2 based interlocking systems for which there are no physical signals. They are replaced by markerboards, and in the control system there are virtual signals associated with the markerboards. Throughout the paper we use the term *signal* as a synonym for *markerboard*.

[4] A network is *loop-free*, if there are no physically possible path through the network containing the same section more than once.

[5] Throughout this paper, as generic model and safety properties, we are using those from [20]. The properties are the *no collision* and *no derailment* properties, shared by the vast literature on interlocking verification.

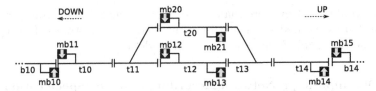

Fig. 1. A railway network layout example. From [18].

it instantiates the generic model and generic safety properties with the network description, and finally it verifies that the instantiated model satisfies the instantiated safety properties, by means of a bounded model checker performing a k-induction proof.

3   A Method for Compositional Verification

To introduce the compositional method, we first need to define what is a *cut* of a network, and how the sub-networks should be generated by the cut.

3.1   Cut Specifications

A *single cut* is a cut that can be performed between any two neighbouring, non-border sections $t1$ and $t2$ in a network N. An example of a single cut is shown in Fig. 2. The *specification* of that single cut is the pair $(t1, t2)$. To divide a network into two parts, it is not always enough to perform a single cut, but a *cluster cut* consisting of several single cuts may be needed. An example of a cluster cut is shown in Fig. 3. The *specification* of a *cluster cut* is the set of specifications of each of its single cuts. A cut is *legal*, if it divides the network into exactly two

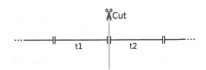

Fig. 2. An example of a single cut. From [8].

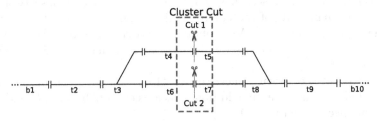

Fig. 3. An example of a cluster cut. From [8].

parts, no route is cut by more than one single cut, and no flank/front protecting elements[6] are separated by the cut from the sections they protect. In this paper we assume that flank/front protection is not adopted.

3.2   Decomposing a Network According to a Cut Specification

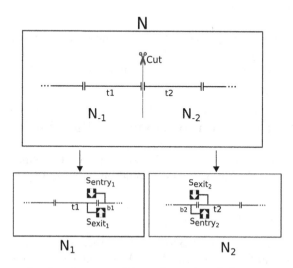

Fig. 4. An example of a decomposition of a network into two networks. From [8].

Given a net N and a legal cut specification, the network can be decomposed into two networks as follows:

- if a single cut is between linear sections $t1$ and $t2$, first divide the network N between $t1$ and $t2$, obtaining two sub-networks N_{-1} and N_{-2}, and then add to N_{-1} and N_{-2} at the respective cut a border section, and also an entry and an exit signal at that border, if there were not already signals placed around the cut. By doing so, two well-formed networks are obtained: N_1 and N_2. Figure 4 shows how a network is decomposed into two networks by a single cut $(t1, t2)$. It can be seen how N_1 is obtained from the sub-network N_{-1} on the left-hand side of the cut by adding a border section $b1$ and border signals s_{entry_1} and s_{exit_1}. N_2 is obtained in a similar way. When it is clear from the context, sometimes we also call the resulting networks N_1 and N_2 *sub-networks*;
- if a single cut is between a linear section $t1$ and a point p, the decomposition is treated as if there was an additional linear section $t2$ between $t1$ and p, and the cut specification was $(t1, t2)$;

---

[6] The notion of flank protection is explained in the end of Sect. 4.2.

- if a single cut is between two points $p1$ and $p2$, the decomposition is treated as if there were two additional linear sections $t1$ and $t2$ between $p1$ and $p2$, and the cut specification was $(t1, t2)$.
- if the cut is a cluster cut, the above rules are simultaneously applied to each of its single cuts.

3.3 Method Steps

Using a legal cut allows to perform compositional verification in these steps:

1. Decompose a network N according to a legal cut specification, achieving two networks N_1 and N_2.
2. For $i = 1, 2$, apply the RobustRailS tool (RR-T) to N_i to instantiate the chosen generic model and generic safety properties and verify that the instantiated model satisfies the instantiated safety properties.

In [8] it is proved that this method is *sound* and *complete*. Soundness means, that in order to prove safety of the model instance for the whole network, it is sufficient to verify safety for the model instances for the two sub-networks formed by a legal cut. Completeness means, that if the safety proof for one of the sub-networks fails, then one can conclude that safety also fails for the full network.

4 A Decomposition Strategy

Using the presented compositional verification method leaves the question: which cuts should be made in order to decompose a network into small networks that are fast to verify? In this section we will exploit the idea of providing a library of pre-verified, elementary networks and a strategy for dividing a given network into sub-networks of which as many as possible are elementary.

4.1 Elementary Networks

As elementary networks we allow the network patterns shown in Fig. 5: (a)–(b) an *elementary linear network*, that is, a sequence of linear sections having only the required signals at the two borders; (c)–(d) an *elementary point network*, that is, one point surrounded by at least two linear sections on each of its three sides, the required signals at the three borders and optionally zero, one, two or three signals directly facing the point. All patterns admit an unbounded number of linear elements at specific positions. In (c) there is only one linear section between the point and each of the three border sections, while in (d), there are two (or more) linear sections between the point and each of the three border sections.

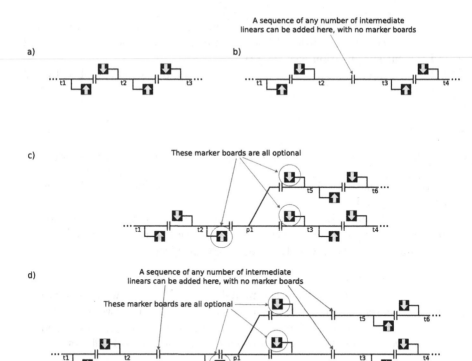

Fig. 5. Patterns for elementary networks.

Model instances of the networks of Fig. 5 have been model checked to be safe, for all the admitted combinations of presence of markerboards, but without the presence of the admitted extra linear sections. Moreover, a result from [8] allows us to add an unbounded number of linear sections at the indicated specific positions without impacting safety. Hence, we can conclude that *model instances for all elementary networks are safe*.

4.2   Decomposing a Network

Given a network, now the idea is to search for places to make legal cuts, one by one, such that the network can be divided into parts that are either *elementary* networks or *non-decomposable* networks (that is, non-elementary networks that cannot be decomposed by any cut(s) without breaking the rules for legal cuts). In the ideal case that the decomposition leads to networks that are all elementary, no additional model checking is needed for verifying the safety of the whole network.

As an example, consider the network shown in Fig. 6. By making the three cuts (two single cuts $(083, PM02U)$ and $(PM02U, PM03U)$ and the cluster cut $\{(802, PM04U), (801, PM04U)\}$) shown by green lines, one by one, one achieves the four elementary networks N_1^1, N_1^2, N_1^3, and N_2^3 shown in Fig. 7.

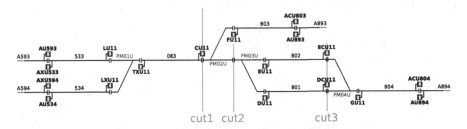

Fig. 6. Cuts shown on a network (LVR1).

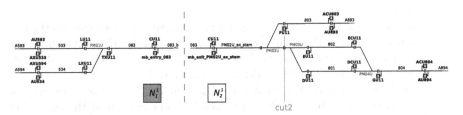

(a) Networks $N_1^1 + N_2^1$ resulting from decomposing the LVR1 network by *cut1*.

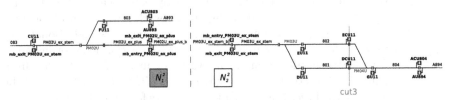

(b) Networks $N_1^2 + N_2^2$ resulting from decomposing N_2^1 by *cut2*.

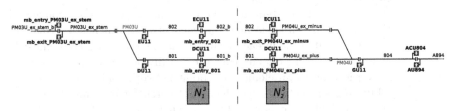

(c) Networks $N_1^3 + N_2^3$ resulting from decomposing N_2^2 by *cut3*.

Fig. 7. Decomposition of the LVR1 network in three steps according to the three cuts shown in Fig. 6. The four resulting green sub-networks N_1^1, N_1^2, N_1^3, and N_2^3 are elementary.

In practice, a possible process of finding such cuts for a loop-free network N is as follows, provided that there are no flank/front protecting elements:

1. Start searching from the neighbour (linear section) l of some border section b of N. The search direction is from l towards the next adjacent element in the direction opposite to b.

2. Follow the sections from l one by one as long as they are linear and do not have any signals attached until one of the following happens:

   (a) If a linear section next to a border is reached, no cut should be made, as the considered network is an elementary linear network.

   (b) If two consecutive, linear sections $l1$ and $l2$ are found, and at least one of them has a signal facing the other, then a decomposition using the cut $(l1, l2)$ should be made. As a consequence, the generated sub-network containing $l1$ will by construction be an elementary linear network. The search for further cuts should then continue from $l2$ in the other sub-network.

   (c) If a point p is found, then we should continue to search for cuts on the two other sides of p. This search depends on from which side p was found: the stem or one of the branching sides. In both cases the search also depends on whether the two other sides are connected or not[7].

       i. If coming from the stem side of p, and the two other sides are not connected, then we should search for cuts in each of the two other sides. The search here is similar to the search starting from a border, except that if a second point is found, a single cut must be made just *before* that point. The two searches may hence lead to totally zero, one or two single cuts, dividing the network into (1) an elementary point network containing p and (2) zero, one or two additional sub-networks in which a search for cuts must be performed. For instance, when searching for a cut in network N_2^1 in Fig. 7(a), starting from $PM02U\_ex\_stem$, a single cut, $cut2 = (PM02U, PM03U)$, will be found in the lower branch, while no cuts are found in the upper branch (as a border is met before any further points or non-border signals), so it results in two sub-networks.

       ii. If coming from the stem, and the two branching sides are connected, then a similar search is made in each of the branches. In this case two single cuts (one in each branch) will be found and these must be combined in a cluster cut (in order to divide the network into two parts) leading to an elementary point network containing p and one additional sub-network to which the search for cuts must be recursively applied. That is e.g. the case when searching for a cut ($cut3$) in network N_2^2 in Fig. 7(b), starting from $PM03U\_ex\_stem$.

       iii. If coming from a branching side of p, and the stem and the other branching side are not connected, searches for cuts in the other branch and on the stem side must be performed in a similar way to case i

---

[7] By *connected* we mean that by navigating the graph of the not yet visited part of the network starting from the two sides we eventually reach a common point.

above. That happens e.g. when searching for the first cut in Fig. 6 starting from linear section 533.

iv. If coming from a branching side of p, and the stem and the other branching side are connected, the search to be performed is similar to case ii, except that in some cases it is not possible to find a legal cluster cut: that happens if a potential cluster cut divides a route into three parts[8], as shown in Fig. 8, where the cluster cut shown by a red, dotted line is found when searching from $L1$ on the upper branching side of point $P1$. In such a case we say that N is *unbreakable* from the border b from where the search started, and we should then start a search from another border to see if a cut can be found from there. If N is *unbreakable* from all borders, it is *non-decomposable*. It is our conjecture that it is always possible to find a border from which it is possible to find a legal cluster cut through the connected sub-component, provided that the network is loop-free. For instance, in Fig. 8, the legal cluster cut $\{(P2, P1), (L24, P4)\}$ shown by a dashed, green line can be found when searching from $L2$. Figure 9 gives an example of a network that cannot be decomposed into elementary networks as the network is not loop-free.

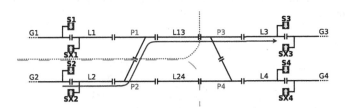

Fig. 8. The cluster cut $\{(P1, P2), (L13, P3)\}$ shown by a red, dotted line is illegal as it divides the route shown as a blue, solid arrow in three parts. The cluster cut $\{(P2, P1), (L24, P4)\}$ shown by a green, dashed line is legal. (Color figure online)

In railway interlocking systems, specific additional mechanisms may be included to enforce safety also in the case in which trains do not strictly respect signals, due to a driver's misbehaviour or accidental inability to brake. In the *Flank Protection* mechanism, points and signals not belonging to the route are properly set in order to avoid hostile train movements into the route at an incident point. In the example of Fig. 10 locking of route r requires the point $t20$ to be in the straight position in order to protect the flank of route r by a train accidentally missing the closed $mb20$ signal. If both point $t20$ and route r lie in the same sub-network when a cut is operated, the extra condition on the point

---

[8] Note that when coming from the stem, we do not have such a problem, as a route cannot pass through a point via its two branches.

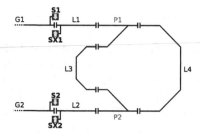

Fig. 9. An example of a non-decomposable network containing a loop.

position has no impact on compositionality: but this is not the case for the drawn cut, which separates the protecting and the protected points. As discussed in [8], in this case compositional verification results do not fully hold, so we consider such a cut as not legal: both elements should instead be in the same sub-network, which is therefore not elementary, since it contains two points. In the presentation of our approach, we have assumed that there is no flank protection. If flank protection was adopted, legal cuts would not be allowed to separate the protecting and the protected points. However, then we would no longer be able to decompose a loop-free network into networks that are all elementary. This also holds for similar protection mechanisms like *front protection* that we do not consider here.

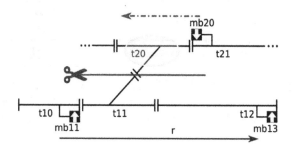

Fig. 10. Cut through a flank protection.

5   Formalisation

The decomposing strategy informally explained in Sect. 4.2 has been formalised as a collection of functions in the formal RAISE Specification Language (RSL) [16]. Below we show sketches of selected parts of that specification.

The specification consists of definitions of the functions and needed data types. There are e.g. data types for representing entities like network layouts and cluster cuts:

```
1  type
2     NetworkLayout = ..., –– network layouts composed of sections and markerboards
3     SecId = Text,              –– unique ids for network sections
4     MarkerboardId = Text,      –– unique ids for markerboards
5     ClusterCut = SingleCut-set, –– a cluster cut is a set of single cuts
6     SingleCut = SecId × SecId,  –– a single cut is a pair of SecIds
7     Direction = UP | DOWN, –– two possible search directions
8     ...
```

```
1  decompose : NetworkLayout × SecId × SecId-set →
2              NetworkLayout-set × NetworkLayout-set
3  decompose(N, b, bs) ≡
4    let cutset = find_cuts(N,b) in
5      if cutset = { {} } –– means N is elementary
6        then ({N}, {})
7      elsif cutset = {} –– means N is unbreakable from b
8        then –– try to search from another border
9          if bs = {} then ({}, {N}) –– no other borders to search from
10         else let b2 • b2 ∈ bs in
11                 decompose(N, b2, bs \ {b2}) –– search from border b2
12              end
13         end
14      elsif card cutset = 1 –– found one non–empty cluster cut
15        then
16          let
17            ccut • ccut ∈ cutset, –– ccut is the found cluster set
18            (N1, N2) = divide(N, ccut) –– divide N into two nets N1 and N2
19                                –– ccut is defined s.t. N1 becomes elementary
20            added_borders = ..., –– set of borders added to N2 during division
21            b2 • b2 ∈ added_borders,
22            (e_ns, u_ns) =
23              decompose(N2, b2, (bs ∩ borders(N2)) ∪ added_borders\{b2})
24          in
25            ({N1} ∪ e_ns, u_ns)
26          end
27      else –– found two cluster cuts having one single cut each
28        –– see text for explanation of what is then done
29        ...
30      end
31  end
```

Fig. 11. Specification of the *decompose* function.

The decomposer has been specified as a recursive function named *decompose* listed in Fig. 11. This function takes as input a network N, a border section b in N (from where a search for cuts should start), and a subset bs of the border sections in N, $b \notin bs$. The set bs is the (current) subset of border sections of N from where there has not yet been made a search. In the first invocation of *decompose*, *bs* should be the set of all borders, except *b*. The function returns the set of elementary sub-networks and the set of non-decomposable sub-networks that *N* can be divided into by following the stepwise process described in Sect. 4.2. Below we will explain the chosen division algorithm for that.

The overall idea of the division algorithm is as follows: in each recursive call of *decompose*, the current network *N* is divided into two (or three) sub-networks, if possible, of which one is elementary, and then it makes recursive call(s) of *decompose* on the one or two other obtained sub-networks. It will not divide *N*, if *N* is already elementary or *N* is unbreakable from *b*. In the latter case it will make a recursive call $decompose(N, b2, bs \setminus \{b2\})$, where it starts from another border $b2 \in bs$, if *bs* is not empty.

The *decompose* function uses an auxiliary function named *find_cuts* (listed in Fig. 12 and explained further below) to find the cluster cut(s) that *decompose* should use (in the current iteration) for cutting the network into some sub-networks. Furthermore, it uses another auxiliary function *divide*($N, ccut$) (see [15], where it is named *decompose*) to divide a network *N* into two sub-networks *N*1 and *N*2, according to a found cluster cut *ccut*. This division is done as informally explained in Sect. 3.2.

When *decompose*(N, b, bs) is invoked, (in line 4) it invokes *find_cuts*(N, b) to find a set *cutset* of next cluster cuts that should be used for cutting the network into sub-networks. Then, depending on the returned set (which by construction will contain zero, one, or two cluster cuts), it will take various actions:

(1) If *cutset* contains one cluster cut which is empty (line 5), it is because *N* is elementary and the function will (in line 6) return *N* as the only elementary network and it will return no non-decomposable networks.

(2) If *cutset* is empty (line 7), it is because *N* is unbreakable from *b*. In that case, (in line 11) a new search (made by a recursive call of *decompose*) is started from one of the other borders *b*2 of *N*, from where there has not yet been made a search, and *b*2 is removed from *bs*. If there was no such other border *b*2, it means that *N* was unbreakable from any border of *N*, and the function will (in line 9) return *N* as the only non-decomposable network and it will return no elementary networks.

(3) If *cutset* contains one non-empty cluster cut *ccut*, it will use *divide*($N, ccut$) (in line 18) to divide *N* into two networks *N*1 and *N*2, where *N*1 will be elementary due to the definition of *findcuts* and *divide*. Then, (in line 23), it will continue making a recursive call of *decompose* on *N*2 from one of *N*2's added borders *b*2, obtaining a set of elementary networks *e_ns* and set of non-decomposable networks *u_ns*. Finally (in line 25), it will add *N*1 to *e_ns*.

(4) In a similar way, if *cutset* contains two cluster cuts (line 26), it will make two consecutive calls of *divide* using these cluster cuts to divide *N* into three networks *N*1, *N*2, and *N*3, of which *N*1 will, by construction, be elementary. Then it will make two recursive calls of *decompose* on *N*2 and *N*3, respectively, obtaining two sets of elementary networks, *e_ns*2 and

e_ns3, and two sets of non-decomposable networks, u_ns2 and u_ns3. Finally, it will return $(\{N1\} \cup e\_ns2 \cup e\_ns3, u\_ns2 \cup u\_ns3)$.

The termination of *decompose* is guaranteed by the fact that each time it is invoked in cases (3) and (4), it is called with smaller networks, and in case (2) the *bs* parameter becomes smaller.

```
1   find_cuts : NetworkLayout × SecId → ClusterCut-set
2   find_cuts(N, b) ≡
3     let
4        dir = find_direction_towards_neighbor_of_border(b, N),
5        l = next_from_linear(b, dir, N)  -- l is the neighbor of b
6     in
7        find_cuts_from_linear(l, dir, N)
8     end,
9
10  find_cuts_from_linear : SecId × Direction × NetworkLayout → ClusterCut-set
11  find_cuts_from_linear(l, dir, N) ≡
12    let next = next_from_linear(l, dir, N) in  -- next section to visit
13      if is_linear(next, N)
14      then
15        if is_border(next, N) then {{}}   -- case 2(a)
16        elsif has_signal(l, dir, N) ∨ has_signal(next, opposite_direction(dir), N)
17            then { { (l , next) } }           -- case 2(b)
18        else -- no signals between l and next
19            find_cuts_from_linear(next, dir, N) -- continue search from next
20        end
21      else -- is_point(next, N), i.e. case 2(c)
22        -- further search depends on from which side the point is met:
23        case get_pointend_entry_given_neighbor(next, l, N) of
24          STEM → find_cuts_from_stem(next, dir, N),
25          PLUS → find_cuts_from_branch(next, dir, PLUS, N),
26          MINUS → find_cuts_from_branch(next, dir, MINUS, N)
27        end
28      end -- if
29    end -- let
```

Fig. 12. Specification of the *find_cuts* function.

find_cuts(N, b) (listed in Fig. 12) takes as input a network N and a border section b of N (from where the search should start) and searches for cuts that can be used to divide the network such that one of the resulting sub-networks is an elementary network containing b. This search is done by invoking (in line 7) another auxiliary function *find_cuts_from_linear*(l, dir, N) (also listed in Fig. 12) to search for cuts from the linear section l next to b in the search direction dir going from b towards l. This formalises step 1 in Sect. 4.2.

find_cuts_from_linear(l, dir, N) (listed in Fig. 12) takes as input a network N, a linear section l of N (from where the search should start), and a search direction dir. It returns a set of "next" cluster cuts that can be found when searching from l in direction dir. This set will by construction contain zero, one, or two cluster cuts. The search is made as described under step 2 in Sect. 4.2, and the returned set of cluster cuts, will contain the cuts found as explained informally for each of the cases 2(a), 2(b), 2(c)i - 2(c)iv in Sect. 4.2.

The function uses two auxiliary functions, $find\_cuts\_from\_stem$ and $find\_cuts\_from\_branch$, to specify the search for case 2(c). They are defined in a similar way as $find\_cuts\_from\_linear$, but not shown here due to space limitations.

6   Experiments

The formal RSL specification of the *decompose* function is executable and has hence been used as an early prototype for a decomposer tool. It has been thoroughly tested to be functionally correct. After that the specification was translated to C++ achieving a second prototype which was also tested. The tests have shown a full agreement between the two prototypes, and have therefore given some confidence in the correctness of the algorithm and of its implementation, although we have not attempted a formal proof thereof.

Furthermore, we have used first the RSL executable and later the C++ executable for making some experiments: for networks of various complexity, we measured the time it takes to automatically decompose a network into elementary networks and we compared this with the time it takes to verify the full network using the RobustRails Tool (RR-T).

Table 1. Verification metrics for the RobustRails Tool (RR-T) and the decomposer prototypes (in RSL and C++) applied to some interlocking examples. Time is measured in seconds.

Example	Linears	Points	Signals	Routes	RR-T Time	RSL Time	C++ Time	Sub-networks
EDL	111	39	126	179	22863	219	1,5	68
LVR1	11	4	18	18	91	7	0,5	4
LVR7	26	12	42	48	49813	9	0,5	13
Tramway line	22	12	20	62	43184	8	0,5	12
Flying junction	24	16	16	40	62172	9	0,7	16

Table 1 shows the metrics for these experiments using the RobustRails Tool (RR-T) and the decomposer prototypes (both the RSL specification and the C++ implementation). The tools have been applied on a benchmark of network layouts considered in some other, past experiments (using the RobustRailS Tool only), some of which were published in previous conference papers [1,2,12,14]. The EDL network is a line in Denmark comprising 8 stations, LVR1 is Binche station in Belgium, LVR7 is Piéton station in Belgium, and the two last networks are inspired by real networks [7]. In the table, columns 2–5 give for each network example its number of linear sections, points, signals, and routes, respectively. Column 6 shows for each network the verification time using the RobustRails Tool and columns 7 and 8 show the average time[9] needed to divide the network into sub-networks using the decomposer prototypes. The last column contains the number of elementary sub-networks obtained. In all cases no non-decomposable sub-networks were obtained. All the experiments were executed on an Intel Core i5 CPU 750 (-MPC-) at 1.20 GHz, 16 GB RAM, Ubuntu 14.04, Linux 3.19.0-25-generic x86 64 (64 bit, gcc: 4.8.2) kernel.

The experiments show a dramatic reduction of the time needed for the verification of a network using our decomposer prototypes compared to time needed when using the traditional monolithic verification by the RobustRails Tool. The considered networks have all been successfully decomposed into elementary networks, in most cases in as many as there were points in the network, that is, in elementary point networks of type (c) or (d) in Fig. 5.

7   Conclusions and Future Work

In this paper, we have exploited a previously defined compositional method for model checking the safety of interlocking systems, by pushing it to the finest granularity level. The said compositional method guarantees that, under given conditions, dividing into two parts a network expressing the interlocking over a complex network layout and then proving safety of the two parts equates to proving safety of the whole network. This provides significant advantages in terms of reduction of state space explosion.

In this paper, we have formally specified in RSL and implemented in C++ an algorithm which automatically divides a network into a number of sub-networks of minimal size by repeatedly applying the above mentioned network division. In the ideal case each of the resulting sub-networks is an instance of one of a limited set of "elementary networks", for which safety proofs have already been given (in less than 3 s) by model checking, once for all. That means, in such a case no model checking is needed. We have successfully applied first the fully automated RSL executable and later also the C++ implementation to decompose into elementary networks several network examples of different complexity, hence proving their safety. In all cases the execution time was a very small fraction of the time needed by a model checker to verify the full network.

Our suggested verification approach will be the subject of further work: For all the case studies, the algorithm succeeded to divide the network into sub-networks that were all elementary. In principle, the algorithm could return one or more sub-networks that cannot be decomposed into elementary networks, but

---

[9] The *decompose* function was repeatedly invoked with each of the network's borders as the border parameter b of *decompose*, and then the average execution time was computed. Note that the invocations with different b on the same network sometimes produce slightly different sets of networks: the cardinalities of the sets of networks returned by two different invocations are the same and networks are usually the same, except that sometimes a linear section may be included in a different sub-network.

we have not found any loop-free networks for which this is the case, provided that there is no flank/front protecting elements. We conjecture that the algorithm is always capable to divide any loop-free network into elementary networks, provided that there is no flank/front protecting elements, but we need to formally prove this conjecture.

A proof of correctness of the algorithm could be a topic for future work: if the conjecture above is proved to hold, the algorithm should be demonstrated to produce a consistent set of elementary networks.

For future work, it could also be interesting to investigate how the topology and the choice of the border from where the search should start impact the execution time of the decomposer prototypes.

We conjecture that the proposed decomposition method can be instantiated with similar benefits in other compositional frameworks, as the one described in [1]: this is another future research direction.

Acknowledgements. The authors would like to thank (1) Jan Peleska and Linh H. Vu together with whom Anne Haxthausen developed the RobustRailS verification method and tools, (2) Hugo D. Macedo, who contributed to the initial work on the applied compositional method, and to (3) Anna Nam Anh Nguyen and Ole Eilgaard for their network cutter tool which we have integrated in our decomposer tool. The contribution by the second and third author was carried out within the MOST – Sustainable Mobility National Research Center and received funding from the European Union Next-GenerationEU (Piano Nazionale di Ripresa e Resilienza (PNRR) – Missione 4 Componente 2, Investimento 1.4 – D.D. 1033 17/06/2022, CN00000023). This manuscript reflects only the authors' views and opinions, neither the European Union nor the European Commission can be considered responsible for them.

References

1. Fantechi, A., Gori, G., Haxthausen, A.E., Limbrée, C.: Compositional verification of railway interlockings: comparison of two methods. In: Dutilleul, S.C., Haxthausen, A.E., Lecomte, T. (eds.) RSSRail 2022. LNCS, vol. 13294, pp. 3–19. Springer, Cham (2022). https://doi.org/10.1007/978-3-031-05814-1_1

2. Fantechi, A., Haxthausen, A.E., Macedo, H.D.: Compositional verification of interlocking systems for large stations. In: Cimatti, A., Sirjani, M. (eds.) SEFM 2017. LNCS, vol. 10469, pp. 236–252. Springer, Cham (2017). https://doi.org/10.1007/978-3-319-66197-1_15

3. Ferrari, A., ter Beek, M.H.: Formal methods in railways: a systematic mapping study. ACM Comput. Surv. **55**(4), 1–37 (2022)

4. Ferrari, A., Magnani, G., Grasso, D., Fantechi, A.: Model checking interlocking control tables. In: Schnieder, E., Tarnai, G. (eds.) FORMS/FORMAT 2010, pp. 107–115. Springer, Heidelberg (2011). https://doi.org/10.1007/978-3-642-14261-1_11

5. Ferrari, A., Mazzanti, F., Basile, D., ter Beek, M.H.: Systematic evaluation and usability analysis of formal methods tools for railway signaling system design. IEEE Trans. Softw. Eng. **48**(11), 4675–4691 (2022)

6. Ferrari, A., Mazzanti, F., Basile, D., ter Beek, M.H., Fantechi, A.: Comparing formal tools for system design: a judgment study. In: Proceedings of the ACM/IEEE 42nd International Conference on Software Engineering, ICSE 2020, pp. 62–74. Association for Computing Machinery, New York (2020)
7. Haxthausen, A.E., Fantechi, A., Gori, G.: Decomposing the verification of interlocking systems. In: Haxthausen, A.E., Huang, W., Roggenbach, M. (eds.) Applicable Formal Methods for Safe Industrial Products. LNCS, vol. 14165, pp. 96–113. Springer, Cham (2023). https://doi.org/10.1007/978-3-031-40132-9_7
8. Haxthausen, A.E., Fantechi, A.: Compositional verification of railway interlocking systems. Formal Aspects Comput. **35**(1) (2023). https://doi.org/10.1145/3549736
9. James, P., Möller, F., Nguyen, H.N., Roggenbach, M., Schneider, S., Treharne, H.: Decomposing scheme plans to manage verification complexity. In: Schnieder, E., Tarnai, G. (eds.) 10th Symposium on Formal Methods for Automation and Safety in Railway and Automotive Systems, FORMS/FORMAT 2014, pp. 210–220. Institute for Traffic Safety and Automation Engineering, Technische Univ. Braunschweig (2014)
10. Limbrée, C., Cappart, Q., Pecheur, C., Tonetta, S.: Verification of railway interlocking - compositional approach with OCRA. In: Lecomte, T., Pinger, R., Romanovsky, A. (eds.) RSSRail 2016. LNCS, vol. 9707, pp. 134–149. Springer, Cham (2016). https://doi.org/10.1007/978-3-319-33951-1_10
11. Limbrée, C., Pecheur, C.: A framework for the formal verification of networks of railway interlockings - application to the Belgian railway. Electron. Commun. Eur. Assoc. Study Sci. Technol. **76** (2018)
12. Limbrée, C.: Formal verification of railway interlocking systems. Ph.D. thesis, UCL Louvain (2019)
13. Macedo, H.D., Fantechi, A., Haxthausen, A.E.: Compositional verification of multi-station interlocking systems. In: Margaria, T., Steffen, B. (eds.) ISoLA 2016. LNCS, vol. 9953, pp. 279–293. Springer, Cham (2016). https://doi.org/10.1007/978-3-319-47169-3_20
14. Macedo, H.D., Fantechi, A., Haxthausen, A.E.: Compositional model checking of interlocking systems for lines with multiple stations. In: Barrett, C., Davies, M., Kahsai, T. (eds.) NFM 2017. LNCS, vol. 10227, pp. 146–162. Springer, Cham (2017). https://doi.org/10.1007/978-3-319-57288-8_11
15. Nguyen, A.N.A., Eilgaard, O.B.: Development and use of a tool supporting compositional verification of railway interlocking systems. Technical report, DTU Compute, Technical University of Denmark (2020). https://findit.dtu.dk/en/catalog/5f181f35d9001d016b4e1f3b
16. The RAISE Language Group: George, C., et al.: The RAISE Specification Language. The BCS Practitioners Series, Prentice Hall Int. (1992)
17. Vu, L.H., Haxthausen, A.E., Peleska, J.: A domain-specific language for railway interlocking systems. In: Schnieder, E., Tarnai, G. (eds.) 10th Symposium on Formal Methods for Automation and Safety in Railway and Automotive Systems, FORMS/FORMAT 2014, pp. 200–209. Institute for Traffic Safety and Automation Engineering, Technische Universität Braunschweig (2014)
18. Vu, L.H., Haxthausen, A.E., Peleska, J.: A domain-specific language for generic interlocking models and their properties. In: Fantechi, A., Lecomte, T., Romanovsky, A. (eds.) RSSRail 2017. LNCS, vol. 10598, pp. 99–115. Springer, Cham (2017). https://doi.org/10.1007/978-3-319-68499-4_7
19. Vu, L.H.: Formal development and verification of railway control systems - in the context of ERTMS/ETCS level 2. Ph.D. thesis, Technical University of Denmark, DTU Compute (2015)

20. Vu, L.H., Haxthausen, A.E., Peleska, J.: Formal modelling and verification of inter-
    locking systems featuring sequential release. Sci. Comput. Program. **133**, Part 2,
    91–115 (2017)
21. Winter, K.: Optimising ordering strategies for symbolic model checking of railway
    interlockings. In: Margaria, T., Steffen, B. (eds.) ISoLA 2012. LNCS, vol. 7610, pp.
    246–260. Springer, Heidelberg (2012). https://doi.org/10.1007/978-3-642-34032-
    1_24

Integral Formal Proof: A Verification Approach Bridging the Gap Between System and Software Levels in Railway Systems

Alexandra Halchin[1]([✉]), Adja Ndeye Sylla[1], Sarah Benyagoub[1],
Abderrahmane Feliachi[2]([✉]), Yoann Fonteneau[2], and Sven Leger[1]

[1] RATP, Val de Fontenay, France
{alexandra.halchin,adja-ndeye.sylla,sarah.benyagoub,sven.leger}@ratp.fr
[2] Prover, 7 Rue Auber, 31000 Toulouse, France
{abderrahmane.feliachi,yoann.fonteneau}@prover.com

Abstract. In modern railway systems, verification of system and software are usually performed independently, even though the refinement from system to software level is covered. However, experience shows that this conventional approach is error-prone and inadequate for complex functions that are increasingly common. Bugs resulting from the gap between system and software levels often go undetected until late in the development process, making corrections costly and raising concerns about other bugs that may have been missed. In an ideal scenario, comprehensive verification would identify such bugs early on, regardless of the gap. This paper introduces a verification approach that intends to bridge the gap between system and software levels through the formal verification of system level safety properties on a model of the software. Its application on a pilot project revealed several safety critical bugs that would not have been detected using the aforementioned activities.

Keywords: Formal verification · System level properties · System of Systems · Environment Model · CBTC

1 Introduction

RATP (Regie Autonome des Transports Parisiens) deploys and operates all metro lines of the Paris area, in addition to other commuting services transporting millions of commuters every day. Passengers safety has always been a high priority for RATP, starting from the early planning phases to the operation and maintenance phases. This attachment to safety has materialised in the establishment of dedicated safety activities and teams having the main task of performing a second independent safety verification of all deployed systems. For this purpose, RATP has developed a verification methodology called PERF to apply formal verification against the deployed software. This methodology allowed RATP and its suppliers to guarantee higher safety levels by discovering unsafe software behaviours before deployment.

The increasing complexity of modern railway systems makes the verification activities more and more tedious. The, usually V-shaped, development process defines rigorous and extensive verification activities from one level to its following level. The refinement of requirements from System level to Software level (through subsystem levels) may introduce some gaps that go undetected by the traceability activities. One of the main reasons of these gaps is the incompleteness of the requirements apportioning. In other words, the composition of subsystem or software requirements is not always equivalent to the refined requirements. This might be due to the fact that requirements (even the vital ones) are described in a functional, i.e. they only describe how the system should behave and rarely explicit how it shouldn't (safety-wise). The behavior might be correctly decomposed functionally, but loopholes are injected in the safety coverage. Another reason of the gap introduced by the refinement is the bias caused by implicit assumptions made during the development and verification activities. These assumptions related to the interfaces of the system and its environment narrow the space of considered behaviors.

RATP deployed several modern signaling systems in the recent years and one common observation is that no matter how perfect verification activities can be at different levels, gaps that exist between levels can be missed. It is well known that early detection of bugs is always better than a later detection, one can emphasize that late detection of problems raises concerns about the presence of other undetected bugs. This kind of issues is unacceptable regarding the high safety expectations at RATP, so a new methodology has been developed in the recent years to close this verification gap. The core idea is to expand the scope of PERF verification, to cover not only the software but subsystem and system levels as well. This paper presents this new verification approach that intends to bridge the gap between system and software levels through the formal verification of system level safety properties on a model of the software. Rather than focusing on one level, this approach is based on the definition of a formalization of the system under verification, along with its interfacing systems, and perform formal verification of high-level safety properties against this model. The most important contribution was probably to find the right balance of abstraction levels to produce a sufficiently complex yet verifiable model. This approach is now being extended to cover all new CBTC projects at RATP.

This paper is organised as follows: next section provides a brief overview of the context and related works. Section 3 introduces the proposed approach more in detail. A real case study is presented in Sect. 4 to illustrate how the approach works. Finally, Sect. 5 concludes this paper with the main results and limitation of the approach.

2   Context

For each deployed system, RATP conducts evaluation activities independent of those of its suppliers to ensure overall system safety. These activities are performed for the system, hardware and software. The system-level assessment activities involves the analysis of the documentation produced by the supplier (responsible for supplying the system and software). This assessment is conducted manually through critical review in order to determine the conformity and completeness of the system specification.

Software assessment is based on formal methods, using the PERF (Proof Executed over a Retro engineered Formal model) approach together with its associated workshop [1,6]. This methodology has been successfully applied to several projects and has consistently produced results that guarantee the correctness of software safety requirements. PERF enables the formal verification of properties on existing software, regardless of the development and verification methods employed by the supplier. This is accomplished by applying formal proof techniques after the design and development phase, even when the software was not meant to be formally verified. HLL [9], the pivot language of PERF, is an asynchronous data-flow language, allowing to specify both system behaviour and safety properties together. This approach strengthens the demonstration of safety objectives and provides a framework for integrated model and program verification developed by different stakeholders using different modelling and programming languages.

At present, software analyses are performed on individual software components, without considering the constraints of the system in which they operate. However, the current methodology and safety properties verified at the software level fail to effectively detect complex anti-safety scenarios that may arise at the system level or as a result of errors when refining the system specification into the software specification.

Taking system constraints into account when doing software validation would allow to integrate the environment in which the software evolves and to identify the properties resulting from this environment that must be satisfied by the software. Therefore, the development of a methodology that allows for higher-level validation at the system level is essential.

Currently, system-level analyses are insufficiently equipped and rely heavily on manual methods. This approach does not effectively identify malfunctions that may be introduced during the production of software specifications from system specifications. Two factors may account for these malfunctions. In a top-down development scenario, the software specification may be accurately summarized from the system specification, but the system specification may contain errors. On the other hand, in a bottom-up development scenario, the system specification may not contain any errors, but the synthesis of the software specification may not be performed correctly.

In order to achieve the overall proof objective, it is essential to use a verification approach that integrates both the system and software levels, thus demonstrating the preservation of safety properties identified at the system level on the software level. Such an approach enables the identification of anomalies and constraints at the system level and ensures that the specified safety requirements of the overall system are met.

However, this combined approach presents unique challenges due to the inherent differences between the system and software levels. At the system level, we often abstract the actual computations, while at the software level, we lack a comprehensive global understanding of the overall system objectives. The limited perspective of the software makes it difficult to verify global abstract safety properties, such as the prevention of train collisions. Similarly, on the system side, ensuring that the detailed implementation of the software guarantees the safety property is hard to achieve. Combining both approaches requires to bridge the gap between the system and software by formalizing all necessary mapping concepts to obtain an integrated model.

2.1 Related Works

The modelling and safety verification of railway systems is an important and active research topic. The most interesting success stories about formal verification cover railway systems, from conventional interlocking to modern signalling systems. The application of formal methods at an integrated level with both system and software models was the target of several initiatives. Unfortunately, the state-space explosion problem has always been a major common obstacle limiting the scalability of these verification techniques. It also impacts the scope of the analysis, which leads to different solutions and trade-offs.

Authors in [7] and [8] have explored the compositional approach to divide the verified scope into smaller pieces that can be analyzed efficiently. However, this approach is only possible if the system and the verified properties can be divided without any information loss. In our scope of CBTC function with system-level safety properties, it appears impossible to define a decomposition that preserves safety.

Another direction was adopted by [2,11] and [12] and others where the formal verification is applied at software level using refined safety properties, usually extracted from software requirements. The limited scope of this verification and its modularity can solve the state-explosion problem. This approach is a good software verification choice, but it does not cover the gap that can be introduced when refining the safety properties or the software requirements.

Finally, some studies such as [3] and [10] already identified the need of safety verification at system level. The verification being conducted on a wider scope, covers the gap that is introduced at subsystem or lower levels. Some directions are provided to close the verification distance to the target software but no concrete application was performed to confirm their feasibility. A high abstraction level is required to avoid the state-space explosion problem, but can introduce new gaps of its own.

Regarding our target of system level verification on a signalling software, the closest work that could be found in the literature was described in [4]. In this work, the authors cover a similar function than the one covered in Sect. 4. The proposed approach can cover most of the gaps that are targeted in our scope of work. However, the paper did not mention any formalization of other real world systems that may interact with the analyzed system. As explained throughout this paper, some unsafe scenarios are hidden during verification because of strong assumptions that can be made on the environment. For example, the paper did not make a clear difference between the real position of a train and its perceived position at ZC level which can lead to considerable mismatches. In other words, the communication between the onboard and the wayside subsystems is supposed to be ideal, with no delays or message loss, which is not the case in real life. In fact, most of the errors our approach captured were related to this kind of asynchronous behaviour.

3   Proposed Methodology

The aim of this work is to verify system level safety properties on the software model to discover hidden and complex scenarios through exhaustive exploration of input domains. In order to avoid obvious state space explosion problems, the proposed methodology relies on a combination of refinement and abstraction to reach an appropriate level of details. The properties are first derived by analyzing system level specifications and are proved to be sufficient for the safety of the target system. Then, they are refined and formalized at subsystem level with software interfaces to enable their verification on the software model.

This verification is done using an environment model that bridges the gap between the system and software levels as well as between the system and its interfaced systems. A first attempt to verify system level properties on CBTC software at RATP was presented in [5]. However, due to the absence of an environment model, the verification scope was significantly limited, even though high-level properties were identified. Indeed, the verification focused on software inputs rather than system-level observables (eg. received location of a train vs its actual position).

Combining the software model with such an environment model has several advantages. First, it prevents from having a high number of false counterexamples that would be time consuming to analyze and discard. Second, this feeds the software with relevant data that correspond to the occurrence of real world or system events and analyze its behaviour when verifying the properties.

For instance, in a software level verification approach, it is common to treat different software inputs as independent which can lead to unrealistic scenarios and generate false counterexamples. To address this issue, constraints are introduced to establish connections between inputs and eliminate these false counterexamples. However, identifying the appropriate set of constraints is often a tedious task and carries the risk of under- or over-abstraction.

In an integrated approach, software inputs are directly linked to the realistic environment model, enabling the abstraction of different equipment behavior. This allows to describe complex inputs sets by accurately capturing asynchronism, temporal considerations, and interactions between equipment. Consequently, it offers a comprehensive understanding of equipment interactions, enhancing comprehension of the system and thus its overall validation.

3.1   System Level Properties Identification and Refinement

The properties are derived from hazard analyses of the target function. This is done at system level by analyzing the feared events of the function and defining a set of properties that catch their occurrence. The aim of this activity is to cover the security needs of the function and ensure the detection of any dangerous situation that may lead to a feared event. For this purpose, it is important to ensure the sufficiency of the properties regarding to the safety of the function.

Performing the analysis at system level has several advantages. This limits the number of properties, shortens the activity related to their formalization and simplifies the counter-examples analysis. Indeed, in most cases, one or two system level properties are enough to catch the security needs of a function. Moreover, when such a property is falsified, the counter-example given by the proof engine can be directly linked to a dangerous situation. This prevents from states where a property is falsified but the safety impact is difficult to figure out.

Once identified, the properties and the system notions on which they rely on are first expressed with software notions. This is done through the software specification and its design principles. For instance, let us consider the following system level safety property: each train must be represented. The refinement activity consists in concretely defining the notion of train representative using notions and objects that are defined by the software. Then, the properties are formalized in HLL and the correctness of this formalization is checked, for instance through critical reviews, before their verification on the software model.

3.2   Software Model

To ensure the correctness of the proof process implemented at the software level with PERF workshop, it is necessary to formalize and prove the software. The PERF verification process consists of transforming the system's source code into a formal HLL model. This involves obtaining a model of the software being studied, either through the use of available translators in the PERF toolkit or by manually modeling the software in HLL. After obtaining the software model, it is important to verify its correctness with respect to the initial source code. This can be achieved by certifying the translator [6] or through validation. In the case of manual formalization, there are several options available, such as critical reviews. It is crucial to minimize the introduction of bugs at each step of the overall method.

3.3   Designing a Real World Environment Model

One of the key aspects of this methodology is the definition of a realistic environment model. This model includes an abstraction of all real world objects, functions, subsystems and systems interacting with the function under study or impacting the safety properties. It serves as a linking "glue" between the software model and the identified system level properties. Indeed, the properties are expressed in terms of real world objects (e.g. trains should never collide, a representation of these objects is crucial) and must be to the transcribed in the software level. As stated earlier, the most notable contribution of this work was find the right balance between complexity and abstraction when defining the environment model. Models that are too complex can hardly be used for exhaustive exploration because of state-space explosion problems. Models that are too abstract scale much better but will very often fail to find any hidden safety issues.

The overall environment model introduced can be divided in four categories:

- **Systems** intended to model external systems that interact with the CBTC system. This includes for instance, the trains, the track-side objects and external interlocking systems.
- **Subsystems** covering and abstraction of CBTC subsystems that are not directly under study but interact with the studied function. For example, when studying a CC function that uses inputs from a ZC, the ZC part producing these inputs is abstracted in a ZC model.
- **Functions** similar to the subsystems but for functions of the subsystem under study that are not part of the studied function. For example, when studying a CC function, we might abstract other CC functions that contribute to the inputs of this studied function.
- **Transversal** including global notions that may affect multiple models. This covers asynchronous communications between CBTC subsystems, cyclic execution of subsystems, continuous evolution of real-world systems as well as continuous interactions between objects. Verification activities either overlook these aspects or analyse them separately from the whole system which can lead to undetected errors. The challenge is of course, to control the complexity of the model while capturing the most important notions.

3.4 Integrating Data

To perform the proof activity, data of the real line is extracted and integrated to the rest of the models (software and environment models). For this purpose, the data is first formalized in HLL. This can be done by a script that takes as input the data provided by the supplier and generates the required HLL format. This data consists of constants and invariants that are used by either by the software or the environment model. Some data required by the environment model cannot be directly extracted from the supplier files. They need to be designed by the teams members and built from other available data. For instance, an invariant that translates abscissas from on segment to another cannot be extracted.

Using real data prevents from finding and analyzing counter-examples that cannot occur in the line due to its configuration. However, real line data is usually voluminous, which can lead to state-space explosion and scaling problems. To be able to find scenarios quicker, simpler virtual layouts are introduced. The idea is to identify particular configurations that will most probably lead to counter-examples. For instance, layouts containing switches, multiple paths between two points or rail loops are considered. Once the system was analyzed on simple layouts and all possible counter-examples were identified, the verification is then performed on the real data to confirm that no additional counter-examples can be found. If not, new simple layouts are introduced to isolated the configuration that led to the counter-example in order to ease the analysis.

3.5   Global Model Integration and Verification

After obtaining the software model, safety properties, environment, and data in HLL language, the components are integrated to validate the system safety properties on the software model. The correctness of properties is proved by using model checking and SAT solving verification techniques.

Safety-related properties are modeled as observers in HLL models. Observers provide a higher level of assurance for software correctness when they are valid, or valuable counterexamples when they are not, enabling further analysis and design corrections. The proof is accomplished using different proof strategies, including lemma writing and counter-example analysis. However, one must be cautious during this activity as distinguishing real counter-examples that may lead to dangerous situations from those obtained due to certain modeling choices can be very tricky.

In the proof activity, it is important to consider the limitation of the model checking technique due to state space explosion, when dealing with large systems. This is a limitation of model checking technique because the state space increases drastically with the number of system variables. To overcome this issue, there are several solutions available, such as abstraction and decomposition of the system into subsystems, which can be applied during the proof process.

4   Application

The first complete application of this new methodology was performed on the train tracking function of a CBTC system deployed by RATP. After a short introduction of the context, this Section will provide some details about the application of different activities introduced in Sect. 3.

4.1   Case Study Description

CBTC (Communications-Based Train Control) is a complex system that ensures a safe and efficient train service through two-way communication between on-board (Carborne Controller) and wayside equipment (Zone Controller).

One critical role of CBTC is Automatic Train Protection (ATP), realized by the safe train separation function, which ensures that trains never collide. Some of the main functions of a CBTC system are train localization, train tracking and MAL (Movement Authority Limit) computation. Localization determines the precise position of trains on the track, while tracking uses this information to create a comprehensive cartography of train movements throughout the network.

The MAL computation uses the cartography to compute the limits within which the train is authorized to operate safely.

In our particular application, the train tracking function is fully implemented in the ZC (Zone Controller) through fixed virtual blocks. This function receives inputs from multiple sources, including Carborne Controllers (CCs), Input/Output Controllers (IOCs), and neighboring ZCs. Using these inputs, it determines the occupancy status of all virtual blocks based on reported train locations (train envelope) and track circuits occupancy (Fig. 1).

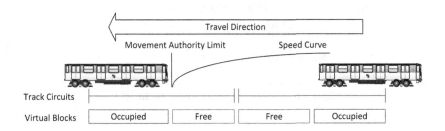

Fig. 1. CBTC notions related to train tracking function

4.2 Identification and Refinement of the Safety Properties

The initial step of this study involves identifying high-level properties that ensure the prevention of safety hazards resulting from errors in the train tracking function. These properties are then refined at the software level and further formalized in HLL to enable their verification.

At system level, the safety properties for train separation functions are concerned with preventing different types of collisions between trains, including head-on, rear-end, and side collisions. In this particular application, the cartography computed by the train tracking function can only lead to potential rear-end collisions. All the other hazards are covered by other functions or subsystems. The system level safety property can be defined as:

Property. *There should be no rear-end collision between trains.*

This property is then refined for the train tracking function level, by identifying all potential mismatches that would lead to the hazard. This was done by analyzing how the cartography is used within the MAL computation function that starts from the estimated rear position of a train and looks for the first obstacle in the direction of travel (see Fig. 1). One possible unsafe situation occurs if the MAL of a following train goes beyond the actual position of the leading train. The reason of such situation can be, for example, that the virtual block under the leading train is wrongly identified as free by the train tracking function. The system level property can be refined for the tracking function to check the absence of this unsafe situation as follows:

Property. *Every train should be represented in the cartography by an occupied virtual block located behind the train's real position.*

This property is then further refined using the different software and system notions leading to the HLL formalisation in Listing 1. This property mixes system notions such as real train position and software notions such as virtual blocks statuses(*is_occupied_vb()*) and localisation report.

```
property :=
    ALL t : TRAINS (
        SOME vb : VIRTUAL_BLOCKS (
            is_vb_behind_train(vb, t)
            ->
            is_occupied_vb(vb)
        ) );
```

Listing 1. Property Formalization in HLL

4.3   Integration of Software Model

This activity is directly inherited from the PERF approach, that is based on a model of the software under verification. The model is either translated directly from the source code of the software or abstracted manually from the software specification. For some cases, complex code portions were abstracted with an optimised version and the equivalence between both representations was demonstrated.

4.4   Definition of the Environment Model

After defining the properties and the software models, an environment model was developed to link the different parts together. All ZC functions that provide inputs to the train tracking function were abstracted from the corresponding subsystem or software specifications. Then impacting subsystems were introduced, which included a CC model, an IOC model and a neighboring ZC model. The CC model provides train estimated locations and the IOC model provides track-related information. Both systems were abstracted from their subsystem specification. For the neighboring ZC there were two options, either using the translated software model or using a separated optimized abstract model.

In order to provide real word information to the different models, trains, track-side objects and external interlocking models were defined. Train positions are used in the properties as well as in the inputs of the CC model. Train speed constrains the movement of trains in the track. The interaction between trains and wayside objects provides inputs to the interlocking and IOC models (e.g. TC occupancy). The asynchronous communication model defines how messages are exchanged between CBTC subsystems. This model supports message loss and deprecation and guarantees that a received message is consistent with the past system state at the time the message was issued.

Since the environment model is a key element of the verification, it was important to ensure that it was correct and that it reveals all possible behaviors of the real system. A validation of the whole environment model was performed by means of cross-reading, intermediate lemmas verification, vivacity checking and specific scenarios exploration.

4.5   Integration of Specific Data

To perform formal verification, the designed models (software, environment and properties) were instantiated with the actual track data extracted from the project database, describing the track objects and their connections. The formal verification was then performed on 3 virtual models and on 8 real instantiated models. The models varied in size and complexity including all relevant track configurations of a metro line.

4.6   Application Outcomes

A number of counter-examples were spotted both on the real and simple layouts. These counter-examples are the reproduction of the known issues on the model but also the discovery of some new complex (but possible) unsafe scenarios. Not all identified scenarios correspond to a bug in the software, three possible reasons were observed:

- Some of the scenarios are confirmed by the supplier as bugs and some changes in the code or in the system specification are done to correct them.
- Some scenarios showed a lack of constraints on the data spotted on simple layouts but not on the real ones. More constraints over the layout data can be added to avoid encountering these issues in a future project.
- Some scenarios involved simultaneous defects from different subsystems with communication delays/messages loss. These scenarios were considered unrealistic by the supplier as there probability was sufficiently low.

5   Conclusion

The approach described in this paper is seen as a promising and successful attempt for system-level verification of safety properties against the target software. In addition to the discovery of complex bugs that were overlooked by conventional verification approaches, this approach led to the identification and discharging of some implicit hypotheses that could lead to an over-constrained system. Similar hypotheses are usually the reason test approaches missing some critical bugs. The approach helped increase the understanding of both the system and software under study and increased the collaboration between system and software verification teams.

Although this study is a successful attempt to perform counter-example exploration of CBTC Systems with a realistic environment, a number of limitations and challenges were identified. Some of them were already addressed in the scope of the first application and will be fed-back to the generic approach. The remaining challenges are currently under analysis for possible solutions and optimizations.

The major obstacle that we usually face in this type of applications is the state-space explosion during the exploration of real layout data. A first solution was to introduce simple layouts representing small but complex configurations. The challenge of course is to find a good trade-off between a sufficiently detailed model and an abstract one. A second solution consisted of using decomposition and abstraction to reduce the complexity of the software model. Other optimisations are currently under consideration, focusing mainly on the proof process.

The second difficulty that emerged from the complexity of the system is the counter-example analysis. The use of system concepts together with software variables makes it difficult to identify the causes leading to the unwanted behaviour. A graphical visualisation tool is being developed in order to make the analysis less tedious and also to make the presentation of scenarios easier.

References

1. Benaissa, N., Bonvoisin, D., Feliachi, A., Ordioni, J.: The PERF approach for formal verification. In: Lecomte, T., Pinger, R., Romanovsky, A. (eds.) RSSRail 2016. LNCS, vol. 9707, pp. 203–214. Springer, Cham (2016). https://doi.org/10.1007/978-3-319-33951-1_15
2. Bonacchi, A., Fantechi, A.: On the validation of an interlocking system by model-checking. In: Lang, F., Flammini, F. (eds.) FMICS 2014. LNCS, vol. 8718, pp. 94–108. Springer, Cham (2014). https://doi.org/10.1007/978-3-319-10702-8_7
3. Comptier, M., Déharbe, D., Perez, J.M., Mussat, L., Pierre, T., Sabatier, D.: Safety analysis of a CBTC system: a rigorous approach with Event-B. In: Fantechi, A., Lecomte, T., Romanovsky, A. (eds.) RSSRail 2017. LNCS, vol. 10598, pp. 148–159. Springer, Cham (2017). https://doi.org/10.1007/978-3-319-68499-4_10
4. Comptier, M., Leuschel, M., Mejia, L.-F., Perez, J.M., Mutz, M.: Property-based modelling and validation of a CBTC zone controller in Event-B. In: Collart-Dutilleul, S., Lecomte, T., Romanovsky, A. (eds.) RSSRail 2019. LNCS, vol. 11495, pp. 202–212. Springer, Cham (2019). https://doi.org/10.1007/978-3-030-18744-6_13
5. Feliachi, A., Bonvoisin, D., Samira, C., Ordioni, J.: Formal verification of system-level safety properties on railway software. In: Congrès Lambda-Mu 20 (2016)
6. Halchin, A.: Development of a formal verification methodology for B specifications using PERF formal toolkit. Application to safety requirements of railway systems. Ph.D. thesis, Institut National Polytechnique de Toulouse (2021). https://www.theses.fr/2021INPT0118, thèse de doctorat dirigée par Aït-Ameur, Yamine et Singh, Neeraj Kumar Informatique et Télécommunication Toulouse, INPT 2021
7. Limbrée, C., Cappart, Q., Pecheur, C., Tonetta, S.: Verification of railway interlocking - compositional approach with OCRA. In: Lecomte, T., Pinger, R., Romanovsky, A. (eds.) RSSRail 2016. LNCS, vol. 9707, pp. 134–149. Springer, Cham (2016). https://doi.org/10.1007/978-3-319-33951-1_10
8. Macedo, H.D., Fantechi, A., Haxthausen, A.E.: Compositional verification of multi-station interlocking systems. In: Margaria, T., Steffen, B. (eds.) ISoLA 2016. LNCS, vol. 9953, pp. 279–293. Springer, Cham (2016). https://doi.org/10.1007/978-3-319-47169-3_20

9. Ordioni, J., Breton, N., Colaço, J.L.: HLL vol. 2.7 Modelling Language Specification. Technical report, RATP (2018). https://hal.archives-ouvertes.fr/hal-01799749

10. Sabatier, D.: Using formal proof and B method at system level for industrial projects. In: Lecomte, T., Pinger, R., Romanovsky, A. (eds.) RSSRail 2016. LNCS, vol. 9707, pp. 20–31. Springer, Cham (2016). https://doi.org/10.1007/978-3-319-33951-1_2

11. Vu, L.H., Haxthausen, A.E., Peleska, J.: Formal modeling and verification of interlocking systems featuring sequential release. In: Artho, C., Ölveczky, P.C. (eds.) FTSCS 2014. CCIS, vol. 476, pp. 223–238. Springer, Cham (2015). https://doi.org/10.1007/978-3-319-17581-2_15

12. Winter, K.: Symbolic model checking for interlocking systems. In: RSRS: Technologies and Systems Engineering, pp. 298–315 (2012)

Halfway Generic Verification of Railway Control Systems

Gustav Zickert$^{(\boxtimes)}$ and Nikitas Stathatos

Prover, Krukmakargatan 21, Stockholm, Sweden
{gustav.zickert,nikitas.stathatos}@prover.com

Abstract. Formal verification of railway control systems, particularly Generic Applications (GAs) and Specific Applications (SAs), is crucial due to their complexity and safety-critical nature. This paper presents a novel framework, Halfway Generic Verification (HGV), applying Software Product Line (SPL) principles for formal verification of railway control systems. The HGV method offers a balanced approach that can verify a broad set of systems derived from the same Generic Design Specification (GDS) in a single computational sweep, retaining feasibility. It also highlights the potential benefits of implementing SPL analysis in modeling and verification of railway control systems, which include enhancing the process of configuration data generation and ensuring the correctness of the GDS and Generic Safety Specification. The effectiveness of the HGV approach is demonstrated with a prototype implementation utilizing the Prover iLock tool.

Keywords: Formal Verification · Generic Application · Software Product Line · Railway Control System · Interlocking · Metaproduct · Variability Encoding

1 Introduction

1.1 Formal Verification of Railway Control Systems

Railway control systems, such as interlockings, are safety critical and complex. Therefore, they require rigorous verification to ensure safe and reliable operation. Formal methods provide cost-effective and safety enhancing means for such verification activities. Consequently, a plethora of formal methods, e.g., Alloy [1], Petri Nets [2], B method [3], etc., are used extensively for verification of railway control systems [4]. The importance of these methods to the railway industry is also reflected by the fact that they are recommended by the CENELEC standards [5].

1.2 Classification of Railway Control Systems

Traditionally, safety critical signaling systems, as well as their related tools and specifications, are classified in terms of the generality of their application domain. In falling order of generality, the corresponding categories are: Generic Product (GP), Generic Application (GA) and Specific Application (SA) [6]. In this paper we will be concerned

© The Author(s), under exclusive license to Springer Nature Switzerland AG 2023
B. Milius et al. (Eds.): RSSRail 2023, LNCS 14198, pp. 178–189, 2023.
https://doi.org/10.1007/978-3-031-43366-5_11

with formal verification of GAs and SAs. For sake of clarity and simplicity of the exposition, we will in this paper use the following rather restrictive and specialized definitions of GA and SA:

By a GA we here mean a collection of generic formal specifications for a family of railway control systems that share common signaling principles. More precisely, we assume that a GA consists of:

1. An Object Model (OM). The OM defines the model ontology in terms of the available classes of objects. This includes declarations of classes representing physical objects (e.g., signals, track circuits and switches) as well as virtual objects (e.g., routes and protection areas), along with their inputs, outputs, internal states, and static relations.
2. A Generic Design Specification (GDS). The GDS, which is only relevant for code generation projects, specifies how each component of a system should operate. More precisely it specifies the temporal first-order logic expressions that define how the internal states are updated. Coupled with configuration data, and an appropriate execution model, the specification should be precise enough to allow for generation of executable code.
3. A Generic Safety Specification (GSS). The GSS specifies static constraints as well as static- and dynamic requirements that are to follow from the constraints. The GSS is assumed to consist of a finite number of first-order temporal logic formulas.

By a SA we mean an individual system that is associated with a combination of a GA and some compatible configuration data. This is the level at which most of the verification and validation work is performed in signaling projects.

1.3 Computerized Railway Control Systems as Software Product Lines

A Software Product Line (SPL) is a family of similar software products [7]. The variability among family members is typically expressed in terms of a set of optional elements, or *features*. Each feature is present in some subset of the SPL. Principles of SPL engineering have previously been applied in the railway industry e.g., for management of rolling stock variability at Alstom, to promote efficient component re-use processes [8]. Another such example presents a method for generating and verifying UPPAAL models based on configuration data and applies it to verification of switch motor controllers [9].

Additionally, and of central importance to this paper, a family of computerized systems corresponding to a given GA may be considered as a SPL [10]. Indeed, following the generative programming paradigm, each SA associated to the GA is typically obtained automatically from a family-wide GDS that prescribe its temporal behavior, together with interlocking-specific configuration data (such as the railyard layout, route tables, etc.).

Formally verifying an entire GA – in the sense of verifying that any executable code generated from the GDS meets the corresponding requirements instantiated from the GSS – is attractive from a business perspective since it may lead to savings in costs and time. Moreover, it increases confidence in the quality of the GDS and facilitates debugging and validating the GSS.

However, it comes with certain computational challenges. Firstly, in the absence of any prior assumptions on the layout, a GA in principle represents an infinite number of

SAs, since there is an infinite number of conceivable configurations. Thus, one is faced with the problem of verifying infinitely many systems against the GSS. Secondly, even if one considers only a finite subfamily of the GA, it typically has a very large number of members. Indeed, the number of systems is generally exponential in the number of optional configuration components. Therefore, the naïve verification approach, i.e., generating and verifying each SA separately, fails in most cases.

In order to overcome these difficulties, alternative verification methods that analyze the SPL as a whole has been put forward in the SPL community [7, 11]. In particular, some of these methods are centered around using *feature variables* to create and analyze *metaproducts* and *metaspecifications* for the SPL under investigation [12, 13]. In this paper we apply these concepts, which will be discussed in greater detail below, to formal verification of families of railway control systems.

1.4 Contributions

Our main contributions are as follows:

1. We present a new application of SPL analysis to formal verification of a family of railway control systems, the members of which originate from the same GDS but differ in their configurations. The resulting framework, which we call *Halfway Generic Verification (HGV)*, enables formal verification of large collections of systems in one sweep, while still retaining computational feasibility. The approach is demonstrated with a prototype implementation based on the Prover iLock tool.
2. We highlight the various uses and benefits offered by the adoption of SPL analysis in modelling and verification of railway control systems:
   a. Verification of a GDS against a GSS for a large family of systems
      (1) This may increase confidence in the correctness of the GDS and GSS.
   b. It supports the configuration data generation process, including:
      (1) Automatic verification of constraint consistency,
      (2) Interactive feedback during manual railyard layout planning.

1.5 Organization of Paper

The rest of the paper is organized as follows: Sect. 2 begins with a general overview of formal methods and their use within the railway industry, with a particular focus on generic system verification. This is followed by a discussion of formal verification of SPLs and an introduction to Prover iLock. In Sect. 3, the proposed approach is described, and a prototype implementation is presented. Finally, in Sect. 4, we provide a conclusion.

2 Background

2.1 Survey of Formal Methods

This section contains a brief, non-exhaustive survey of formal methods relevant for verification of rail systems of various degrees of generality.

Alloy [14] arguably supports both application types (GA and SA), and it comes with a toolset for modeling and analyzing complex systems, such as railway systems.

The Alloy Analyzer tool provides a graphical representation of the model, allowing the visualization of the system behavior and identification of potential issues. Once constraints and assertions have been specified in relational logic, the Alloy Analyzer finds and visualizes valid instances that satisfy the constraints, as well as counterexamples to the assertions. This language has been used for modelling interlockings [15] and in railway case studies such as the hybrid ERTMS/ETCS Level 3 study [16]. Alloy is not primarily developed for code generation or verifying a fixed, given, executable code, but rather for testing designs, analyzing, and verifying (potentially non-deterministic) specifications. Also, this language has limited support for real-time modeling and complex state transitions.

Based on graphical representation of transition systems in the form of graphs, a Petri net [2, 17] is a mathematical modelling technique that allows for simulation of system behavior to identify potential issues. It can also be used for the visualization of issues such as requirement counterexamples, which helps to identify design flaws and understand why a requirement was not fulfilled. Petri nets have also been applied to railway systems [18]. However, once a system grows in complexity and size, Petri nets may become difficult to understand.

B [3] and Event-B [19] are based on theorem proving and model checking. These methods can be combined with tools such as Atelier B [20], Rodin [21] and ProB [22] that are useful for specification, verification, and animation of models. These tools give support for graphical visualization of the system structure, execution trace, behavior animation and identification of errors and inconsistencies. However, they lack support for real-time and concurrent systems. In addition, formal verification may require that several of these tools are used in conjunction, which may in turn necessitate time-costly configuration efforts.

2.2 Formal Verification of SPLs using Configuration Lifting

Formal methods have been used for analysis of SPLs in several contexts [7, 11–13, 23, 24]. Here we focus on a particular kind of formal SPL analysis that is based on configuration lifting [12], also known as variability encoding [13]. This is the process by which, for each optional feature of an SPL, a free Boolean variable - a *feature variable* - is added to the code base as well as to the specifications. The intended semantics of a feature variable is that its value equals True if the corresponding feature is present in some possible product. The end result is a metaproduct capable of simultaneously simulating all products of the SPL. Hence, by formally verifying the metaproduct against the corresponding metaspecifications, in effect one verifies all products of the SPL.

2.3 Prover iLock and PiSPEC

Prover has developed a tool, called Prover iLock [25], specifically designed for designing, testing, verifying and visualizing railway control systems. This tool uses the PiSPEC language [26], an object-oriented Domain-Specific Language [27] that is based on many-sorted first-order logic complemented with a notion of discrete time. Prover iLock automatically analyses PiSPEC models and verifies that a system meets its safety requirements using various proof strategies, such as model checking. In Prover iLock, verification and simulation are usually done at the individual system (SA) level.

A GA captures a set of signaling principles and is implemented as a Prover iLock package [28]. A SA, on the other hand, is developed in a Prover iLock project and represents an individual control system. The most common SA configuration setup involves drawing the railyard in the layout editor based on the schematic plan and reading any relations and parameters that are not computable based on the geography from configuration files.

3 Halfway Generic Verification

3.1 Overview of Proposed Method

The proposed method assumes as input a GA, denoted GA_i, consisting of OM_i, GDS_i, and GSS_i, together with some configuration data C_i. Following metaproduct principles and taking inspiration from some capabilities of the Alloy language and associated tools (see Sect. 2.1 above), the core of the HGV method is the following three-step recipe for transforming the given input, i.e., GA_i and C_i to a new GA and new configuration data, denoted GA_o and C_o respectively.

1. Introduce new *"potential" object classes* to the OM. Each such potential object class inherits properties from some object class already present in OM_i, but additionally has a special Boolean feature variable Exists. The semantics of this variable is that its value equals True if and only if its owner object instance is present in the system. During formal verification, the Exists variable is free in the initial time step but is then forced to be constant in time.
2. Align the OM, GDS and GSS with the modifications introduced in the first two steps. This is accomplished by restricting the scope of any quantification that appears in any expression in the GA to existent objects. Here "expression" refers to temporal first-order logic expressions that define static relations (OM), internal states (GDS) and requirements (GSS).
3. Replace some (user specified) object instances in C_i with corresponding potential object instances.

The simple but powerful observation that underlies the HGV method is that: *Verifying an SA that results from this procedure is equivalent to verifying the collection of systems it encodes.* In principle the method is applicable to any finite family of configurations, however in practice it may become cumbersome to formulate appropriate constraints on the valid configurations if the track layout varies a lot between the family members. Moreover, if a very large number of feature variables is added to the model, the verification will become computationally infeasible.

Additionally, one may also add new static (i.e., time independent) constraints, involving the Exists variables, to the GA. This can be used to specify the valid configurations by disallowing certain combinations of objects from existing. Furthermore, when coupled with visualization of counterexamples to those constraints, it enables real-time user-friendly support for SA configuration. Similarly, it can be useful to add new static requirements that can be formally verified to follow from the constraints.

3.2 Prototype Implementation of HGV using Prover iLock

We have implemented a prototype of the HGV method for an interlocking system using PiSPEC and Prover iLock. Although, as mentioned above, we have been taking inspiration from some capabilities of Alloy, our implementation relies solely on Prover iLock.

As input GA, denoted by GA_i in the above, we used specifications for a toy interlocking system. The input object model OM_i included basic interlocking object classes such as SIGNAL, ROUTE, PROTECTION_AREA, SWITCH, BALISE, etc. The input data C_i was similarly based on a toy railyard drawn in the layout editor of Prover iLock; the latter is depicted in Fig. 1. This layout illustrates tracks T (continuous lines separated with brackets), switches sw, balises (black squares) and signals.

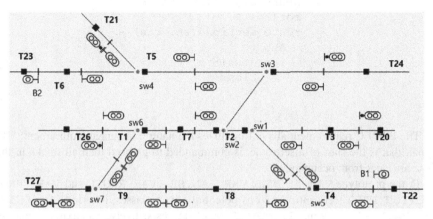

Fig. 1. Schematic drawing of the railyard used in the prototype.

In Prover iLock, some objects such as signals and balises are placed manually on the railyard layout by the user, while other objects such as routes and protection areas are generated according to user-specified rules or input data (e.g., tables). In the prototype discussed here, routes were automatically generated for all pairs of co-directed signals with no other co-directed signal in between them, and a single, minimal, protection area was generated for each "switch-position pair" (normal and reverse) and for each signal.

As an example of a Boolean variable from the GDS_i representing an internal state that is updated in each time cycle, consider the following PiSPEC definition of the CommandedProceed variable that belongs to the SIGNAL type:

```
CommandedProceed :=
  SOME rt (
    start_signal(rt, SELF) &
    ready_to_proceed(rt)
  );
```

This generic definition states that, at each time step in the system execution or verification, a signal is commanded by the interlocking to display the proceed aspect if and only if it is the start signal of a route that is ready to proceed. The "rt" keyword is declared as a "quantifier variable" in the ROUTE class, hence the scope of the "SOME" quantifier is the set of routes. The GSS$_i$ consisted of *dynamic* (i.e., time-dependent) requirements on the behavior of the interlocking. The following is an example of such a requirement:

```
GSS_04 :=
    ALL si
    ALL rt
    ALL rts (
        CommandedProceed(si)&
        start_signal(rt, si) &
        set(rt) &
        route_sections(rt, rts) ->
            ALL tc (
                tracks(rts, tc) ->
                    Clear(tc)
            )
    );
```

The PiSPEC requirement above formalizes the natural language requirement: "If a signal, that is the start of a set route, is commanded to proceed then all tracks in this route are clear from occupancy."

In the prototype VAR_SIGNAL, VAR_BALISE, VAR_ROUTE and VAR_ PRO-TECTION_AREA were introduced as potential object classes, inheriting from SIG-NAL, BALISE, ROUTE and PROTECTION_AREA, respectively. An auxiliary function exists (note the lower case "e") was introduced to the SIGNAL, BALISE, ROUTE and PROTECTION_AREA classes, with definition X.exists= X.Exists, if X is an instance of potential object class and X.exists= True otherwise. The GA specifications were processed by a Python script that restricted the scope of all quantifications to existent objects, by inserting exists functions at propriate places. The updated generic definition of the CommandedProceed variable reads:

```
CommandedProceed :=
    SOME rt (
        rt.exists &
        start_signal(rt, SELF) &
        ready_to_proceed(rt)
    );
```

Similarly, the updated definition for generic requirement GSS_04 reads:

```
GSS_04 :=
  ALL si (
     si.exists ->
        ALL rt (
           rt.exists ->
              ALL rts (
                 CommandedProceed(si) &
                 start_signal(rt, si) &
                 set(rt) &
                 route_sections(rt, rts) ->
                    ALL tc (
                       tracks(rts, tc) ->
                          Clear(tc)
                    )

              )

        )
  );
```

Next, C_i was modified by replacing some instances of SIGNAL with an instance of VAR_SIGNAL, and analogously for BALISE (c.f. Fig. 2.). Using Prover iLock we then formally verified the operational logic of the resulting SA against GSS_0. No constraints were put on the feature variables corresponding to VAR_SIGNAL and VAR_BALISE. Contrarily, no independent feature variables were used for instances of VAR_ROUTE and VAR_PROTECTION_AREA. Instead, their existence was *defined* in terms of existence of VAR_SIGNAL instances. Thereby, in effect, the original generic design GDS_i was formally verified against the GSS_i for all SAs that may be obtained by including or not including each instance of VAR_SIGNAL and VAR_BALISE. The prototype layout had 29 instances of those two object classes (marked in red in Fig. 2.), which corresponds to the simultaneous verification of $2^{29} \approx 5 \times 10^8$ systems.

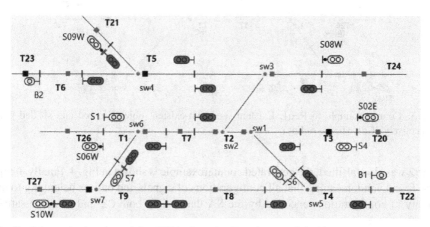

Fig. 2. Schematic drawing of the HGV-adapted railyard. Potential objects are depicted in red. (Color figure online)

In order to demonstrate another application area of the HGV framework, in a separate experiment we also introduced completely new *static properties* (constraints and requirements) to the GA. These involved the feature variables and expressed time-independent properties and relations of the system, such as the relative location of wayside objects in the railyard. We then verified that certain sets of constraints were consistent, and that, for all configurations covered by the HGV-adapted SA, certain sets of static requirements follow from some set of constraints.

For an example of this, consider the following three static properties (two constraints and one requirement) from the prototype (to save space we provide only natural language versions):

- C1: All switches have a balise.
- C2: All routes that do not contain any switch contain a track circuit with a balise.
- Req0: All routes pass over some balise.

With C1, C2 and Req0 as starting points, we considered the following "derived requirements":

- Req1: There is no configuration satisfying C1 and C2.
- Req2: C1 implies Req0.
- Req3: C1 and C2 together imply Req0.

Req1 was falsified and a counterexample was generated, c.f. Figure 3. Note that this counterexample is a witness of the consistency of the conjunction of C1 and C2.

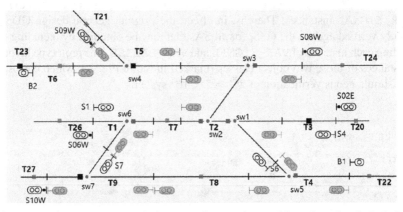

Fig. 3. Counterexample to Req1. Existent- and non-existent objects in red and shaded grey, respectively. (Color figure online)

Req2 was also falsified; the generated counterexample is shown in Fig. 4. Finally, Req3 was found valid, meaning that all configurations of signals and balises belonging to the family of configurations encoded by the SA that satisfy both C1 and C2, also satisfy Req0.

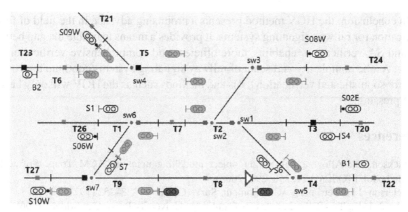

Fig. 4. Counterexample to Req2. Existent- and non-existent objects in red and shaded grey, respectively. The route that does not pass over a balise is shown in purple. (Color figure online)

4 Conclusion

The application of formal verification techniques to railway control systems is a critical and demanding field that can benefit from the integration of various approaches and disciplines, such as SPL engineering, formal verification methods, and the specifics of railway system operation and design.

In this paper, we have proposed and elucidated the HGV method, an approach that merges principles of SPL engineering and formal verification methods to create a comprehensive framework for the rigorous evaluation of railway control systems.

The main strengths of our proposed method are the ability to verify large collections of systems in one pass, maintaining computational feasibility, and its flexibility in accommodating the particular requirements and configurations of different railway control systems. This innovative approach extends the capabilities of SPL analysis into the realm of railway control system verification, expanding its application and showing potential for further research and practical applications in this domain.

Our primary aim with the HGV method is to enhance the verification process's overall effectiveness and robustness, leading to a significant increase in confidence regarding the correctness of the GDS and GSS of railway control systems. Furthermore, our method offers support in generating configuration data and provides interactive feedback during the manual railyard layout planning process, thus ensuring that the resulting systems perform as intended in real-world scenarios.

A prototype implementation of the HGV method demonstrated its efficacy and practical applicability. The prototype was based on the Prover iLock tool; however, the HGV framework can be adopted by other object oriented signaling tools that adhere to the SPL paradigm. The method was able to effectively handle a toy model for interlocking systems, illustrating its potential for real-world use cases. However, it's important to recognize that the HGV method represents just one step towards efficient large-scale GA verification. As with any new method, further development and refinement will be necessary to fully realize its potential.

In conclusion, the HGV method presents a promising advance in the field of formal verification for railway signaling systems. It provides a means to bridge the gap between GA and SA verification, enabling more efficient and comprehensive verification processes. As the complexity and scale of railway signaling systems continue to grow, the need for sophisticated verification tools and methods such as the HGV will only become more pressing.

References

1. Jackson, D.: Alloy: a lightweight object modelling notation. ACM Trans. Softw. Eng. Methodol. (TOSEM) **11**, 256–290 (2002)
2. Peterson, J.L.: Petri nets. ACM Comput. Surv. (CSUR) **9**, 223–252 (1977)
3. Abrial, J.-R.: The B-Book, vol. 146. Cambridge University Press, Cambridge (1996)
4. Boulanger, J.-L. (ed.) Formal Methods Applied to Industrial Complex Systems. Wiley-ISTE (2014)
5. CENELEC. Railway applications – The specification and demonstration of reliability, availability, maintainability and safety (RAMS), Part 1: Generic RAMS Process, EN 50126-1:2017, European Committee for Electrotechnical Standardization
6. CENELEC. Railway applications – Communication, signalling and processing systems – Safety related electronic systems for signalling, EN 50129:2003, European Committee for Electrotechnical Standardization
7. Meinicke, J., Thüm, T., Schröter, R., Benduhn, F., Saake, G.: An overview on analysis tools for software product lines. In: Proceedings of the 18th International Software Product Line Conference: Companion Volume for Workshops, Demonstrations and Tools-vol. 2 (2014)
8. Góngora, H.G.C., Ferrogalini, M., Moreau, C.: How to boost product line engineering with MBSE - a case study of a rolling stock product line. In: Boulanger, F., Krob, D., Morel, G., Roussel, J.-C. (eds.) Complex Systems Design & Management, pp. 239–256. Springer, Cham (2015). https://doi.org/10.1007/978-3-319-11617-4_17
9. Proença, J., Borrami, S., Sanchez de Nova, J., Pereira, D., Nandi, G.S.: Verification of multiple models of a safety-critical motor controller in railway systems. In: Collart-Dutilleul, S., Haxthausen, A.E., Lecomte, T. (eds.) RSSRail 2022, pp. 83–94. Springer, Cham (2022). https://doi.org/10.1007/978-3-031-05814-1_6
10. Vu, L.H., Haxthausen, A.E., Peleska, J.: A domain-specific language for generic interlocking models and their properties. In: Fantechi, A., Lecomte, T., Romanovsky, A. (eds.) RSSRail 2017, vol. 10598, pp. 99–115. Springer, Cham (2017). https://doi.org/10.1007/978-3-319-68499-4_7
11. Thüm, T., Apel, S., Kästner, C., Schaefer, I., Saake, G.: A classification and survey of analysis strategies for software product lines. ACM Comput. Surv. (CSUR) **47**, 1–45 (2014)
12. Thüm, T., Schaefer, I., Apel, S., Hentschel, M.: Family-based deductive verification of software product lines. In: Proceedings of the 11th International Conference on Generative Programming and Component Engineering (2012)
13. Post, H., Sinz, C.: Configuration lifting: verification meets software configuration. In: 23rd IEEE/ACM International Conference on Automated Software Engineering (2008)
14. Jackson, D.: Alloy: a language and tool for exploring software designs. Commun. ACM **62**, 66–76 (2019)
15. Svendsen, A., Møller-Pedersen, B., Haugen, Ø., Endresen, J., Carlson, E.: Formalizing train control language: automating analysis of train stations. In: Comprail (2010)
16. Cunha, A., Macedo, N.: Validating the hybrid ERTMS/ETCS level 3 concept with electrum. In: Butler, M., Raschke, A., Hoang, T.S., Reichl, K. (eds.) ABZ 2018. LNCS, vol. 10817, pp. 307–321. Springer, Cham (2018). https://doi.org/10.1007/978-3-319-91271-4_21

17. Hack, M.H.T.: Petri net language (1976)
18. Giua, A., Seatzu, C.: Modeling and supervisory control of railway networks using Petri nets. IEEE Trans. Autom. Sci. Eng. **5**, 431–445 (2008)
19. Abrial, J.-R.: Modeling in Event-B: System and Software Engineering. Cambridge University Press, Cambridge (2010)
20. Boulanger, J.-L.: Formal Methods Applied to Complex Systems: Implementation of the B Method. Wiley, Hoboken (2014)
21. Abrial, J.-R., Butler, M., Hallerstede, S., Hoang, T.S., Mehta, F., Voisin, L.: Rodin: an open toolset for modelling and reasoning in Event-B. Int. J. Softw. Tools Technol. Transfer **12**, 447–466 (2010)
22. Leuschel, M., Butler, M.: ProB: a model checker for B. In: Araki, K., Gnesi, S., Mandrioli, D. (eds.) FME 2003. LNCS, vol. 2805, pp. 855–874. Springer, Heidelberg (2003). https://doi.org/10.1007/978-3-540-45236-2_46
23. Apel, S., Speidel, H., Wendler, P., Von Rhein, A., Beyer, D.: Detection of feature interactions using feature-aware verification. In: 26th IEEE/ACM International Conference on Automated Software Engineering (2011)
24. Lauenroth, K., Pohl, K., Toehning, S.: Model checking of domain artifacts in product line engineering. In: 24th IEEE/ACM International Conference on Automated Software Engineering, Auckland, New Zealand (2009)
25. Borälv, A.: Interlocking design automation using prover trident. In: Havelund, K., Peleska, J., Roscoe, B., de Vink, E. (eds.) FM 2018. LNCS, vol. 10951, pp. 653–656. Springer, Cham (2018). https://doi.org/10.1007/978-3-319-95582-7_39
26. Borälv, A., Stålmarck, G.: Formal verification in railways. In: Hinchey, M.G., Bowen, J.P. (eds.) Industrial-Strength Formal Methods in Practice, pp. 329–350. Springer, London (1999). https://doi.org/10.1007/978-1-4471-0523-7_15
27. Fowler, M.: Domain-Specific Languages. Pearson Education (2010)
28. A. B. Prover Technology. Prover iLock Software User Guide. ILOCK-SUG 5.24 (2023)

Formal Model and Visual Tooling

Modelling, Visualisation and Proof of an ETCS Level 3 Moving Block System

Michael Leuschel[1]([⊠])[iD] and Nader Nayeri[2]

[1] Institut für Informatik, Universität Düsseldorf, Universitätsstr. 1, 40225 Düsseldorf, Germany
michael.leuschel@hhu.de
[2] Ground Transportation Deutschland GmbH, Stuttgart, Germany
nader.nayeri@urbanandmainlines.com

Abstract. This work aims to formally ensure the safety of modern moving block systems. For this a proof model was developed in Event-B which captures several safety critical aspects. The new model identifies several key concepts, that are at the heart of the mathematical safety proof and which should later be at the heart of the safety case for a moving block system with trackside train detection. Some of the key concepts were inspired by earlier CBTC models and adapted for ETCS moving block, and a few novel key concepts were developed to deal safely with delays of train position reports and trackside train detection.

The invariants of the proof model have proven mathematically with the Rodin toolset, thereby establishing safety properties of the modelled system. The proof model can also be animated and visualised using the PROB validation tool. By necessity, the proof model abstracts away from irrelevant details and still has some restrictions in scope (such as linear topology). Nonetheless, even with current restrictions, the key concepts already proved valuable when reasoning about safety of moving block systems. In the article we also present our modelling and tooling methodology, outlining the importance of complementing proof with animation. We also explain the importance of inductive properties and argue that a train-centric approach is more promising for proof of a moving block system than a track-centric approach.

1 Introduction

B was originally developed by Jean-Raymond Abrial in the 1990s and has now been used for over 25 years in the railway sector [9] (see also [19,36]). Currently the B Method is used in three distinct ways for safety critical systems:

- B for software (classical B [2]): here an abstract specification of a component is successively refined until one reaches an implementation level (called B0), where automatic code generators can be applied. Examples of this are the *Paris Métro Line 14* [16], the New York Canarsie Line [17] and around 95 installations of Alstom's U400 CBTC (Communication-Based Train Control) system, which contain code generated from verified classical B models.

B. Milius et al. (Eds.): RSSRail 2023, LNCS 14198, pp. 193–210, 2023.
https://doi.org/10.1007/978-3-031-43366-5_12

- B for system modelling (Event-B [3]): here B is used to model an entire system, not just an individual component. The goal is to verify critical properties at the system level and understand why a system behaves correctly.
- B for data validation: here properties about data and system configurations are specified in B. These properties can then be checked automatically (and reliably) on concrete data, resulting in validation reports.

For this work, we focus on the second application, using Event-B for safety cases for railway applications. Several railway examples can be found using Event-B for system modelling, notably the academic interlocking model in Chapter 17 of Abrial's book [3] on Event-B, and a much more detailed model [8] including feature management. On the industrial side, ClearSy has used Event-B in at least two previous projects [13,35] (Flushing Line for New York City Transit Authority and Octys for the Parisian Autonomous Transport Administration RATP) to perform a safety analysis of CBTC metro systems. Safety analyses of Alstom's U400 Zone Controller have also been carried out [14]. ClearSy is using this approach also for mainline systems, namely the new Hybrid ERTMS Level 3 signalling on the Marseille to Ventimiglia line.[1]

Within Thalesthe approach was previously used for Hybrid Level 3 [1] fixed virtual block systems [22]. There a formal model was developed that helped uncover over 30 errors in the original EUG specification and to various real-life demonstration by running the model in real-time using PROB [30]. The formal model was used as a demonstrator and presented at the 2018 Innotrans trade fair.However, the purpose of the model was not to conduct a formal proof; the errors were uncovered using animation and model checking. Other models for Hybrid Level 3 with Event-B were developed [15,20,33], within the scope of the ABZ 2018 case study [25]. While [33] was able to prove several properties using Event-B, some important aspects were not proven. Indeed, we believe that the Hybrid Level 3 [1] specification is not well suited for a formal correctness proof in general, nor for an inductive correctness proof within the B-method in particular (we return to this in Sect. 3 below). In this article, we focus on modelling a European Train Control System (ETCS) level 3 *full moving block* system with Trackside Train Detection (TTD), as specified in [38]. The modelling is done in Event-B, inspired by the previous successful applications of Event-B to CBTC systems in [13,14,35]. Motivated by the successful use of animation and visualisation in [22], we also strive to make the formal models amenable to animation. One goal of this work is to answer these key questions:

- Can we develop Event-B models for both proof and animation and is it beneficial to do so? Which methodology should be used to develop such models?
- Can the CBTC knowledge and insights be transferred to a moving block ETCS system?

---

[1] https://www.clearsy.com/en/ertms-en/.

2   Modelling Methodology

Before explaining specifics of the formal proof model, we elaborate on a few general principles we have employed in this and other projects.

2.1   Verification Techniques: Proof Is Essential

Verification of formal models can be done in three ways: 1) formal proof (e.g., [3]), 2) explicit model checking [26], or 3) symbolic model checking [5,11].

While model checking can scale for verifying concrete instances of interlocking systems, (see, e.g., [6,7,23]), it does not yet scale for moving block systems. One reason is that train positions need to be modelled much more precisely, leading to a considerably larger state space that has to be verified. Setting aside scalability, ideally one wants to establish a safety case independent of the topology. This can only be done with proof. As such we see **proof** to be essential for establishing the safety of moving block systems in particular and safety critical systems in general.

2.2   Complementing Proof with Model Checking

Proof is rarely fully automatic and it is easy to make mistakes either in the proof itself or in the formulation of the properties in the model. Even experienced formal methods practitioners take time to analyse a failed proof, trying to decide whether the model needs changing or whether it is just the proof that needs to be done differently.

Hence **model checking** is a good complement to automatically check a system on small instances and find issues quickly. Indeed, if the model checker finds an error we know the model needs to be changed and we also obtain a counterexample that can be used to diagnose the problem.

2.3   Combining Proof and Animation

When doing mathematical proof it is essential that the axioms from which proof starts are consistent. Otherwise anything can be proven and a proof is worthless.

In classical B for software, an inconsistency in the axioms (aka PROPER-TIES clause of B) would eventually be detected when implementing a system or checking the axioms during data validation [31]. While this is quite late (and can thus be expensive), at least the issue would be uncovered. In system modelling, however, there is not necessarily a refinement chain from the high-level specification to some concrete implementation. As such, inconsistencies in the axiomatisation may not be detected at all!

Hence, particularly for systems modelling, **animation** is essential for its role in ensuring that the axioms are consistent. Indeed, an animator like PROB will check the axioms in the initial setup phase, before performing the first animation steps. In our experience, this check has detected numerous inconsistencies in the axioms both in academic and industrial models.

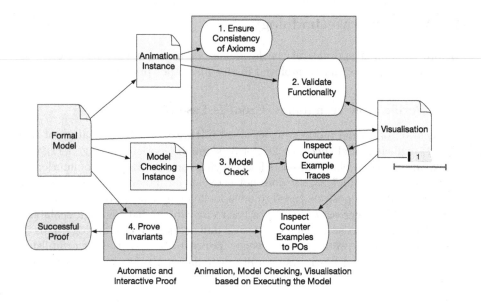

Fig. 1. Tooling Methodology

Animation is also a good complement to model checking, which may give false confidence (one should be skeptical when the model checker reports that your model is correct too quickly) and will only look for the very specific errors you have thought of. In fact, an animator will allow a user to interactively explore the behaviour of a model (i.e., controlling the non-determinism in the user interface). A such one can check that the model dynamics meet expectations, and one often uncovers issues that one did not think of before (and hasn't expressed formally yet as invariants or temporal logic formulas).

Adapting a quote from Leslie Lamport ("Formal mathematics is nature's way of letting you know how sloppy your mathematics is" [28, page 2]) we state that:

> Animation is nature's way of letting you know how sloppy your formal mathematics is.

2.4   Challenges in Combining Proof, Animation and Model Checking

There are also considerable challenges when combining proof and animation. Formulas that help conducting proof (e.g., universal quantifications over large or infinite domains) can make animation difficult or impossible. Still, thus far we have always managed to overcome these issues. Complicated formulas can be moved to the theorems (aka ASSERTIONS) section, which are not checked during constant setup. We have also added a feature to mark some properties with a "prob-ignore" pragma. The PROB animator will skip such properties, but it will mark them as "not fully checked". One should thus still use the tool to validate such properties for a finite subset of parameters. In our experience, there are only a few of those "difficult" properties.

There used to be a considerable debate in the formal methods community whether specifications should be executable [21] or not [24]. While [24] is certainly right to point out the tension between proving and execution, some of the examples and arguments in [24] relate to imperative or functional languages, not to the constraint-logic programming foundation of tools such as PROB. E.g., PROB executes the "non-executable" perfect square example from [24] with ease, finding all perfect squares in 1..10000 in about 0.002 s. While the article [24] makes the plea that "the positive advantages of specification should not be sacrificed to the separable objective of prototyping" our plea is that "the positive advantages of animation should not be sacrificed to the separable objective of proving". One could argue that sometimes it is impossible to write a natural model that is amenable to proof and animation. For example, sometimes a proof model may use an infinite or very large domain (e.g., for positions of the train). This means that the model per se may not be animatable, but one can often reduce the size for animation by providing an instance or refinement of the model. This is what we did for our model, by providing several concrete track topologies for animation (see Fig. 1). Thus far we have never encountered a situation that was not "fixable".

3   Principles of the Moving Block Model

Scope. The aim of this model is to establish the safety principles of a full moving block train control system for ETCS. We are thus not aiming for hybrid level 3 in the middle of Fig. 2, where track sections are divided into virtual subsections of fixed size and location. We are aiming to analyse a full moving block system, where there is no fixed granularity of zones that can be allocated to trains. We still want to cater for the possible existence of trackside train detection devices (**TTD**s), which can detect the presence of trains on certain fixed sections of track, see [38, page 10]. We, however, assume that our trackside system called TRACKSIDE, encompasses both train protection and route protection functions as in traditional signalling systems. It should be pointed out that no routes are modelled.

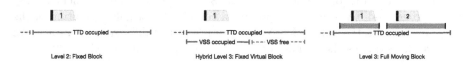

Fig. 2. ETCS Level 2, Hybrid Level 3 and Level 3

Finding Key Properties. Conducting a formal proof of a system often relies on finding and formulating certain **key properties** of the system.

These key properties must be strong enough to establish safety of the system, but weak enough so that they can be proven. Such proofs tend to be done by induction (see, e.g., Sect. 3.2 of [13]):

– we have to establish that the property holds initially
– we have to prove that when the property holds for some time point, that it holds after any possible next event.

We call a property that satisfies these two points **inductive**. Note that typical safety properties themselves do **not** satisfy the latter requirement and are thus not inductive: i.e., the fact that two trains are not in collision at time t does in no way guarantee that they will not collide immediately thereafter.

HL3 VSS Status Is Not Inductive. Finding the key properties is thus difficult and often requires many iterations of modelling and proof. Maybe surprisingly, the key concepts in the hybrid level 3 [1] specification are not inductive. [1] has a "track-centric" approach and relies on four different kinds of status (free, occupied, unknown, ambiguous) for the various virtual subsections (VSSs) of the track. For example, [1] contains these two possible track statuses:

– "unknown" when there is no certainty about whether the VSS is "occupied" or not.
– "ambiguous" when the VSS is known to be occupied by a (connected) train, but when it is unsure whether another (not connected) train is also present on the same VSS.

However, the knowledge about the status of each subsection of the track is **not** sufficient to always correctly determine the status in the next cycle of the system. For example, given the knowledge that a VSS is "ambiguous" and the knowledge that a connected train leaves the VSS, we do not know whether the VSS stays "ambiguous" (if another connected train is on the section) or switches to "unknown". The track status knowledge is not amenable to an inductive correctness proof; the VSS status information is too weak to allow to preserve it upon updates.

The hybrid level 3 specification [1] solves these issues by additional timers, the value of those timers contains additional knowledge and help determining the correct updates of the status of a VSS. Dealing with such timers is very error-prone, and it is difficult to provide a completely formal description of the meaning of a status value of a VSS in terms of possible train positions. We believe this explains the number of issues found by formal modelling [22].

3.1 Key Concepts Explained

Thus, in our model we do not use track-centric key concepts based on track status, but a train-centric approach. In other words, our model (and TRACK-SIDE) keeps track of a variety of **protection zones** which are associated with individual trains and not with track sections.

The overall safety of the system follows from the fact that the TRACKSIDE keeps safe train images covering at all time points the real train position of all trains.

The last point is very important: an essential safety concept is the train image, and not the status of track sections. As such the modelling is quite different than, e.g., the one performed in the hybrid level 3 principles paper [1].

Key Concept 1: TRAINPZ At the heart of the modelling is the train protection zone (TRAINPZ) concept. Every train, registered or not, has an associated TRAINPZ. However, this is a virtual proof concept as the trackside does not directly know the TRAINPZ of the trains. The TRACKSIDE only knows of the existence of registered trains and does not know how many unregistered trains there are.

The TRAINPZ always encompasses the associated train's physical location on the track. This is captured in these safety invariants in Table 1. However, the TRAINPZ covers more than just the current location of the train: it covers *all the controlled or uncontrolled movements* that the train can make in the future, without any further communication between train and TRACKSIDE. In other words, the TRACKSIDE cannot prevent the train from moving backwards or forwards within its TRAINPZ. These movements cover the following practical events:

– shortening or lengthening of trains due to acceleration, deceleration or slopes,
– rollback and roll forward,
– controlled moving forward to the movement authority (MA).

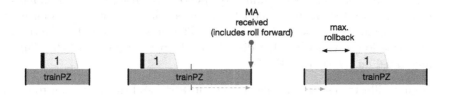

Fig. 3. Movement of a registered train within its TRAINPZ

On the one hand, the proof model assumes that a train will never leave its TRAINPZ. On the other hand, the proof model allows a train to freely move within its TRAINPZ. The proof model makes some assumptions about these possible movements of a train within its TRAINPZ. More precisely, we assume that rollback and roll forward are bounded by a maximal value. These assumptions are important, e.g., to adequately treat trackside train detection (TTD) devices, as we explain below. Indeed, these assumptions are also used in practice by the TRACKSIDE to infer upper and lower bounds for the TRAINPZ (even though the TRACKSIDE does not know the precise TRAINPZ of trains). Indeed,

Table 1. Some invariants related to TRAINPZ

@safetyPZ
$\forall t1, t2.t1 \in activeTrains \wedge t2 \in activeTrains \wedge t1 \neq t2 \Rightarrow$ $trainPZ(t1) \cap trainPZ(t2) = \emptyset$
All TRAINPZs are pairwise disjoint.
@trainPZ_safe_rear
$\forall tr.tr \in activeTrains \Rightarrow trainPZ\_rear(tr) \leq train\_rear(tr)$
@trainPZ_safe_front
$\forall tr.tr \in activeTrains \Rightarrow train\_front(tr) \leq trainPZ\_front(tr)$
All trains are always fully contained in their TRAINPZs.

- knowing that the *train location* lies within some interval is *not an inductive property* (i.e., without further knowledge about the train's speed, acceleration, movement authority, etc., we have no way of knowing where the train will be located next),
- while knowing that the TRAINPZ lies within some interval *is an inductive property*, and the extensions of the TRAINPZ can be monitored by the TRACK-SIDE.

The proof model also distinguishes between unregistered and registered (connected) trains. For registered trains the TRAINPZ can change as follows:

- the TRAINPZ of a registered train can be **extended** at the front, this corresponds to receiving an MA. This is illustrated in the middle of Fig. 3.
- the TRAINPZ of a registered train is **reduced** at the back when a train moves forward. Note that the proof model contains a constant RollbackDistance for the "maximum rollback" and roll forward. The model enforces that the train's back location stays within that distance of the back of the TRAINPZ. This is illustrated on the right in Fig. 3.

Figure 4 illustrates the interplay of the TRAINPZ and the maximum rollback when TRACKSIDE processes TTD freeness. In Fig. 4 the TTD1 is marked as free (e.g., detected by axle counters or a track circuit). This, however, does **not** mean that the entire area of TTD1 is guaranteed to remain free, as the TRAINPZ of train 1 could still reach back into the area of TTD1; TRACKSIDE thus cannot prevent train 1 from rolling back onto TTD1 within its TRAINPZ. However, TRACKSIDE **does** know that there is a maximum rollback and hence does know that there is a maximum reach of the TRAINPZ back onto TTD1. In other words, the gray area on the left in Fig. 4 is guaranteed not to contain the TRAINPZ of train 1.

Key Concept 2: REGPZ The next important concept is the TRACKSIDE protection zone REGPZ for every registered train. This is a zone managed and known

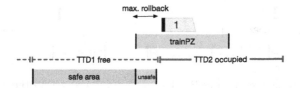

Fig. 4. TTD freeness in relation to TRAINPZ and maximum rollback

by the TRACKSIDE. This zone completely covers the TRAINPZ of the associated
train, and *not just* its current position. This is very important: as Fig. 4 shows,
just requiring that a REGPZ covers the train's current position would *not* be an
inductive property necessary for a successful proof.

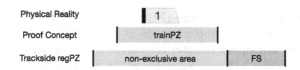

Fig. 5. The REGPZ for registered trains in relation to the TRAINPZ

As Fig. 5 shows the REGPZ is split into two parts:

- the non-exclusive area (NEA), where the train is allowed to move at its own
  "risk", this area is not guaranteed to be free of other trains. This concept
  covers OS (On-Sight) and SR (Staff Responsible) modes. This area is necessary to cater for splitting or joining trains and also directly after registering
  of trains, when it is unclear whether other unregistered trains can be close to
  the train (e.g., on the same TTD).
- the FS (Full Supervision) area where the train can move forward without
  risking encountering any other train or obstacle.

A REGPZ is always non-empty and must always fully cover the TRAINPZ of
the associated registered train. The FS part, however, can be empty. The NEA
part contains at least one "unit" of measurement; this also enables joining two
registered trains (the train behind can obtain an OS MA for the last "unit of
measurement" to connect the trains).

An REGPZ can be reduced at the back, based, e.g., either on TTD freeness
or train position reports. The model requires to prove that such reduction still
safely covers the train's TRAINPZ. A REGPZ can extended at the front, either
in an NEA or a FS fashion.

There are also events that allow to extend the TRAINPZ of registered trains
within the REGPZ. These events correspond to the train receiving an MA from
the TRACKSIDE.

Fig. 6. The extension of a TRAINPZ due to an MA issued within the REGPZ. On the left the TRACKSIDE issues an MA, on the right the train actually receives the MA.

Fig. 7. The reduction of a REGPZ due to a train position report or a free TTD report

Key Concept 3: Zones for Unregistered Trains. The next important concept are the non-identified protection zone NIPZ. These zones are managed by TRACKSIDE and are meant to cater for unregistered trains or other obstacles. Such zones are similar to the zones described in Fig. 1 of [13].

The TRACKSIDE, by the invariants, knows that any part of the track not covered by a NIPZ is free of unregistered trains. Together with the REGPZ zones, the TRACKSIDE can thus safely detect parts of the track are free, and that unless it issues MAs, these zones will stay free.

3.2 Major Challenge: Proving Preservation of Invariants in the Presence of Delays

We first concentrate on the reduction of zones at the back by the TRACKSIDE when receiving new information. This information can either come from TTD's or from trains. The reduction at the back corresponds to the train having moved forward and we can free an associated zone (NIPZ or REGPZ) at the back. In our approach the actual duration of the delay is actually irrelevant, as long as the information can still be safely applied:

- if the information is still applicable, we simply reduce the zone at the back for NIPZ and REGPZ.
- if the information is no longer applicable it is discarded.

Below we show, how we decide whether information is still applicable and how we have formally proven that the zone reductions are safe.

Figure 8 shows two scenarios. At the start (on the left) TTD1 has become free in the physical reality but the message has not yet arrived at TRACKSIDE. In scenario 1 the train rolls back and occupies TTD1 again and the free message is now processed by TRACKSIDE: TRACKSIDE reduces the REGPZ, taking the rollback into account (see Fig. 4). In scenario 2 the train is moving forward towards its MA (end of TRAINPZ). Even if the freeness information arrives very late, the action taken by the TRACKSIDE is identical: the same safe reduction of the REGPZ occurs as in scenario 1. Also note that if the TTD freeness information gets lost, the TRACKSIDE information remains safe.

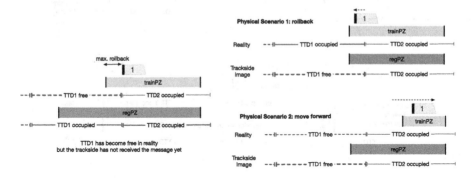

Fig. 8. The safe reduction of REGPZ due to a free TTD report with two different delays

To conduct the successful proof in the model it is crucial that between a) the TTD freeness occurring and c) the arrival of the message the affected protection zone (REGPZ or NIPZ) was *not modified*. Figure 9 shows one scenario where a REGPZ has been modified between the point that the physical freeness occurred and the TTD freeness message is processed. This leads to an erroneous reduction at the bottom of the figure, where the train is no longer covered by its REGPZ.

The proof model uses this approach to dealing with delays:

– when a physical event like TTD freeness or sending of a TPR (train position report) occurs, the model executes a "virtual" event which marks existing zones (REGPZ or NIPZ) as safe for reduction
– the invariants of the model ensure that the potential reduction remains safe, as long as the message is in transit and the affected zone has **not been modified,**
– when the TTD freeness or TPR report arrives, the TRACKSIDE can safely reduce the affected zones which have not been modified. This event contains in its guard a check that the zone is safe. Later implementations (aka refinements) of this event will have to prove that this guard holds. The guard is thus a documentation of the condition that ensures safety of any implementation. There are various ways this guard can be satisfied in practice, e.g., by remembering how long ago a zone was changed and by having time stamps for the TTD free and TPR events.

Thus in essence, a safe implementation of a TRACKSIDE will need to ensure that a TTD freeness or TPR event occurred physically **after** the last time an affected zone was changed.

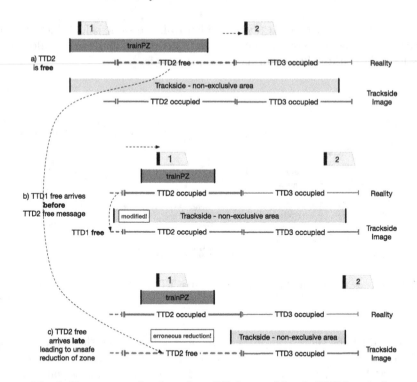

Fig. 9. Erroneous reduction of REGPZ due to delay in TTD2 arrival

3.3 Visualisation

Also, it is usually worthwhile to add **visualisation** to animation. While this adds some initial effort, it is quickly recovered by much more quickly spotting mistakes. For example, in the picture on the right of Fig. 2 one can immediately spot that train 2 is preceding train 1 and both are located on the same track section. This situation would be far from obvious when looking at a textual representation of the model's state (e.g., $trainFront = \{tr1 \mapsto 25, tr2 \mapsto 44\}, trainRear = \{tr1 \mapsto 22, tr2 \mapsto 39\}, ..., ttdLeft = \{ttd1 \mapsto 0, ttd2 \mapsto 20, ttd3 \mapsto 48\}, ttdRight = \{ttd1 \mapsto 19, ttd2 \mapsto 47, ttd3 \mapsto 69\}$).

Visualisation also makes the models amenable to validation by domain experts, unfamiliar with the formal notation used. This was the case for the HL3 models [22] that could be animated and inspected by domain experts.

In our case the visualisations were done with the VisB [37] plugin of PROB in a generic way. For examples trains and zones (protection zones, movement authorities, ...) were drawn using SVG (scalable vector graphics) polygons with coordinates derived from the formal model.

3.4   Tooling Decisions: Proof and Platform

For Event-B one can either use the commercial Atelier-B tool or the Rodin toolset [4]. The former has a textual syntax and more powerful proof interface, e.g., allowing the addition of new proof rules. On the other hand, the Atelier-B proving interface is more difficult to master. Rodin provides a more intuitive proof interface, where many actions can be carried out by clicking on symbols in the hypotheses or goals. On the downside, the modelling language of Rodin is more restricted as far as statements and components are concerned.

We have conducted initial modelling efforts in the more flexible Atelier-B/PROB syntax, and once the components and concepts had stabilised, we translated the model to a linear refinement chain in Rodin (see also [32]). Note that we could build on the experience of a preceding project, where we had developed a first moving block model.

The proof effort was reasonable. We constructed 10 iterations of the Rodin model over the course of 14 months. Iteration 5 for example had 271 proof obligations, 197 proven automatically, 71 manually. Three proof obligations related to initialisation were not proven but checked by PROB by starting the animation. Iteration 8 had 380 proof obligations, iteration 10 had 423. The last iteration has 7 refinement levels (i.e., one abstract machine and 6 refinements), as well as one additional refinement containing instantiations for animation, see Fig. 1.

The provers were sometimes a bit weak for expressions using intervals in combination with minimum and maximum values. Here we used PROB's Disprover [27] to uncover required hypotheses for proof to go through. We actually developed a new improved exportof proof obligations from Rodin so that the counterexamples can be inspected and visualised in detail (see bottom of Fig. 1). One sees the counterexample which invalidates the proof goal, satisfies all selected hypotheses but violates at least one global hypothesis.

4   Scope, Uses, Future and More Related Work

The proof model aims to formally analyse and ensure the safety of moving block systems. The model was developed in Event-B and its scope covers these aspects:

- Movement of multiple trains on a linear track section, including rollback and forward (Sect. 3.1).
- Joining and splitting of trains.
- Train registering and deregistering with TRACKSIDE.
- TRACKSIDE issueing movement authorities to registered trains
- TRACKSIDE maintaining a safe image of the track's occupation using:
  - Identified zones for registered trains (Sect. 3.1),
  - Non-identified zones for unregistered trains and obstacles,
  - Safe processing of updates from trackside train detection (TTDs) and train position reports (TPRs), safely dealing with delays.
  - Invariants to guarantee that the image is a safe over-approximation of the real occupation at any time.

Thus far our Event-B model has been used internally for

- uncovering and visualisation of tricky danger scenarios and communication with domain experts in ETCS railway systems.
- The derived key properties provide guidelines for later implementation of moving block systems,
- the guards of the TRACKSIDE events in the model contain the necessary operational conditions to ensure safety.

4.1 Possible Future Extensions

Below is a summary of possible ways to extend and improve our proof model.

- *Integrity loss* can be considered a special case of splitting a train. A corresponding event (to provoke integrity loss) is present in the current model, but is disabled. Correct processing of integrity loss will require adapting some invariants and adding train integrity status information to TPR messages.
- To support *non-linear topologies* new events and invariants will need to be added at higher refinement level. To be generic, we should also model that trains can appear at points and that trains can disappear at points (moving to and from other parts of the topology). This is already prepared in the latest version of our model by its support for joining and splitting trains, but will require updating invariants and proofs for NIPZ zones.
- Allowing *bi-directional movement* is feasible and one would have to add a direction for every train and a direction for every zone.

In the future it would also be interesting to check whether we can produce a provably correct variation of Hybrid Level 3 [1] virtual fixed blocks by a form of data refinement, i.e. projecting our protection zones on the virtual sub sections.

4.2 Changes Compared to Previous Models

The proof model was inspired by an earlier CBTC proof model [35] developed by ClearSy for Thales Toronto, as well as a moving block model developed by the authors. Some of the key concepts were taken from [35], but there are significant changes:

- There is a *single* model for all proof aspects (not a union of various sub-models as in [35]),
- The model can be animated and visualised, avoiding inconsistencies or errors in the safety proofs,
- The TRACKSIDE has no separate interlocking component,
- There are no complex physical movement functions for trains (the new proof model uses a simpler modeling approach, allowing trains to move freely in their TRAINPZ, see Sect. 3.1). We decided to try a simpler model of the train movement, to ease proof and maintenance of the model. The approach is more general and turned out to be sufficient for establishing safety. (It is, however, always possible to add more detailed movement descriptions as B refinements later.)

- There is a non-exclusive (NEA) area where safety invariants are relaxed to allow joining and splitting of trains (joining and splitting is probably not catered for in the CBTC models).
- The new proof model has, however, a more principled way of dealing with delays.

5   Conclusion

The essential goal of the proof model is to ensure that the moving block TRACK-SIDE computes a safe internal image of the external world. It is secondary what this safe image is used for, be it collision freeness, derailment or other safety hazards.

- The formal model contains a gluing invariant, which formulates very precisely the meaning of the image inside of TRACKSIDE. It provides the exact relationship between the internal information and the physical position of trains and the physical status of the infrastructure.
- The model is very precise about the time points for which the internal information is valid. Delays between the image and the physical world are not "swept under the carpet". The formal model provides conditions under which the safety of the image is maintained by any update and action.

The proof model uses a new refinement technique to deal with arbitrary delays, by adding virtual events and temporary invariants that are preserved until the end of the delay. In summary, we have achieved the following:

- We have ported some of the ideas and concepts from CBTC models to a (simplified) generic moving block model.
- We were able to create a formal model suited for rigorous formal proof and animation and visualization.
- We successfully combined sub-models into a single overall model, that can be used as demonstrator or shown to domain experts.
- We established the absence of collisions (despite delays in position reports).
- Parts of the model were formally proven for all topologies. Train image and protection zones are vital concepts and scale to inductive formal proof.

The take away conclusions of this work are:

- We are confident that a proven formal model for moving block can be developed with sufficient precision for ETCS.
- Reusing experience from CBTC (and also HL3) is possible, key concepts and components are now known. We argue for a train-centric approach with inductive key properties rather than the track-centric approach of [1].
- The key to a good design and good safety case are inductive concepts, which have a clear and precise link to the physical reality, are robust wrt delays and which can be understood by stakeholders and (future) engineers alike.

- It is important to complement formal proof with animation and it is possible, given current tooling, to develop a formal Event-B model that can serve multiple purposes: as safety proof, as an executable reference specification understandable by domain experts, and as a demonstrator for experimentation and field tests.

Acknowledgement. We thank anonymous referees for their useful feedback.

References

1. Hybrid ERTMS/ETCS Level 3. Principles Ref: 16E042, Version: 1A, EEIG ERTMS Users Group, 123–133 Rue Froissart, 1040 Brussels, Belgium (2017)
2. Abrial, J.-R.: The B-Book. Cambridge University Press, Cambridge (1996)
3. Abrial, J.-R.: Modeling in Event-B: System and Software Engineering. Cambridge University Press, Cambridge (2010)
4. Abrial, J.-R., Butler, M., Hallerstede, S., Voisin, L.: An open extensible tool environment for event-B. In: Liu, Z., He, J. (eds.) ICFEM 2006. LNCS, vol. 4260, pp. 588–605. Springer, Heidelberg (2006). https://doi.org/10.1007/11901433_32
5. Biere, A., Kröning, D.: SAT-based model checking. In: Handbook of Model Checking, pp. 277–303. Springer, Cham (2018). https://doi.org/10.1007/978-3-319-10575-8_10
6. Borälv, A.: Case study: formal verification of a computerized railway interlocking. Formal Aspects Comput. **10**(4), 338–360 (1998)
7. Breton, N., Fonteneau, Y.: S3: proving the safety of critical systems. In: Lecomte, T., Pinger, R., Romanovsky, A. (eds.) RSSRail 2016. LNCS, vol. 9707, pp. 231–242. Springer, Cham (2016). https://doi.org/10.1007/978-3-319-33951-1_17
8. Butler, M., et al.: Formal modelling techniques for efficient development of railway control products. In: Fantechi, A., Lecomte, T., Romanovsky, A. (eds.) RSSRail 2017. Lecture Notes in Computer Science, vol. 10598, pp. 71–86. Springer, Cham (2017). https://doi.org/10.1007/978-3-319-68499-4_5
9. Butler, M., et al.: The first twenty-five years of industrial use of the B-method. In: ter Beek, M.H., Ničković, D. (eds.) FMICS 2020. LNCS, vol. 12327, pp. 189–209. Springer, Cham (2020). https://doi.org/10.1007/978-3-030-58298-2_8
10. Su, W., Chen, J., Khan, S.: Insulin pump: modular modeling of hybrid systems using event-B. In: Butler, M., Raschke, A., Hoang, T.S., Reichl, K. (eds.) ABZ 2018. LNCS, vol. 10817, pp. 403–408. Springer, Cham (2018). https://doi.org/10.1007/978-3-319-91271-4_31
11. Chaki, S., Gurfinkel, A.: BDD-based symbolic model checking. In: Handbook of Model Checking, pp. 219–245. Springer, Cham (2018). https://doi.org/10.1007/978-3-319-10575-8_8
12. Marques-Silva, J., Malik, S.: Propositional SAT solving. In: Handbook of Model Checking, pp. 247–275. Springer, Cham (2018). https://doi.org/10.1007/978-3-319-10575-8_9
13. Comptier, M., Deharbe, D., Perez, J.M., Mussat, L., Pierre, T., Sabatier, D.: Safety analysis of a CBTC system: a rigorous approach with event-B. In: Fantechi, A., Lecomte, T., Romanovsky, A. (eds.) RSSRail 2017. Lecture Notes in Computer Science, vol. 10598, pp. 148–159. Springer, Cham (2017). https://doi.org/10.1007/978-3-319-68499-4_10

14. Comptier, M., Leuschel, M., Mejia, L.-F., Perez, J.M., Mutz, M.: Property-based modelling and validation of a CBTC zone controller in event-B. In: Collart-Dutilleul, S., Lecomte, T., Romanovsky, A. (eds.) RSSRail 2019. LNCS, vol. 11495, pp. 202–212. Springer, Cham (2019). https://doi.org/10.1007/978-3-030-18744-6_13

15. Dghaym, D., Dalvandi, M., Poppleton, M., Snook, C.F.: Formalising the hybrid ERTMS level 3 specification in iUML-B and event-B. Int. J. Softw. Tools Technol. Transf. **22**(3), 297–313 (2020)

16. Dollé, D., Essamé, D., Falampin, J.: B dans le transport ferroviaire. L'expérience de Siemens transportation systems. Technique et Science Informatiques, **22**(1), 11–32 (2003)

17. Essamé, D., Dollé, D.: B in large-scale projects: the Canarsie line CBTC experience. In: Julliand, J., Kouchnarenko, O. (eds.) B 2007. LNCS, vol. 4355, pp. 252–254. Springer, Heidelberg (2006). https://doi.org/10.1007/11955757_21

18. Fantechi, A., Lecomte, T., Romanovsky, A.B.: (eds.) Proceedings RSSRail 2017, LNCS 10598. Springer, Cham (2017). https://doi.org/10.1007/978-3-319-68499-4

19. Ferrari, A., et al.: Survey on formal methods and tools in railways: the ASTRail approach. In: Collart-Dutilleul, S., Lecomte, T., Romanovsky, A. (eds.) RSSRail 2019. LNCS, vol. 11495, pp. 226–241. Springer, Cham (2019). https://doi.org/10.1007/978-3-030-18744-6_15

20. Fotso, S.J.T., Frappier, M., Laleau, R., Mammar, A.: Modeling the hybrid ERTMS/ETCS level 3 standard using a formal requirements engineering approach. Int. J. Softw. Tools Technol. Transf. **22**(3), 349–363 (2020)

21. Fuchs, N.E.: Specifications are (preferably) executable. Softw. Eng. J. **7**(5), 323–334 (1992)

22. Hansen, D., et al.: Using a formal B model at runtime in a demonstration of the ETCS hybrid level 3 concept with real trains. In: Butler, M., Raschke, A., Hoang, T.S., Reichl, K. (eds.) ABZ 2018. LNCS, vol. 10817, pp. 292–306. Springer, Cham (2018). https://doi.org/10.1007/978-3-319-91271-4_20

23. Haxthausen, A.E., Nguyen, H.N., Roggenbach, M.: Comparing formal verification approaches of interlocking systems. In: Lecomte, T., Pinger, R., Romanovsky, A. (eds.) RSSRail 2016. LNCS, vol. 9707, pp. 160–177. Springer, Cham (2016). https://doi.org/10.1007/978-3-319-33951-1_12

24. Hayes, I., Jones, C.B.: Specifications are not (necessarily) executable. Softw. Eng. J. **4**(6), 330–338 (1989)

25. Hoang, T.S., Butler, M., Reichl, K.: The hybrid ERTMS/ETCS level 3 case study. In: Butler, M., Raschke, A., Hoang, T.S., Reichl, K. (eds.) ABZ 2018. LNCS, vol. 10817, pp. 251–261. Springer, Cham (2018). https://doi.org/10.1007/978-3-319-91271-4_17

26. Holzmann, G.J.: Explicit-state model checking. In: Handbook of Model Checking, pp. 153–171. Springer, Cham (2018). https://doi.org/10.1007/978-3-319-10575-8_5

27. Krings, S., Bendisposto, J., Leuschel, M.: From failure to proof: the PROB disprover for B and event-B. In: Calinescu, R., Rumpe, B. (eds.) SEFM 2015. LNCS, vol. 9276, pp. 199–214. Springer, Cham (2015). https://doi.org/10.1007/978-3-319-22969-0_15

28. Lamport, L.: Specifying Systems: The TLA+ Language and Tools for Hardware and Software Engineers. Addison-Wesley, Boston (2002)

29. Limbrée, C., Cappart, Q., Pecheur, C., Tonetta, S.: Verification of railway interlocking - compositional approach with OCRA. In: Lecomte, T., Pinger, R., Romanovsky, A. (eds.) RSSRail 2016. LNCS, vol. 9707, pp. 134–149. Springer, Cham (2016). https://doi.org/10.1007/978-3-319-33951-1_10

30. Leuschel, M., Butler, M.J.: ProB: an automated analysis toolset for the B method. STTT **10**(2), 185–203 (2008)
31. Leuschel, M., Falampin, J., Fritz, F., Plagge, D.: Automated property verification for large scale B models with ProB. Formal Asp. Comput. **23**(6), 683–709 (2011)
32. Leuschel, M., Mutz, M., Werth, M.: Modelling and validating an automotive system in classical B and event-B. In: Raschke, A., Méry, D., Houdek, F. (eds.) ABZ 2020. LNCS, vol. 12071, pp. 335–350. Springer, Cham (2020). https://doi.org/10.1007/978-3-030-48077-6_27
33. Mammar, A., Frappier, M., Fotso, S.J.T., Laleau, R.: A formal refinement-based analysis of the hybrid ERTMS/ETCS level 3 standard. Int. J. Softw. Tools Technol. Transf. **22**(3), 333–347 (2020)
34. Mazzanti, F., Basile, D.: A formal methods demonstrator for railways. ERCIM News **121**, 2020 (2020)
35. Sabatier, D.: Using formal proof and B method at system level for industrial projects. In: Lecomte, T., Pinger, R., Romanovsky, A. (eds.) RSSRail 2016. LNCS, vol. 9707, pp. 20–31. Springer, Cham (2016). https://doi.org/10.1007/978-3-319-33951-1_2
36. ter Beek, M.H., et al.: Adopting formal methods in an industrial setting: the railways case. In: ter Beek, M.H., McIver, A., Oliveira, J.N. (eds.) FM 2019. LNCS, vol. 11800, pp. 762–772. Springer, Cham (2019). https://doi.org/10.1007/978-3-030-30942-8_46
37. Werth, M., Leuschel, M.: VisB: a lightweight tool to visualize formal models with SVG graphics. In: Raschke, A., Méry, D., Houdek, F. (eds.) ABZ 2020. LNCS, vol. 12071, pp. 260–265. Springer, Cham (2020). https://doi.org/10.1007/978-3-030-48077-6_21
38. X2Rail-3. Advanced signalling, automation and communication system (IP2 and IP5). Deliverable D4.2: Moving block specifications. Part 2 - System definition. Technical report (2020). https://projects.shift2rail.org

A Tool-Chain for the Verification of Geographic Scheme Data

Madhusree Banerjee[2], Victor Cai[2], Sunitha Lakshmanappa[2],
Andrew Lawrence[2(✉)], Markus Roggenbach[1], Monika Seisenberger[1],
and Thomas Werner[2]

[1] Swansea University, Swansea, Wales, UK
{m.roggenbach,m.seisenberger}@swansea.ac.uk
[2] Siemens Mobility Limited, Chippenham, England, UK
{madhusree.banerjee,victor.cai,sunitha.lakshmanappa,andrew.lawrence,
wt.werner}@siemens.com

Abstract. The Engineering Data Preparation System (E-DPS) is a
tool-chain produced by Siemens Mobility Limited for digital railway
scheme design. This paper is concerned with the creation of a tool able
to formally verify that the scheme plans follow the design rules required
for correct European Train Control System (ETCS) operation. The E-
DPS Checker encodes the scheme plan and signalling design rules as an
attributed graph and logical constraints over that graph, respectively.
Logical constraints are verified by the E-DPS Checker using the satisfiability modulo theories solver Z3. This approach verifies the configuration
of ETCS for a particular scheme and reduces the amount of principles
testing and manual checking required. The E-DPS Checker is currently
being developed to EN50128 basic integrity and has been applied to verify the correctness of a number of real-world scheme plans as part of the
development process.

1 Introduction

Railway verification with formal methods has a long history [8]. Often, verification concerns the dynamic aspects of rail movement. However, there are also
verification challenges with regards to the static design of railways. Given the
topological track layout in form of a track plan, a scheme plan provides a signalling design (that can include elements of conceptual nature, e.g., routes, as
well as where to place track side equipment, e.g., balises). In this paper, we consider the question of how to verify if scheme plans follow a set of design rules,
which arise from railway standards and safety concerns. We formally represent
both, scheme plans and design rules, and implement a tool chain to automatically verify if a scheme plan complies with the desired properties. As a speciality,
we also represent counterexamples in a visual way, with a view to bridge the gap
between the shape of the formal verification result as a logical formula and the
domain specific language of railways.

B. Milius et al. (Eds.): RSSRail 2023, LNCS 14198, pp. 211–224, 2023.
https://doi.org/10.1007/978-3-031-43366-5_13

Scheme plans were originally created by survey with engineers measuring the track layout and the location of equipment by hand. Modern surveys are performed using a LIDAR scanning train which generates a highly accurate digital map of the railway. The detailed map is encoded in a file format that is easy for both humans and machines to process. The existing process for checking is laborious, the data and changes are manually reviewed by inspecting the files. This is made worse by the fact that the scheme design follows an iterative process, in which a human reviewer may end up checking the same files repeatedly. As human beings are weak at performing repetitive tasks with subtle differences between each required check, fatigue can set in and the possibility for human error increases.

Modern railway signalling systems, such as the European Train Control System (ETCS), are designed using accurate geographical maps of the railway derived from scheme plans. The maps contain the topology of the tracks, positions of signalling equipment, and conceptual constructs such as train routes. The safe operation of the signalling systems requires that the geographic maps, and the signalling schemes that they represent, reflect the safety principles of the system. The combined safety target for the system under discussion in this paper is SIL 2. Our formal method tool forms part of the safety argument for this level. It serves as an independent and diverse check at reasonable cost.

In this paper we will consider two, medium-size, real world examples of scheme plans, one which is an extension to an existing development, and one which is a new development. One of these plans has about 300 passive position beacons (so-called balises). If one was to naively checking if all pairs of balises would fulfil one layout criterion, one would have to perform nearly one hundred thousand checks. The challenge is to design a tool-chain which is capable of automatically verifying such number of checks within an acceptable time, say, within less than one hour per scheme plan. Figure 1 presents our tool-chain.

Our tool-chain takes as an input a scheme plan and formally represents it as a labelled graph in SMT-Lib2 [4]. The next step is to identify for which elements of the scheme plan a specific design rule applies: a design rule can be seen as a pattern, which can be instantiated using these elements. Each instantiation yields a check which is passed on to a verification process with the SMT Solver Z3 [15] at its heart. After possibly several calls to Z3, this process produces a three-valued output of Fail/Pass/Unknown. In case the check fails, we produce a visualisation of a counter example. The final output is a report comprising of all results of the checks for one rule.

As SMT solving is Siemens' chosen proof technology for many verification tasks, it was natural to utilise SMT solving also for geographic scheme data verification. With the prover Z3 there is a tool available that has been developed up to industrial standards.

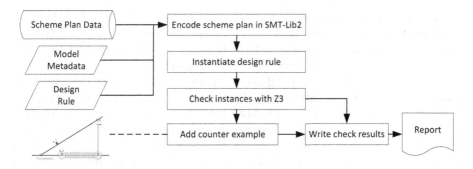

Fig. 1. Geographic Scheme Data Verification Tool-Chain

As a multitude of properties shall be encoded, the decision was to build a human-readable domain specific language on top of SMT-Lib2 rather than having a possibly easier to solve Constraint Satisfaction Encoding for each property. Here, we are (perhaps) trading the possibility to validate property encodings for verification speed. The same holds for the possibility to rely on Z3's graph search as underlying proof method.

1.1 Related Work

Formal methods have been applied to verify both traditional and more modern signalling systems. For instance, the specification of ETCS has been verified in [16], and the European Rail Traffic Management System in [6]. [9] investigates how static checking of interlocking control tables can complement model-checking approaches. In [10], Idani et al. developed an approach to modelling railway topologies and signalling systems. Similarly to them, our work involves both graphical DSLs and formal methods, but they check *dynamic* properties while our work verifies *static* properties of the infrastructure.

In [3,13], the authors perform data validation using the OVADO tool, based on the B-method. For data description, they rely heavily on the B-method's set theory and first-order logic. However, as they perform static validation, the B-method's abstract machine notation plays less of a role. They model a scheme plan as a one-dimensional Cartesian coordinate system, in which balises, signals, points, track circuits, blocks, etc. are placed. They are modelling informal requirements such as "each zone must be connected". Depending on the CBTC equipment investigated, its multiplicity in the design, and the number of properties to be verified, the validation times range from minutes to several hours. The OVADO tool might be capable of validating the properties we are interested in, however as discussed above, it would not fit into the Siemens ecosystem of verification tools. The verification times we achieve appear to be better, as they are in the range of minutes only, however we achieved them on hardware advanced over a decade.

In [14], Luteberget developed a tool suite named *Junction*, which features verification of infrastructure data for consistency and compliance with rules and regulations encoded in a knowledge base. Runtime for verification tasks is in the order of seconds. This is for a workflow in which one new element is placed into a scheme plan, and it is verified if the placement of this element complies with the rules. We took inspiration from this work for visualising counterexamples. One difference is that, like the OVADO tool [3], we are using first order logic to express properties, while Luteberget is restricted to Horn clauses. In our verification practice we found some design rules that appear to require existential quantification and thus require first order logic. The workflow to be supported at Siemens differs from the one by [14]. There is a need to verify a whole scheme plan after its design rather than to verify 'on the fly' when adding a new element. Again, our choice of technology is driven by the need to have a uniform formal methods framework: Siemens Mobility has started to build several tools around SMT solving.

1.2   The Paper's Scientific Contributions

In our paper, we provide a holistic view of how to bring together different techniques (DSLs, SMT solving, transformations, counter example visualisation) for efficient data verification. In particular, we

- formulate a DSL on top of SMT-Lib2, utilising type classes capturing the signalling elements and mapping them to topological constructs;
- define an iterative process calling unsat-checks based on proof generation capabilities of the underlying SMT solver;
- report on a unique process on how to ensure that safety properties have been faithfully encoded in FOL; and
- design a counterexample display chosen by the instrument of a focus group and integrated it into the Siemens Engineering Data Preparation System (E-DPS).

1.3   Organisation of the Paper

In Sect. 2 we briefly discuss the topics of scheme plan representation and SMT solving. In Sect. 3 we give some example design rules and detail the formalisation process that represents them in first order logic. In Sect. 4 we describe rule instantiation for a scheme plan and how to address our verification challenge using SMT solving. In Sect. 5 we present how counterexamples found in the verification process can be visualised for rail engineers. In Sect. 6 we provide performance results.

2   Background

The E-DPS system utilises several representations for processing scheme plan data. The model on which we perform automated reasoning (cf. Scheme Plan

Data of Fig. 1) is the so-called node edge model (NEM, cf. Definition 1) which allows for automated translation to SMT-Lib2 (see Sect. 2.1). An NEM is an attributed graph, where generic attributes store data associated with the various scheme plan elements. Figure 2 shows such an NEM with two balises placed on a passing loop. The balises are represented as position objects, which have a location within the topology. All objects in the model are attributed with additional information, including the type of the signalling object, its identifier, and any other data that would be contained within the scheme plan.

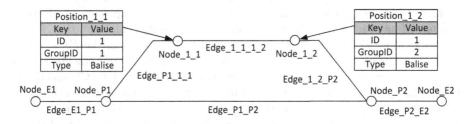

Fig. 2. Example of an NEM containing nodes attributed with balise information.

Definition 1 (Node Edge Model). *A node edge model is a triple (N, E, P) where N, E, and P are sets of nodes, edges and positions, respectively. Edges have a weight $length(e)$. Every position p has an associated $node(p)$. Nodes, edges and positions are referred to as object types in the model and can be attributed with additional information.*

2.1 SMT Solving

The Boolean satisfiability problem (SAT) [7] is foundational to theoretical computer science. It can be stated as follows: given a Boolean formula φ does there exist a model M assigning truth values to the variables of φ such that φ evaluates to true? Tools to solve this problem are commonly referred to as SAT solvers. Typically, SAT solvers produce either a satisfying assignment in the case that φ is satisfiable or a derivation demonstrating that φ is unsatisfiable.

Satisfiability modulo theories (SMT) is a generalization of SAT to solve additional types of problems. In SMT solving, the Boolean formula φ is replaced with a many-sorted first order logic formula over a set of theories T, e.g., for numbers, arrays, and strings. The result of SMT solving is three valued: *satisfiable*, if the solver could find a model, *unsatisfiable*, if the solver could show that there is no model, and *unknown*, if the solver's proof procedures were unable to come to a decision within the user-defined timeframe.

E-DPS Checker uses the SMT-Lib2 [4] standard to encode scheme plans and desirable properties. SMT-Lib2 is tool independent. For SMT solving, E-DPS Checker currently uses Z3 [15] developed by Microsoft Research. As an industrial user we want to use tools that are widely adopted and offer a degree of stability. For performance reasons, in the E-DPS Checker we disable the ability of Z3 to generate a model, i.e., a *satisfiable* result, and can only obtain either *unsatisfiable* or *unknown* from an instance check with of Z3 (cf. Fig. 1).

3   Design Rules and Their Formalization

The Radio Block Centre (RBC) is one of the many safety-critical components of ETCS level 2. Data preparation for the RBC includes the provision of a scheme plan, detailing, e.g., the specific locations of balises. The placement of track equipment must meet strict layout requirements to ensure safe operation. There are various sources of these layout requirements. For example, the *Futur* series of RBC designed by Siemens comes with vendor-specific requirements. These ensure the correctness of product-specific implementation of ETCS functions. Other examples are project or area specific requirements that are determined by local infrastructure managers or standard bodies. In the following we provide two example rules concerning the placement of balises. *The BG-03 design rule*[1] states that design placement of balises should avoid points and crossings. Designed spacing shall be constrained by:

1. 1.0 m between balise and point toes.
2. 1.0 m between balise and point frog.
3. 1.4 m lateral separation between a balise on one path and the centre line of the other path.
4. No balises between the toe and frog of set of points.

The rationale for this rule is as follows. If a balise is present very near to a point node or a diamond node, then the metal in the point may interfere with the reading of the balise. Also, the lateral separation between two balises should be greater than 1.4 m. As, if the two balises are placed too close to each other, then the train can read the information from the wrong balise which can lead to wrong-side failure and in turn could also lead to collision between trains.

The BG-05 design rule[2] states that the designed minimum spacing between adjacent balise groups shall be constrained by: MIN_BG_SEPARATION between adjacent end balises, one at each end of the two groups. MIN_BG_SEPARATION is a numeric value which describes the minimum distance which must be present between adjacent end balises, one at each end of the two groups. This rule shall prevent trains from missing a reading, as could happen if adjacent end balises of two balise groups are placed too close to each other. Additionally, balises are expensive and there is an engineering trade off to be made between the accuracy of train positioning and cost.

---

[1] The lateral separation part is derived from [2] Subset-036 v3.1.0 Table 1 'One Balise and one Antenna Unit'. The other parts are derived from [2] section 5.7.10.

[2] This requirement originates from subset-040 (Dimensioning and Engineering rules) [1] section 4.1.1.from the ETCS specification documents.

Our process of formalising properties consists of several steps, that finally lead to an XML file of design rules, see Fig. 1. In the first step, railway engineers perform a refinement of the *source requirements*, which usually come in the form of text documents. In this step, they re-describe the desired behaviours or restrictions in terms of the data structures or functions of the target RBC or interlocking. This yields an *intermediate document*.

In the second step, software engineers provide a clear mapping between the terms of the intermediate document and NEM elements. Using the BG-05 requirement as an example, the terms 'balise group' and 'balise' correlate to the 'BaliseGroup' and 'Balise' object types of the NEM.

The requirements of the intermediate document are still given as natural language descriptions, which – for the sake of formal verification – need to be captured in an unambiguous mathematical notation. Here, we chose many-sorted first order logic which enables us to define operators over the generic sorts of the NEM. These operators include, e.g., distance which is a function representing the distance between two positions or nodes; and adjacent, which is a predicate that indicates that there is a path between two objects with no other objects of the same type on that path.

To determine which balise pairs should be checked for BG-05, we need to consider several conditions: balises b, b' should not be in the same balise group; b, b' should be at the ends of their respective balise groups; and b, b' should be adjacent. These considerations finally lead to our formalisation of BG-05:[3]

$$\forall b, b' \in \mathbf{Set_{Balise}}.\text{adjacent}(b, b') \rightarrow \text{balise\_group\_id}(b) \neq \text{balise\_group\_id}(b') \rightarrow$$
$$\text{distance}(b, b') \geq \mathbf{MIN\_BG\_SEPARATION}$$

Such design rule formulae are stored as an XML file for use by the checker tool, cf. Fig. 1. Modelling assumptions and mappings are recorded in an accompanying document. In a final step, the railway engineers who authored the intermediate document review the formalisation. This includes checking example schemes plans that are expected to pass or fail the design rules.

4   Verification Approach

The verification process starts by encoding both the scheme plan and the design rule into SMT-Lib2 internally inside the checker. Each element of the scheme plan is encoded as an NEM object in SMT-Lib2 representation. The transformation process is complex with several stages and additional entities. Here, we provide the core constructions. Once encoded, the design rules are instantiated for a particular scheme plan, removing the quantifiers and constructing a number of design rule instances. Following the instantiation, the checker performs an iterative deepening search to analyse the instances with reachability axioms, cf. Fig. 1.

---

[3] Due to our definition of adjacency (no intermediate balise objects), we do not need a specific 'end balise' relation in the formalisation of this design rule.

4.1 Quantifier Instantiation and Sub-formulae Elimination

Our E-DPS Checker carries out a number of pre-processing steps in C# prior to executing the SMT solver, see step "Instantiate the design rule" in Fig. 1. Quantifiers fall into the semi-decidable fragment of first order logic and therefore in general are hard to reason about for SMT solvers. When the value of the quantified variable is from some finite domain like a finite set then it is possible to iterate over all concrete values of the variable and write an equivalent logical expression without the quantifier: $\forall x (x \in S \to P(x))$ can equivalently be replaced by $\wedge_{t \in S} P[t/x]$. Formulae with false premises are trivially true and can be eliminated from any conjunction: $P_1 \wedge \ldots \wedge P_{n-1} \wedge (\bot \to P_n)$ can equivalently be replaced by $P_1 \wedge \ldots \wedge P_{n-1}$. In practice, our E-DPS Checker generates a set of formulae referred to as assumptions during model translation. These are used during the false premise elimination phase to reduce the number of checks required from the order of hundreds of thousands to thousands of checks.

4.2 Reachability

A large number of the design rules formalized as part of the checker development require that signalling elements have either a minimum or maximum separation and are referred to as reachability constraints. The standard way to reason about reachability is to use a breadth-first search algorithm to find the shortest path between two nodes. The E-DPS Checker takes a declarative approach that simulates the performance benefits of breadth-first search. It uses SMT solving to construct a traversal tree starting from the source node of the search and incrementally deepens the tree until it can infer the required information. This has taken inspiration from iterative deepening depth-first search [11] which is an approach to simulate the behaviour of breadth-first search with a depth-first search algorithm. It has as an additional benefit that Z3 computes a witness to the design rule in the form of a traversal tree or path, which would be missing if an imperative algorithm was used.

Definition 2 (Traversal Tree). *A* k-*traversal tree* traversal_tree$_k(n_0, n_{end})$ *from a source node* n_0 *to a destination node* n_{end} *is the set of all path segments up to length* k. *A path segment in this context may end on the destination node or earlier.*

In our first attempt, we naively formalized the standard definition of reachability, however, this caused the SMT solver to blindly generate all paths from a source node to the destination and was highly inefficient. The initial focus of the checker was to prove reachability constraints with minimal separation with other kinds of properties being in scope over the longer term. To this end, we have developed an axiomatisation of reachability that could infer minimal separation by only analysing the immediate vicinity around the source node.

Definition 3 (Reachability). *We define a k-shortest segment in a k-traversal tree as:*

$$\forall k.\, \forall n_0, n_e.\, \forall p \in \text{traversal\_tree}_k(n_0, n_e).\, \forall q \in \text{traversal\_tree}_k(n_0, n_e)$$
$$(\text{length}(p) \leq \text{length}(q)) \rightarrow p \in \text{shortest\_seg}_k(n_0, n_e)$$

Distance is defined using 3 axioms, here we only present the axiom for validating minimum separation, the other axioms follow a similar pattern. The axiom states that if we have a k-shortest segment p and the end of the segment is not the destination node, then we can infer that the distance between n_0 and n_e is at least $\text{length}(p)$: $\forall k.\forall n_0, n_e.\forall p \in \text{shortest\_seg}_k(n_0, n_e)\,(\text{end}(p) \neq n_e \rightarrow \text{distance}(n_0, n_e) \geq \text{length}(p))$.

The impact of this axiomatisation is that the majority of checks can be achieved through a low-bound in less than a second per instance.

Lemma 1 (Monotonicity of Minimum Separation). *The minimum separation axiom is monotonic: if the two nodes are inferred to be minimally separated at k then minimum separation would also hold at all subsequent $k' > k$:*

$$\forall k, n_0, n_e.\exists p \in \text{shortest\_seg}_k(n_0, n_e)(\text{end}(p) \neq n_e \wedge \text{distance}(n_0, n_e) \geq \text{length}(p))$$
$$\rightarrow \exists q \in \text{shortest\_seg}_{k+1}(n_0, n_e)\,(\text{distance}(n_0, n_e) \geq \text{length}(q))$$

The other reachability axioms have similar correctness arguments.

4.3   Instance Checking Process

The E-DPS Checker runs an iterative process of quantifier instantiation as shown in Fig. 3 to infer whether a given design rule instance holds, resulting in one of three overall results for a design rule **Manual Check Required/Pass/Fail**. A result of **Manual Check Required** indicates that the solver was unable to decide one or more instances, however the rest of the instances complied with the design rule. A **Pass** requires that all design rule instances were successfully validated, whereas a **Fail** indicates that there were one or more instances where a counter example was produced demonstrating that the design rule does not hold. Checking the individual instances one at a time increases the performance, the model axioms are only instantiated with the instances being checked and the topological constructs under the bound of the search. The process starts by assigning 1 to the bound k and takes as input the SMT-Lib2 representation of the NEM model and design rule instances. Then up to three runs of Z3 are made:

Bug-finding Pass: Checks whether the design rule instance is incompatible with the encoded node edge model. If the SMT solver returns unsat then there exists a counter example which can be discovered by the counter example pass. The checker has inferred that the instance does not comply with the design rule.

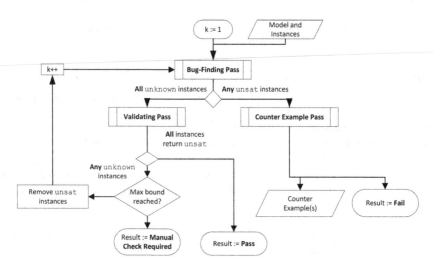

Fig. 3. Instance Checking Process

Validating Pass: Checks whether the negated design rule instance is incompatible with the encoded node edge model. If the SMT solver returns unsat then the design rule instance and the model are compatible. The checker has inferred that the instance complies with the design rule.

Counter Example Pass: Generates an unsat core which forms a counter example indicating which model elements caused the violation of the design rule.

If the bound has not been reached, then all the validated instances are removed, the current value of the bound k is incremented, and the process is rerun. The maximum bound is a user configurable constant.

5   Counterexample Visualisation

Our tool-chain has the capability to visualise counterexamples, see the box "Add counterexample data" in Fig. 1. The instance checking process, see Fig. 3, triggers construction of a counter example if an inconsistency has been found. Here, we instantiate the quantifiers as much as necessary to produce the first counterexample. In principle, the unsat core produced as witness might consist of many clauses. However, as we are focusing on constants only, experience suggests that its size does not pose a problem.

Through a focus group study [12] with the intended user group of railway engineers, we determined of how to visualise counterexamples and accompany them with an explanatory text, see Fig. 4 for a typical example of our final design: on the left, it shows a scheme plan with a wrongly placed balise (4.3), in the middle it shows the visualisation of the counter example highlighting in NEM the nodes involved (in blue) and the distance that needs changing (in yellow), on the right a text provides an explanation of the mistake.

Original Scheme Plan	Counter Example	Explanatory Text
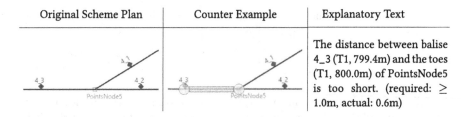		The distance between balise 4_3 (T1, 799.4m) and the toes (T1, 800.0m) of PointsNode5 is too short. (required: ≥ 1.0m, actual: 0.6m)

Fig. 4. Counterexample Visualisation for a violation of the BG-03 design rule

In case the algorithm in Fig. 3 returns that a design rule is incompatible with a given scheme plan, the *Counter Example Pass* generates a so-called unsat core[4] from which we extract information about the found counterexample. For instance, the unsat core for the violation shown in Fig. 4 looks as follows:

```
(distance_to_distancebound_2 def_edge_T1_node_4_3_PointsNode5
def_pointsnode_PointsNode5 def_position_Balise_4_3 rule2)
```

The transformation from such an unsat core to its visualisation involves several steps. Thanks to a consistent naming scheme of the axioms in SMT-Lib2 it is possible to identify which elements of the NEM are violating a rule. For instance, labelled elements of the scheme plan have axioms names with the prefix def_. Thus, by parsing the above unsat core, we know that the violating elements are PointsNode5 and the balise 4_3, and that the violating distance involves the edge called T1_node_4_3_PointsNode5.[5] This allows us to produce explanatory text. This information is also stored in an XML report, which is read and rendered by the E-DPS Editor. Here, an XAML file contains a specification of how to display the various elements contained in such a report.

6 Analysis of Performance on Real World Examples

To analyse performance of the automated checks, we have applied balise group placement rules BG-03 and BG-05 against real-world example railway scheme plans.[6] Our real-world railway scheme plans include all the physical components (tracks, signals, points etc.) as well as the logical components like routes, subroutes and locking conditions. For the performance analysis we have considered two real-world railway scheme plans, one example from new development (ND) and another an extension to an existing development (ED). Below are the features of the example railway scheme plan considered for the performance analysis:

---

[4] Given an unsatisfiable Boolean propositional formula in conjunctive normal form, a subset of clauses whose conjunction is unsatisfiable is called an unsatisfiable core.

[5] In more complex scheme plans, the connection between the violating elements can consist of several edges, in our example it involves only one edge.

[6] The following is the configuration of the machine used to run the automated tests: ZBook Fury 15 G7 Mobile Workstation, Microsoft Windows 10 Enterprise OS, x64-based PC, Intel®Core™ i7-10850H CPU @ 2.7GHz with 6 cores.

Railway Scheme Plan	Tracks	Signals	Block Markers	Points	Balises
ND	10	27	21	12	72
ED	42	44	0	32	237

The following table documents the run-tine of automated testing for checking of the design rules for real-world railway scheme plans. Timing is provided in seconds.

Railway Scheme Plan	Design Rule	Automated Check (s)
ND	BG-03 (part 1)	32
ND	BG-03 (part 2)	64
ND	BG-05	192
ED	BG-03 (part 1)	34
ED	BG-03 (part 2)	85
ED	BG-05	208

These times are sufficiently small to make the tool useful in the context of the envisioned workflow at Siemens, where verification shall run as a background service rather than live during editing. There is room for improvement on verification times, in particular quantifier instantiation is not optimal yet.

One benefit with automated checking is that it reduces the time to perform the checks compared to a manual approach. A further benefit is that it is guaranteed that all the faults will be found by automated checking. A human checker might overlook a combination. Also, human errors due to repetitive work are eliminated. Furthermore, automated checks cater for re-design of scheme plans. Though in the examples of ED and ND, the automated checking did not reveal any new mistakes, it is often the case that errors in scheme plans are found at later stages of the scheme design and were costly to resolve. Automated checking guarantees that errors are found early on.

7 Summary and Future Work

We have presented a tool-chain that scales to the verification of static properties of real-world scheme plans. The tool-chain is based on SMT solving and utilizes the Z3 solver. Thanks to optimisations of properties and the strategy of which properties to check first, verification time is kept small. The formal method is made applicable by counterexample visualisation, developed involving railway engineers as end users.

Parallel deployment with the manual process is future work. We plan to utilize satisfiability modulo monotonic theories [5] for model generation, currently Z3 is unable to generate such models. This will extend our approach to automated test data generation and automatic scheme plan design. Design rule instantiation currently relies on the trustworthiness of the C# code, further investigation of the interplay between pre-computing solutions and checking solutions is desirable. Another approach to further increase integrity will be to pursue proof checking and proof reconstruction.

Acknowledgement. The authors would like to thank Peter Woodbridge, Simon Chadwick and Mark Thomas for providing valuable advice and feedback. Erwin R. Catesbeiana (Jr) enlightened us on the intricacies of inconsistency.

References

1. Dimensioning and Engineering rules. Technical report. https://www.era.europa.eu/system/files/2023-01/sos3_index013_-_subset-040_v340.pdf
2. FFFIS for Eurobalise. Technical report. https://www.era.europa.eu/system/files/2023-01/sos3_index009_-_subset-036_v310.pdf
3. Abo, R., Voisin, L.: Formal implementation of data validation for railway safety-related systems with OVADO. In: Counsell, S., Núñez, M. (eds.) SEFM 2013. LNCS, vol. 8368, pp. 221–236. Springer, Cham (2014). https://doi.org/10.1007/978-3-319-05032-4_17
4. Barrett, C., Fontaine, P., Tinelli, C.: The SMT-LIB Standard: Version 2.6. Technical report, Department of Computer Science, The University of Iowa (2021). https://smtlib.cs.uiowa.edu/papers/smt-lib-reference-v2.6-r2021-05-12.pdf
5. Bayless, S., Bayless, N., Hoos, H., Hu, A.: SAT Modulo monotonic theories. In: Proceedings of the AAAI Conference on Artificial Intelligence, vol. 29, no. 1 (2015)
6. Berger, U., James, P., Lawrence, A., Roggenbach, M., Seisenberger, M.: Verification of the European rail traffic management system in real-time Maude. Sci. Comput. Program. **154**, 61–88 (2018)
7. Biere, A., Heule, M., van Maaren, H., Walsh, T. (eds.): Handbook of Satisfiability - Second Edition, Frontiers in Artificial Intelligence and Applications, vol. 336. IOS Press, Amsterdam (2021)
8. Fantechi, A.: Twenty-five years of formal methods and railways: what next? In: Counsell, S., Núñez, M. (eds.) SEFM 2013. LNCS, vol. 8368, pp. 167–183. Springer, Cham (2014). https://doi.org/10.1007/978-3-319-05032-4_13
9. Haxthausen, A.E., Østergaard, P.H.: On the use of static checking in the verification of interlocking systems. In: Margaria, T., Steffen, B. (eds.) ISoLA 2016. LNCS, vol. 9953, pp. 266–278. Springer, Cham (2016). https://doi.org/10.1007/978-3-319-47169-3_19
10. Idani, A., Ledru, Y., Ait Wakrime, A., Ben Ayed, R., Bon, P.: Towards a tool-based domain specific approach for railway systems modeling and validation. In: Collart-Dutilleul, S., Lecomte, T., Romanovsky, A. (eds.) RSSRail 2019. LNCS, vol. 11495, pp. 23–40. Springer, Cham (2019). https://doi.org/10.1007/978-3-030-18744-6_2
11. Korf, R.E.: Depth-first iterative-deepening: an optimal admissible tree search. Artif. Intell. **27**(1), 97–109 (1985)
12. Krueger, R.A.: Focus Groups: A Practical Guide for Applied Research. Sage Publications, Thousand Oaks (2014)
13. Lecomte, T., Burdy, L., Leuschel, M.: Formally checking large data sets in the railways (2012)

14. Luteberget, B.: Automated reasoning for planning railway infrastructure. Ph.D. thesis, Faculty of mathematics and natural sciences, University of Oslo (2019)
15. de Moura, L., Bjørner, N.: Z3: an efficient SMT solver. In: Ramakrishnan, C.R., Rehof, J. (eds.) TACAS 2008. LNCS, vol. 4963, pp. 337–340. Springer, Heidelberg (2008). https://doi.org/10.1007/978-3-540-78800-3_24
16. Platzer, A., Quesel, J.-D.: European train control system: a case study in formal verification. In: Breitman, K., Cavalcanti, A. (eds.) ICFEM 2009. LNCS, vol. 5885, pp. 246–265. Springer, Heidelberg (2009). https://doi.org/10.1007/978-3-642-10373-5_13

Author Index

B. Milius et al. (Eds.): RSSRail 2023, LNCS 14198, pp. 225–226, 2023.
https://doi.org/10.1007/978-3-031-43366-5

Printed in the United States
by Baker & Taylor Publisher Services